THE DANCER

AND

THE DEVIL

STALIN, PAVLOVA, AND THE ROAD TO THE GREAT PANDEMIC

JOHN E. O'NEILL

SARAH C. WYNNE

REGNERY
HISTORY
Washington, D.C.

Regnery History™ is a trademark of Salem Communications Holding Corporation
Regnery® is a registered trademark and its colophon is a trademark of Salem Communications Holding Corporation

ISBN: 978-1-68451-254-6
eISBN: 978-1-68451-283-6

Library of Congress Control Number: 2021949636

Published in the United States by
Regnery History
An imprint of Regnery Publishing
A division of Salem Media Group
Washington, D.C.
www.Regneryhistory.com

Manufactured in the United States of America

10 9 8 7 6 5 4 3 2 1

Books are available in quantity for promotional or premium use. For information on discounts and terms, please visit our website: www.Regneryhistory.com.

The Dancer and the Devil

To Gareth Jones and Dr. Li Wenliang who gave their lives
to report the truth, as well as to the millions of other victims of
communism, known and unknown, from poison, disease, and
other means. May God hold them one and all, including warmly
our dear friends, in the hollow of his hand.

To our children and grandchildren—may they grow up
in the world of Anna Pavlova and Liu Xiaobo, not the world
of Stalin, Putin, and Xi.

There are others from China and Russia who assisted in the creation,
research, writing, and editing of this book. Because of the reach and
ruthlessness of the Putin and Xi governments and the contents of this
book, their names are not mentioned here. There would be no book,
however, without them. They are truly (like Anna Pavlova, Gareth
Jones, and Dr. Li Wenliang) what Emily Brontë called "chainless
souls." Marxism, because of the hypocrisy implicit in an irrational
system which claims to promote equality but actually ends in slavery
and the rule of tyrants like Stalin, Putin, and Xi, necessarily requires
deniable and anonymous weapons of death like poisons and bioweapons to eliminate opponents and truth tellers. And so, there are casual-
ties in Marxism's century-long war on free thought. Artists, religious
figures, writers, poets, actresses, and even dancers die inexplicably of
mysterious causes or simply disappear forever. But standing aside history are always new free thinkers who will sacrifice their lives for the
truth. God protect them one and all. Our thanks to them.

This is the story of brave souls who were lights illuminating the road
to the great pandemic. Marxism could not debate or control them,
so it killed them with deniable weapons. The story would not be
known without these truth-tellers.

"Yes, as my swift days near their goal:
'Tis all that I implore;
In life and death a chainless soul,
With courage to endure."
—Emily Brontë, "The Old Stoic"

"God is on your side? Is he a conservative?
The Devil is on my side, he's a good communist."[1]
—Joseph Stalin to Winston Churchill
1943 Tehran Conference

As he was being taken to jail ostensibly for failing to report
to Russian law enforcement while in critical condition from a
Putin-directed poisoning, Russian reformer Alexei Navalny said,
"Putin's only method is killing people. He pretends to be a great
geopolitician [but] he will go down in history as a [miserable
little] poisoner."[2]
—Alexei Navalny
February 3, 2021

"For more than a year, the Chinese Communist Party (CCP)
has systematically prevented a transparent and thorough
investigation of the COVID-19 pandemic's origin, choosing
instead...deceit and disinformation...."[3]
—United States Department of State Fact Sheet
January 15, 2021

"When Vice Premier Sun Chunlan visited [Wuhan]...she was
heckled. Some residents shouted "It's all fake!" from their
apartment windows."[4]
—Wall Street Journal
January 22, 2021

CONTENTS

CHAPTER ONE

Pavlova's Candle in the Wind

The Dying Swan

The Dying Swan is a four-minute solo dance which was choreographed by the great Russian dancer Mikhail Fokine with one ballerina in mind. That dancer was Anna Pavlova, still widely regarded as the greatest of all ballerinas, who performed *The Dying Swan* over four thousand times, from Paris to New York, from Mexico to Australia.

Grainy film from the silent era gives us a glimpse of Anna Pavlova on stage. As the swan, Pavlova raises her tremulous arms and gazes upward, as if begging the heavens for her life. Her arms wave and flutter, only for her to be pulled, time and again, to the ground by her failing body. A contemporary French critic wrote, "faltering with irregular steps toward the edge of the stage—leg bones quiver like the strings of a harp—by one swift forward-gliding motion of the right foot to earth, she sinks on the left knee—the aerial creature struggling against earthly bonds; and there, transfixed by pain, she dies."[1]

The Dying Swan touches the thin line between life and death, between the spiritual and the physical. It is to some a tragic funeral dance of death, to others a dance at the gate to resurrection. For Anna Pavlova, Fokine, and other Russian exiles, it became a way to memorialize the life they had known in their Russia, before the Bolshevik Revolution. By 1930, the performance had also become for these expatriates a way of grieving for a homeland in which so many friends, so many artists, and so many faceless millions were being shot or starved to death by the regime of Joseph Stalin.

It was also an act of resistance, both to commemorate those dead and to carry on the culture of the old Russia that Stalin labored to destroy at home and abroad. Anna and her coterie of Russian exiles knew that Stalin's wrath did not end at the border. Around Europe, Russian artists, performers, and impresarios who had defied the regime by refusing summons to return to the Soviet Union were dying from mysterious causes. Healthy people, in the prime of their lives, were suddenly taking ill and dying within hours.

This book is more than a history of these exiled Russian artists and their persecution by Stalin. It is the examination of historical and current mysteries with the tools of the detective and an attorney's eye for evidence that seals guilt. More than once, Anna Pavlova told her friends that a "sword of Damocles" hung over her head. Just before Christmas, 1930, an audience packed into the Golders Green Hippodrome in London to watch Pavlova perform *The Dying Swan*. Pavlova likely also danced her own great ballet composition *Autumn Leaves* set to the music of Chopin, describing a beautiful flower killed by the evil North Wind.

It was to be the last public dance by history's greatest ballerina.[2]

The Mysterious Death of Anna Pavlova

Pavlova died in the early morning hours of January 23, 1931, at age forty-nine. Hers was the first of many deaths of great diva celebrities in the twentieth century—Jean Harlow, Marilyn Monroe, Lady Diana—

spectacles that left the public both enchanted and grieving. Though largely forgotten in popular memory today, the death of Anna Pavlova shocked the world.

Her death, as Churchill's description of Russia itself, was a riddle, wrapped in a mystery, inside an enigma. Pavlova had been in Paris for several days rehearsing for her 1931 tour of European countries and the United States.[3] After taking lunch in her hotel room, Pavlova boarded a train for the Netherlands, where she was scheduled to appear at The Hague. She became ill soon after departure. She struggled to breathe, and her lungs began to fill with fluid.[4] Once in her room at the Hotel Des Indes in The Hague, Pavlova sent for her personal physician from Paris, who joined the Dutch physicians who hovered over her.[5] Although she told the doctors and her husband, Victor D'André, that she had been "poisoned" by the food in Paris, no one took her words seriously.[6] Instead, her doctors treated her for pneumonia. When that failed, they treated her for bacterial blood poisoning.[7] As the doctors failed to find a cause, they were reduced to treating symptoms. Despite their efforts, injecting her with serum and draining fluid from her lungs, nothing they did helped.[8] With death closing in, Anna Pavlova made her company swear to go forward with the scheduled opening performance of her tour on the following night. Around midnight, she called for the costume that she had worn so many times as the dying swan.[9] Too weak to speak further, she raised her hand as if making the sign of the cross, and died.

On the following night, true to her company's promise and her command, the show went on before a weeping audience. Anna's part was played by no one; a spotlight followed her marks on the stage. And when Anna's signature *Dying Swan* was played with the spotlight shining where she should have stood, the audience, led by the king and queen of Belgium, was moved to tears. Royals and commoners stood as one, openly crying.

The death of Anna Pavlova was front-page news all over the world—except in the Soviet Union, which earnestly ignored the fact that the most famous daughter of Russia had just died. Her sudden death was mysterious enough to provoke a Dutch police investigation, which yielded nothing except the clearing of her husband who had been in London when she first became ill.[10] The fact that such an alibi was required for Victor D'André demonstrates that the Dutch detectives believed there was reason to suspect Pavlova's death was a homicide. Various unlikely causes for her death were proposed. She had stood briefly in the rain a few days before her death. Perhaps that had caused an unknown respiratory ailment? Her death was ultimately ascribed to pleurisy. That she suffered from inflammation of the lungs was certain. But these were fatal symptoms without a certain cause. As recently as 1996, the Dutch surrealist artist and writer Jean Thomassen dealt with Pavlova's mysterious death, concluding it could not have been pneumonia and instead ascribing the death to contaminated surgical instruments which caused blood poisoning.[11]

Pavlova's London mansion, Ivy House, and her costumes were auctioned off to the highest bidder. Famous for populating her estate's lake with swans, Anna had a favorite: her devoted swan Jack who loved Anna, fiercely guarded her, and was often photographed with her at Ivy House. He disappeared after Anna's death. Anna passed into legend, the subject of a biography by the great ballerina Margot Fonteyn and an inspiration to a legion of little girls, including Audrey Hepburn.[12] Homages to Anna Pavlova are many, such as "Fred's Steps," a ballet sequence created by Sir Frederick Ashton, head of the Royal Ballet, commemorating his inspiration in 1917 at age thirteen in Lima, where he saw Pavlova perform.[13] From time to time, dancers and admirers of many nations find their way to Ivy House. They leave flowers and notes. Even now, nearly ninety years after her exit, the great, now legendary, Pavlova is invariably included in lists of history's greatest dancers—usually at the top.

Ashes and Porcelain

The Golders Green Hippodrome, once advertised by a marquee gaudy with electric bulbs, is now a Protestant megachurch. Anna Pavlova is interred a five-minute walk away at the Golders Green Garden and

Crematorium in the north of London. The twelve-acre Garden of Rest, which surrounds the crematorium, is among the most beautiful cemeteries in London, planted nearly one hundred years ago by the garden designer William Robinson. Designed primarily in a wild English cottage garden style, but with a Japanese garden pond and impressive monuments, it includes almost five hundred British dead from the First World War.

The ashes of many of England's most famous entertainers also rest there, including writer H. G. Wells, actors Peter Sellers and Sir Cedric Hardwicke, and musician and drummer Keith Moon of The Who. Except for the rather dreary Communist Corner (reserved for leaders of Britain's Communist Party), Golders Green is a lighter and happier place for internment than under a stepping stone in the dark shadows of Westminster Abbey.

On a shelf in a niche sits a marble urn containing the ashes of Anna Pavlova. It is marked only with her name in Russian and English and an inscription of the date of her death. In contrast to many pretentious statues like that of a dour Sigmund Freud, Pavlova's urn is joined only by a beautiful porcelain swan protectively guarding her ashes and a porcelain ballerina representing a dancer at final rest. These simple objects were once accompanied by the ballet slippers in which she danced around the world, but these and much else were stolen long ago.

A visitor cannot help but feel a sadness tinged with rage over Pavlova's ashes, the feeling of a great dance performance prematurely interrupted. Walk to Ivy House, where Pavlova established her ballet school and appeared in pictures worldwide with her pugnacious but protective swan Jack, and one will find a bronze statue depicting Pavlova as a ballerina *en pointe*, arms outstretched and looking up as if about to fly to a far different place than Golders Green.[14]

For decades, the Russian government sought the return of Pavlova's ashes, as it had once pursued Pavlova herself in life and later, her estate.[15] Recently a publication of the Russian government picturing Pavlova's ashes described her as first among the most famous and greatest of Russians whose remains are still located outside of Russia.[16] In 2000, Russian officials, joined by Dutch Pavlova fans, were within a few days of transporting her ashes to Moscow when Pavlova's friends and relatives succeeded in blocking the transfer. Moscow was a city with little connection to Pavlova, who had danced with the long-gone Imperial Ballet in the once great Mariinsky Theater in Saint Petersburg, then the center of the ballet world.[17]

Pavlova's friends and admirers in Hollywood, where she had visited and briefly starred in a silent film, mourned her mysterious death the following year on film. *The Grand Hotel* (1932) is centered around the story of a doomed Russian ballerina, clearly patterned after and inspired by Pavlova. Only the great Greta Garbo could play the ballerina, whose lover in the movie was Anna's close personal friend John Barrymore. At the film's end, the ballerina goes to the Vienna train to meet Barrymore, who, unbeknownst to her, has been murdered. She is clearly doomed as well, but her precise end in the movie is left a mystery, as in life. *The Grand Hotel* won the 1932 Academy Award for Best Picture, but no other awards—the only film ever to do so. Perhaps this recognition was the Academy's way of underscoring unanswered questions. Like *The Grand Hotel's* mystery, Pavlova's friends and admirers insisted that her death was as much a mystery as a misfortune.

Destruction of the Cathedral of Christ the Saviour

As Anna Pavlova was dying, Stalin was planning the destruction of the most renowned church in the Christian Orthodox world, Moscow's Cathedral of Christ the Saviour. Next to Pavlova, it was the clearest symbol to the world of Old Russia, and thus a threat to Stalin's campaign to erase Russia's historic culture and replace it with Soviet agitprop.[18] Situated near the Kremlin with a vast golden dome visible throughout the city, the church was built to commemorate the salvation of Russia from Napoleon. It was designed in the style of the Hagia Sophia in Istanbul, the center of the Christian Orthodox world for a thousand years until its conquest by the Turks in 1453. The *1812 Overture* by

Tchaikovsky was first written and performed for the church's completion. Through the hunger and grief of World War I and the trauma of the Bolshevik revolution, the great golden dome of the church on Moscow's skyline reminded all of both another time and the promise of future redemption. A month after Anna died in The Hague in January 1931, the Soviet security organ, OPGG, planned for workers in Moscow to quickly remove the golden dome before demolishing the church.[19] With this demolition, Stalin believed that even the memory of Old Russia and the hope for a future reversion to religion would disappear. Stalin was, of course, disastrously wrong. The church was rebuilt, almost identically, by the Russian Orthodox Church between 1995 and 2000.

There is no evidence that anyone outside Russia at the time connected the two events—the mysterious death of the world's greatest ballerina in The Hague and the ensuing destruction of Russia's greatest church in Moscow—even though they involved the loss of two of the most important symbols of historic Russia. To understand the how and why of Pavlova's mysterious death, it is necessary to understand the connection between these events and what Pavlova's life represented to Russia and the world. To solve the mystery of her premature death, it is necessary to understand the dark motives of the dictator Stalin.

The Great Cathedral was an obvious, even necessary, target for Stalin and his regime. It was visible from many windows in the Kremlin, that rambling, ancient collection of palaces and buildings built by the Romanov dynasty. In an office there in the ironically named "Palace of Amusement" sat the man who ordered the destruction of the Great Cathedral. Stalin also ordered destruction of Russia's most famous historic structure, the so-called Gate of Resurrection topped by the Iberian Chapel, where Russians entering today's Red Square had prayed for four hundred years. He had no need of a Gate of Resurrection since Stalin had decreed that he would kill God so completely that even the word "God" would be forgotten in Russia by 1937.[20] In a century of carnage, Stalin would exceed Hitler and rival Mao as the century's most successful killer, ordering the murder of tens of millions of human beings.

Stalin, wrecker of cathedrals, was perhaps the only person in the world who would have smiled at the death of the beloved ballerina. One of communism's most prominent critics, George Orwell, would later capture the mentality of Stalin and his obsession with what could have been dismissed as mere "cultural" milestones and personalities: "Who controls the past controls the future; who controls the present controls the past."

What sledgehammers and explosives did to a church that represented the past, poison did to Russian expatriates who had become inconvenient reminders of the glories of pre-Soviet Russia. Stalin invested heavily in labs dedicated to the dark art of poisoning opponents of the regime while maintaining the appearance of death by natural causes. At his direction, a dozen or more Russian expatriates in Paris and other cities in Western Europe were poisoned, adding credibility to an overwhelming circumstantial case that Pavlova herself was poisoned on Stalin's orders.

In time, Stalin's poison labs and his network of assassin-poisoners had become an entrenched, institutionalized scientific and military enterprise. As we will see, Stalin himself likely became a victim to his own chemical weapons of stealth. But Stalin's legacy continued in a growing science and substructure of labs dedicated to developing untraceable poisons and new bioweapons.

Stalin's labs live on today in Putin's Russia, which dispatched operatives to poison Ukrainian leader Viktor Yushchenko, ex-Russian agents in the UK, and Russian opposition leader Alexei Navalny. His labs and their technology are shared with other Communist states, a toxic legacy that has long outlived Soviet communism. These projects endure in the form of hideous human experiments being conducted today in the concentration camps of North Korea, and in the very public killing of the "dear leader's" brother in an airport in Kuala Lumpur.

And, as we shall see, the spirit of Stalin persists in the People's Republic of China, where the military is aggressively exploring toxins and biological weapons. We will make the case that the coronavirus pandemic was not a natural transference of a disease from a still mythical animal to man, but a blunder committed by either the military or civilian labs in Wuhan. The Chinese Communist Party is responsible for the release of the coronavirus, leaving the cities of the world with empty streets and closed shops during the COVID-19 pandemic and killing millions of people.

From the death of Anna Pavlova to today, Stalin has cast a shadow over the world with his enduring ideology and famous followers—each dedicated to his memory, his methods, and even his tools of death. They have become the absolute leaders of nations and are among the most powerful men in the world. Murder is perpetuated by them, sometimes individually, sometimes in groups, and sometimes in entire races and religions. Stalin's ruthless ideology and strange fascination with (and use of) poisons and bioweapons are an evil legacy that is felt by everyone on Earth today, including you, dear reader. The road to the great pandemic running through Wuhan and now killing in every city in the world began a century ago, in 1921, in Moscow.

As Stalin said, a single death can be a tragedy, but a million deaths is just a statistic.[21] The tragedy of Anna Pavlova is the origin story for stealth murder, a tragedy that leads to the sad "statistics" of the present.

CHAPTER TWO

The Impresario and the Swan

The best history of ballet, *Apollo's Angels*, proposes that ballet periodically swoons to near death, until, like *Sleeping Beauty*, it is redeemed with a great talent's kiss.[1] There is little doubt that for a time in the 1920s, those saving ballet were two Russian émigrés: the impresario Sergei Diaghilev and the dancer Anna Pavlova, both of whom were the face of Russia to the world.

As different as they were in style, outlook, morals, and temperament, they were both formed by their apprenticeships in the legendary Mariinsky Theater and Imperial Russian Ballet of Saint Petersburg, where Pavlova trained and where Diaghilev honed his singular talent. By the late 1800s, the center of the ballet world had moved from France to Russia with productions like *Sleeping Beauty*, *The Nutcracker*, and *Swan Lake*.

Diaghilev and the Ballet Russes

Diaghilev was never a dancer, composer, or choreographer. He was from the start a producer who understood the essence of integrating music, performance, and visuals into an awesome spectacle. A biography of Diaghilev by Sjeng Scheijen portrays with encyclopedic detail the life of this extraordinary genius, with a friend's conclusion that the producer "was a terrible and charming man who could make stones dance."[2]

Diaghilev, the child of a once-wealthy, then bankrupt, Russian family, was eternally in debt, though in his lifestyle he was eternally rich. He coasted on his skill in attracting, usually on the strength of a promise (that often went unfulfilled) of future payments to the most gifted composers, choreographers, dancers, and designers of his day. He combined superb taste with a lack of means, but proved time and again that he was unrivalled in discovering and cultivating the most talented composers and dancers. He was an expert at finding and highlighting sometimes controversial geniuses. He first made Stravinsky and Prokofiev famous— arguably the two greatest composers of the twentieth century. Diaghilev populated his ballets with undiscovered dancers and choreographers like Serge Lifar, Vaslav Nijinsky, and George Balanchine. He also conceived using artistic geniuses like Pablo Picasso, Georges Braque, and Henri Matisse for set and costume design, joined by a young, unknown Coco Chanel.

In 1909–10, Diaghilev began the Ballet Russes in Western Europe (primarily in Paris, London, and Monte Carlo) in order to bring together Russian and European talent in a combination of classic Russian and French ballets, alternating with new, revolutionary creations. His productions instantly became the talk of the art world. His initial ballets featured Anna Pavlova, but as his productions became more novel, abstract, and less dancer-oriented, Diaghilev and Pavlova grew estranged from one another. Diaghilev's productions (a total company of as many as one hundred forty) featured more and more novel sets, elaborate plots, and fresh music. To Pavlova, in this distracting milieu, dancers became dehumanized props. It is possible to see her point of view while appreciating the novelty and artistry of Diaghilev's creations. The Ballet Russes productions were among history's most impressive ballets featuring revolutionary productions like 1913's *The Rite of Spring*, which left its Paris audience openly fighting over the merits of Vaslav Nijinsky's loud and stomping choreography that drowned out Igor Stravinsky's orchestral concert work, which was itself dissonant to ears tuned to classical melody. It was a multi-media show featuring great sets, costumes, staging, and dancing at art's cutting edge. Diaghilev's shows were the most dynamic live artistic entertainment in the world for almost twenty years. Because of their immense size, the productions and their elaborate sets moved mostly by train between Paris, London, and Monte Carlo. There was another reason for Diaghilev's keeping his productions in a close radius—he avoided passenger ships because he was deathly afraid of the sea.

Anna Pavlova and the Mariinsky Theater

To gaze on the five-foot-tall Anna Pavlova was to wonder how so much dynamism could be packed into such a short, thin frame. The illegitimate child of a laundry worker, she was the most unlikely of ballerinas. Lacking polish and connections, Pavlova was rejected by ballet school as undersized. But by dint of her work ethic and natural genius for dancing, she was eventually accepted for training by the Russian Imperial Ballet. Later, when she was famous, she would remember her mother's swaddling her as an infant in swan's down, a tender memory she would draw on when she became the most well-loved and famous of swans.

The great Mariinsky Theater in the late nineteenth and early twentieth century was dominated by the renowned ballet master Marius Petipa. He was perhaps ballet's most gifted choreographer, the creative genius who collaborated with others to create *The Nutcracker, The Pharaoh's Daughter, Don Quixote*, and *Sleeping Beauty*. Petipa, born in 1818, had danced and grown up with the beautiful French ballerinas of the Romantic period. They were long gone, and aged Petipa was perhaps the last leaf on the tree from that long-ago artistic period of the 1840s. Since those days, beginning in the 1860s, Petipa had developed a powerful Imperial Ballet School in Saint Petersburg. Well into his eighties, he encountered a new ballerina whom he must have regarded as God's gift to an ancient ballet master. Her name was Anna Pavlova, and he loved her from the first time he saw her dance.

She was far from a master. Pavlova was at first somewhat awkward, a less than confident dancer, but he saw in her passion the glories of the past. She reminded him of the age of the great Romantic ballerinas of his youth in Paris, where expression and emotion counted for as much as execution. From the beginning, Anna had an almost magical ability to express profound emotional and spiritual feelings not only with her face, but with the movement of her body. Petipa's diary reflects his disdain for some very talented, but very self-possessed, ballerinas of the Imperial Ballet. From the beginning, however, he admired Pavlova and how her character, spirit, emotion, and determination showed in her dance. If the stage or walls of the venerable Mariinsky Theater, still standing in Saint Petersburg, could tell a story, they would surely tell of the ancient ballet master's first meeting, coaching, and ultimate worship of the young Pavlova.

It was at first a great struggle. She did not have the raw power and strength of other famous ballerinas. After a series of embarrassing accidents (she landed once in a conductor's box), she finally began to heed the advice of her teachers that her weakness was in fact her strength. Anna Pavlova began to use her frailty, emotion, and delicacy in her dance, developing a style never fully replicated, one that moved audiences to believe they were actually glimpsing her inner soul. It was this quality that drew Mikhail Fokine to create for her his seminal work, *The Dying Swan*, in 1905. As the Swan, she became the most famous dancer, not only in Russia, but eventually in the entire world.

With the retirement and then death of her beloved mentor Petipa, Pavlova's ties to the Imperial Ballet and to Russia weakened. After nearly a decade at the Imperial Ballet in Saint Petersburg performing at the Mariinsky Theatre—then the center of ballet—it was time for the Swan to fly beyond Russia. She began to tour, first appearing abroad in Paris with Diaghilev's Ballet Russes in 1909.

Anna Pavlova was from the very first minute magic to all who saw her. In Paris, a commentator said that it was as if God had secretly given her wings.[3] Sculptors, painters, and composers competed to capture the movement of this divine creature. After a performance in Bombay, a critic averred that Pavlova was not one of the best dancers of this world because she could not be of this world.[4] Yet another admirer stated, "Her most wonderful gift was her ability to vivify and spiritualize by the help of a poetic feeling which never left her."[5] In New York, it was said she was a "Goddess, immaterial, light as swan's down," and a song to put behind us the wounds of the world.[6]

In that less cynical world of the early twentieth century, there was much more room for expressing romantic ideals. The word, "ethereal," now seldom used, was often applied to Pavlova, meaning her performances were almost spiritual ceremonies that seemed to point to the heavenly.

Pavlova would perform *The Dying Swan* throughout the world in venues ranging from great opera houses to music halls. The artistically restless Diaghilev kept disrupting his own masterworks, with the goal of finding new ways to mesmerize and enchant the public. His dancers were constantly competing for attention with stage art and impressive backdrops. Their performances were parts subordinate to a greater whole—what we today would call an *experience*. Ballet Russes eventually dropped classical ballet performances like *Swan Lake* altogether and explored the energy and new sensibilities of modern dance. Pavlova loved the classical music of traditional ballet and the choreography of her mentor Petipa. Although her own style was somewhat unconventional, she did not approve of the radical changes embraced by the Ballet Russes. As their artistic disagreements became rancorous, Pavlova refused the lead in Diaghilev's brilliant 1910 *The Firebird* and left the

Ballet Russes. Instead of returning to the Imperial Ballet, Pavlova, at some risk to her pocketbook and reputation, started her own competing dance company.

Anna Pavlova danced primarily in short extracts from the great ballets. In time, as she traveled, she opened to new forms. In the later years of her career, Pavlova incorporated compositions from Mexican, East Indian, and Japanese dance. But fundamentally she remained unlike her former mentor, Diaghilev. Pavlova's focus was always on the dance rather than the great multimedia shows of the Ballet Russes. Victor D'André, her husband, said that Pavlova, who otherwise had gone silent on Diaghilev, began crying quietly as a spectator in London watching the Ballet Russes. She was disturbed at the way Diaghilev reduced talented dancers to props.[7] But Pavlova was also innovative where Diaghilev was traditional. As unconventional as he was, Diaghilev remained conservative in his choice of what constituted a proper venue. He sniped at Pavlova for lowering the dignity of ballet by appearing in venues like theaters, where on other nights one would find a musical or vaudeville routine.

From our vantage point, we can appreciate them both. The great division between Diaghilev and Pavlova actually enriched the world with two very different styles and locales of performance.

In Paris, Monte Carlo, and London, the Ballet Russes produced the most avant-garde performances of the age, combining stage art by the greatest artists with compositions by the best composers and costumes at the cutting edge of design—art and music in a way that had never been done before. Each season's new compositions, whether *The Firebird* or *The Rite of Spring*, were the talk, if not the scandal, of the artistic community.

Pavlova loved to travel. Her company, not confined to war-torn Europe, crisscrossed the world, spending the years of World War I in North and South America, dancing selections from many classic ballets, as well as their own compositions.[8] They were celebrated in many countries as the first classical ballet company ever to perform in Ecuador, Burma, Australia, and Panama. They enchanted audiences from Japan, where she incorporated classical Japanese dance, to Mexico, where she brought peasant dances to the stage.[9] Pavlova displayed a natural understanding of publicity, dancing with elephants at the Hamburg Zoo and posing with camels in Egypt for pictures sent all over the world. She hired a renowned agent, Sol Hurok, and seems to have followed his advice.

She once said her prayer was her dance, and her mission was to seed the entire world with ballet.[10] With the world made accessible by fast passenger ships, she became one of the first and most famous international celebrities.[11]

Accounts from many countries report that she had a smile that captured all who saw her and a magnetic presence. Like Madonna in the eighties, she was everywhere. She was a fashion model for Best + Company. She compiled a fortune recommending shoes, waxes, and soaps. She was the "peerless Pavlova" with her own windows at Selfridges and endorsed Baldwin and then Bechstein pianos.[12] Pavlova went from the Met in New York City and the Royal Opera House in London to a mouse-infested theater in Jackson, Mississippi.[13] When asked why she went to marginal venues in out-of-the-way places, she said, "If I do not go there, how will people ever see me?" In Chicago it was said, "Pavlova doesn't need a floor. For 15 minutes she did not touch it.... You thought she was a butterfly."[14]

Her headquarters was her home on four acres in London called Ivy House. There she also taught ballet to new students and kept her trademark swans. She endowed charities for children, Russian refugees, and aspiring ballerinas.[15] Like her namesake swans, she spread her wings and toured the entire world, bringing ballet to Africa and the Pacific islands. New Zealanders still argue over who named the dessert Strawberries Pavlova for her. One poll shows it to be Australia's most popular dessert.[16] Everywhere she was celebrated.[17] In the same way that Tiger Woods brought golf from country clubs to the masses, Pavlova brought ballet from the elite to the millions.[18] Whether dancing with Zulu warriors or learning classical Japanese dances, she was the Babe Ruth and

Johnny Appleseed of ballet. On the European continent there were Pavlova dolls and porcelain figures everywhere.

Along with her natural magnetism and legendary dedication, she possessed two other foundational qualities. One, she had a personal sense of dance as spiritual, as an expression of the sacred. Like other great dancers, her dance seemed to leave the physical plane, expressing the deepest spiritual and religious emotions. She bared her soul in dance, and her followers felt hers was the noblest of souls. Obviously no prude and deeply physical, she also was spiritual in a way once common among Russian Orthodox believers. That spirituality reflected itself in her dance and the need to spread it everywhere on earth and across oceans and mountains from Buenos Aires to Tokyo.

Her second foundational quality was courage. Any ballerina who performs in front of an audience knows that an awkward fall on opening night could color her entire career. But Pavlova, who rose from poverty and left her comfortable position as a premier grand ballerina with the Imperial Ballet and then the Ballet Russes, gambled her credibility and renown to dance in the West with her own company and democratize the ballet. She ignored criticism from Diaghilev and others and continued to take her dance to wherever it was in demand. For those who felt ballet required more dignity, Pavlova showed that dignity was portable.

In 1916, she starred in a silent film advocating the overthrow of the established order. She also danced several times despite warning of great danger if she appeared.[19] Her small frame carried the bravest of hearts. The diminutive ballerina struggling against death itself as the Dying Swan and displaying truthfully her own inner courage captured the hearts of the world. She became larger than ballet itself.

CHAPTER THREE

The Last Ball and the Day of the Soviets

The Romanov dynasty ruled for more than three hundred years. In the nineteenth century, the sprawling, developing country of Russia and the young United States were both rising nations shaped by their frontiers. As Russia expanded east past the Ural Mountains to the Pacific, the United States expanded west to the same ocean. The great sin of slavery in the United States was matched by serfdom in Russia, enslaving men to soil, with both practices ending at around the same time. Only a short time after the completion of the Transcontinental Railroad, Russia completed the much longer Trans-Siberian Railroad running through its heartland to the Pacific. Both nations were industrializing, building vast wealth on the backs of shamefully treated workers. The vibrant culture of Longfellow and Mark Twain was more than matched by that of Tolstoy and Tchaikovsky, creators of *Anna Karenina* and the *1812 Overture*.

But there were two critical differences. First, the United States occupied a continent buffered by two oceans without powerful rivals. Russia, meanwhile, was threatened from the east and west by the two most aggressive and powerful nations of that time: Germany and Japan.

Second, the United States, from birth a republic, was far more resilient and adaptable to the waves of change that came with the early twentieth century. Russia's Romanov dynasty was crusty, repressive, and made only faltering steps toward meeting growing cries for representative government. This frail, outdated monarchy, resting on the outdated belief that the tsar's power came from God, could not withstand the internal pressure of civil unrest and external pressure from a militant Japan in 1904 and a militant Germany in World War One. It was doomed to crack like a Fabergé egg in a vise.

The Start—The Imperial Ball of 1903

From the Rome of Petronius to the court of Versailles under Louis XIV, the height of an era, or a premonition of its end, is sometimes connected with memories of a party. At the Tour D'Argent restaurant in Paris, a table under glass marks the legendary "Dinner of the Three Emperors," which brought together King William I of Prussia, Tsar Alexander II of Russia, his son the tsarevich (later Alexander III), and Otto von Bismarck for a sixteen-course meal served with eight wines over eight hours. Older Americans wistfully remember John F. Kennedy's days of Camelot by his 1962 dinner for Nobel Peace Prize winners at the White House. When exiled Russians were asked about their last and most vivid memories of the *ancien régime* after its fall, despite as much as a half-century of exile, they invariably described the Imperial Ball of 1903, held in the Winter Palace of Saint Petersburg in February.

Beginning in the 1840s, the Winter Ball was a Romanov tradition to celebrate the New Year and the anniversary of their long rule. The celebrations consisted of opulent parties, performances, and dinners that

became more lavish and complex with time, culminating in what would be the regime's last ball.[1]

The ball was attended by approximately four hundred invited guests dressed in the elaborate costumes of seventeenth century Russia, commemorating the two hundred ninetieth anniversary of the Romanov dynasty. The costumes are still widely studied today for their beauty and innovation and included jeweled designs by Peter Carl Fabergé, history's greatest jeweler.[2] The costumers of a *Star Wars* film drew inspiration from the fanciful costumes of the 1903 Winter Ball.[3] The Empress Alexandra's dress alone, if designed today, would cost at least ten million Euros.

The main event was the masquerade ball, which opened with a polonaise and featured room after room of sumptuous foods and music. But the celebrations began the evening before, with selections from the opera *Boris Godunov* and a new star, Anna Pavlova, not yet a prima ballerina, dancing selections from *Swan Lake* under the direction of her mentor, Marcus Petipa. Grand Duke Boris Vladimirovich, a noted warrior and more noted philanderer, called Pavlova, "my little angel," but made no progress with her.[4] The following evening, now a guest at the ball, young Pavlova appeared in a stunning red, white, and gold bejeweled traditional Russian costume created by the Imperial Ballet. She wore an ornate Russian headdress that has been recreated many times for display.

It is sometimes said that "each age is a dream that is dying or one that is coming to birth."[5] The great Imperial Ball was both a dying dream and one being born. For Pavlova, it marked a transition from talented student to famous performer. It was for her a presentation ball before society. For Imperial Russia, it was the last bright glint of a setting sun. Within a year of the opulent, never-repeated ball, the Japanese Empire suddenly and without a declaration of war attacked and almost destroyed Russia's Pacific Fleet. On land and sea, the Japanese revealed Imperial Russia to be an inept paper bear. The final humiliation was the Russian defeat in the great naval battle of Tsushima, where superior Japanese

tactics eliminated with little loss Russia's most modern ships. Over 10,000 Russian sailors died or were captured, and its great battleships were destroyed—at a cost of only 117 Japanese sailors. The ensuing peace, largely on Japanese terms, was deeply humiliating to Russia. That humiliation in turn brought to the surface long, festering resentments fueled by the concentration of power and wealth in a few hands, now revealed to be toothless and incompetent.

Anna Pavlova, only newly accepted into the Imperial Ballet, was swept up in the reformist currents of the age. At great risk to her career and her life, she led a strike of the Imperial Ballet's performers demanding political reform. A member of the ballet, Sergei Legat, tortured into denouncing the strike, committed suicide. Pavlova presented a large wreath at his funeral with the inscription, "To the first victim at the dawn of freedom of art from the newly united ballet company."[6]

The Romanovs and the Empire did not heed Pavlova or other reformist voices. On Sunday, January 22, 1905, a large, unarmed religious procession led by an Orthodox priest, Georgy Gapon, approached the Winter Palace to deliver a petition to the tsar as their father and head of their Church. The Imperial Guard opened fire without warning, killing and wounding hundreds. This atrocity destroyed any remaining affection the Russian people had for the Romanovs. For many Russians, the tsar was no longer either their spiritual or political father. The death of Old Russia began in the bloody snow of that day. While Pavlova, Petipa, and her friend the gifted choreographer Michael Fokine wept for their friends and for Russia itself, the Bolsheviks, Lenin, and Stalin rejoiced in the chaos caused by the Bloody Sunday slaughter.[7]

In the following decade, Russia lost millions in the First World War, where courageous troops were no match for superior German armament, tactics, and leadership. Some of those pictured at the last Imperial Ball died in the Pacific War and many more in World War One. When the Bolsheviks later gained absolute power in Russia, one's appearance in the many public photographs of the Great Imperial Ball, if discovered, was a ticket to a quick death sentence. The ball marked in its own way

the beginning of the end for Imperial Russia, but only the end of the beginning for Anna Pavlova. The graceful polonaise that had opened the Imperial Ball was stilled. The Danse Macabre, the dance of death, had begun.

Even the thickheaded Romanovs realized that after the ravages of the Japanese War and the political mayhem that had followed, it would be indiscreet to hold another ball. The majority of the four hundred merrymakers and their families would be killed within fifteen years. The remainder would flee for their lives into exile.

The Collapse

In 1914–1917, Imperial Russia was ground down by the better-led and better-supplied forces of Germany and Austria-Hungary. Pavlova and Diaghilev spent the war years outside of Russia—Diaghilev mostly in France, and Pavlova touring in Europe, the United States, and South America. Starvation and death were everywhere in Russia. Imperial Russia, which had helped save Europe from Napoleon and defeated the Swedes and Turks, did not survive the conflict, and with it died the living link to the rich lore of the Don Cossacks and Alexander Nevsky. The culture which had birthed Tchaikovsky, Rimsky-Korsakov, Dostoevsky, and Tolstoy was, for a time, no more. The remnants of Russia's historic culture were scattered among refugees in Western Europe, China, and the United States. To much of the world, Pavlova and her rival Diaghilev's Ballet Russes were all that was left of a Russia killed by the Bolshevik Revolution.

Diaghilev and Pavlova were both initially sympathizers with the Revolution. In 1916, Pavlova lived briefly in Hollywood, where she appeared in her only movie, *The Dumb Girl of Portici*. Her performance was recently heaped with highest praise in a retrospective by the *New Yorker*, which proclaimed Pavlova's singular feature film role to be history's greatest single performance by a motion-picture actress.[8] In the movie, she portrays a revolution against nobility in a sympathetic light,

presaging and perhaps encouraging the brewing Russian Revolution. Although it is a silent movie from film's earliest days, in it one can see Pavlova's amazing ability, like Greta Garbo's, to convey deep emotion with subtle gestures of the face, hand, and body.

In Paris, Diaghilev's Ballet Russes unfurled red flags in 1917 and some performances featured the "Song of the Volga Boatsmen," a revolutionary hymn as the Revolution occurred.[9] It didn't take long for artists and intellectuals in Europe to become disillusioned, however, by the 1917 Revolution and the Soviet slaughter that followed. Choreographers, dancers, artists and musicians, music-makers and dreamers of dreams joined large numbers of Russians seeking escape from the Red prison, fleeing certain oppression and likely death for the uncertainty of the West.[10]

The Russian government slowly collapsed first into a provisional government led by parties of the left and then into a Soviet Bolshevik government headed by Lenin. The Romanovs stayed in Russia until it was too late to escape and ultimately moved to Yekaterinburg in the Urals, where Nicholas, Alexandra, their four daughters and son were accompanied by a doctor, nurse, and two others. By this time, the Bolsheviks had assumed complete control. On the orders of Lenin approved by the Party, the family and their servants were awakened around eleven o'clock at night on July 17, 1918. They were taken to a small room and after waiting for an hour, a heavily armed group of twelve men entered.[11] The thugs opened fire—killing Nicholas but only wounding his wife and children, who were partially protected by jewels which Alexandra had sewed into their clothing. The brutal gunmen wounded at least two of their own cohort with ricochets. When the smoke cleared, the butchers went back to work, shooting and stabbing the Romanov children. A few children still stubbornly breathed when others appeared dead, so they were each shot again in the head. Their bodies were then stripped so as to make identification impossible, thrown in a mineshaft, retrieved and burned, and then reburied in a secret location. Afterwards, Russia announced it had no knowledge of what had happened to the little family

and their staff. The Romanov executioners were themselves executed—at least two at Sukhanovka Prison—to maintain the lie.[12] There were no witnesses.

In 1919, Robert Wilton, an English reporter for the *London Times* inspected the rooms where he believed the Romanovs had been killed. He found bullet holes everywhere, many blood stains, and crude pornographic drawings of Alexandra and her young daughters. In the absence of their bodies or witnesses, the Soviets claimed to have no knowledge of where the Romanovs went or what fate befell the family. The Soviet Union was silent on their fate for more than seventy years. Other than Wilton's evidence, there was no definitive proof of what happened to the Romanovs until after the collapse of the Soviet Union. In 1990, Wilton's evidence of location coupled with DNA technology enabled identification of the family and their servants who were reburied in Saint Petersburg. But for DNA evidence, their final fate would never have been known with certainty.

Before leaving Saint Petersburg in 1914, Pavlova was told by Tsar Nicholas that he deeply regretted never having seen her dance *The Dying Swan*. He extracted her promise that she would return to Saint Petersburg and the Mariinsky to dance *The Dying Swan* for his family. Pavlova, of course, would not be able to live up to that promise, as there was soon no royal family. Pavlova would never again dance in the Mariinsky, let alone set foot on Russian soil.

The murders of July 17, 1918, set the tone for everything to come, not just for the Soviet Union, but for many Communist and neo-Leninist regimes in the future. The pattern was to be repeated in Russia under Vladimir Putin, in North Korea under Kim Jong-un, and in the People's Republic of China under Chairman Mao and Xi Jinping. That pattern is as simple as it is brutal: Horrific crimes are mercilessly committed in secret with massive efforts to conceal them, often including the secret execution of the executioners themselves. As opponents disappear, they become non-persons who never existed at all. Their disappearances, whether in Moscow or Wuhan, are unexplained and irrelevant. These

are followed with denial of wrongdoing and claims of an absence of knowledge, even when confronted with incontrovertible evidence. And any reminder of the old regime, like the Romanovs' memory, is to be destroyed beyond recognition.

Pavlova and Diaghilev would soon become Old Russia's preeminent remaining human symbols after the slaughter of the Romanov family.

CHAPTER FOUR

Their Greatest Days: 1910–1920

"The appeal of Pavlova is to all; because it is the appeal of perfection to humanity."[1]
—*Evening Standard and Saint James's Gazette*

T he decade surrounding the Great War brought the greatest days of Pavlova and of Diaghilev's Ballet Russes. Like the flight of the Swan, Pavlova was alight and aloft on ships and trains traveling everywhere, becoming one of the first truly international entertainers.

In 1919 in Mexico, Pavlova produced in the most unusual of locations in one of the single greatest nights in the history of ballet. Mexico was in revolutionary turmoil. Francisco Madero, who sought to bring freedom and democracy to Mexico, was slaughtered by the tyrant Huerta, who in turn was overthrown by President Carranza. A long struggle culminated in the death of revolutionary Emiliano Zapata shortly before Pavlova's arrival with her company of forty-four dancers, musicians, and others in Veracruz, where they were warned of the very dangerous conditions in Mexico and urged by the American Counsel to terminate their plans to perform in Mexico City. Pavlova and her company refused and instead journeyed to Mexico City on a train with more than two hundred armed soldiers riding on the tops of the railway cars.[2]

Upon their arrival in Mexico City, they were presented with the most unlikely of ballet locales: the Plaza de Toros, the famous bullring of Mexico City. After some practice, they gave a performance at night in the bullring attended by 32,000, rich and poor, peon and shop owners alike. It was the first classical ballet performance ever held in Mexico. Illuminated by searchlights and fires, Pavlova, according to her husband, danced as she had never danced before.[3] When she began *The Dying Swan*, she could feel a change in the music. Looking over in surprise, she saw that Pablo Casals, the world's most gifted cellist and musician, had risen from the audience to play. This was to be, as a matter of general opinion, the greatest of her 4,000 performances of *The Dying Swan* and, given the many threats on her life and the vast crowd, a near miracle that it was not a real, final performance of a dying swan. To conclude, she and the company had choreographed a performance of Jarabe Tapatío—the Mexican Hat Dance—which had traditionally been scorned by the Mexican upper classes. As they performed it brilliantly, the Mexican audience threw sombreros onto the stage in the traditional sign of appreciation. It was an incredible display of genius, compassion, artistry, and courage.

For a few minutes, the terrible hate of the Mexican Revolution was gone, and the audience sat together as proud Mexicans. In a subsequent meeting, President Carranza thanked Pavlova, predicting that in a few years Mexico would be a united, peaceful country. Sadly, it was not to be. Carranza was assassinated, and the hopes and dreams of that wonderful night dissolved in a continuing downward spiral of violence and corruption. But Pavlova danced the Mexican Hat Dance in performances all over the world from Rangoon to Berlin. It became Mexico's national dance in 1924. In Mexico City today, the Ballet Folklorico still dances the Jarabe Tapatío, first choreographed and then danced that night a century ago by Pavlova.

After her performance in the Mexican bullring and in following years, Pavlova and her small company danced in forty-four different countries, before emperors and common folk. Pavlova, driven by a love of ballet which she saw as spiritual, popularized it in places it had never been and among people who had never heard of it.[4] Pavlova was truly a missionary of this great art form. Wherever she went, she produced instant crowds, and audiences appeared eager to say they had seen her.

Diaghilev's Greatest Days

If Pavlova brought classical ballet to the most unconventional places, Diaghilev did exactly the opposite. He brought the most imaginative and unconventional new ballets to the most conventional of venues in Paris, Monte Carlo, and London.[5]

Because of Diaghilev's fear of the ocean, he limited his trips largely to Europe, although sometimes he sent his company to the United States or South America without him. As Pavlova toured worldwide, Diaghilev and the Ballet Russes remained at the cutting edge of the intellectual world of Europe. A brilliant showman, after the revolutionary effects of *The Rite of Spring* produced fights in the audience, Diaghilev's 1917 *Parade* had a score that included gun shots and typewriter keys clacking. All of Paris awaited each ballet season wondering what surprise Diaghilev would unveil. Although unable to recruit Pavlova later for his company, he otherwise had his pick of the greatest musicians like Prokofiev and Stravinsky, choreographers, painters Henri Matisse and Georges Braque for magical sets, and Coco Chanel for costumes.[6] Diaghilev's genius lay in part in producing cross-collaborations by the most renowned artists of the age. To be in a Ballet Russes production was in those days a hand-print on the sidewalk of history.

Picasso prepared the sets for six Ballet Russes productions.[7] Despite the high art, there was, to be fair, a kitsch aspect to these productions. Chanel is oft quoted as saying, "Diaghilev is Russia for foreigners."[8] With his massive company of one hundred forty to two hundred fifty, the Ballet Russes was a multi-media experience of art, costume, magic, and dance not unlike what the Cirque du Soleil is today.[9] It was clearly the greatest such show of its time—a collection of geniuses with Diaghilev as its leader. To the world outside enslaved Russia, it was Russia. And as Pavlova traveled all over the world, the Ballet Russes, through extraordinary imagination and recognizing no boundaries, became the world's ultimate symbol of artistic freedom.

The Ballet Russes in its twenty years from the 1909 performances in Paris to Diaghilev's 1929 death was fundamental to all ballet and continues to exercise foundational influence. Its new ballets were so innovative, inspired, and marked by genius that they are performed over and over to this day, much like the earlier immortal Russian ballets. Like the arguments over which movie or play was the greatest of all time, there is no consensus over which of Diaghilev's creations was the most important. Many would single out three ballets as among his most esteemed work.

The Firebird (1910)

The Firebird, a new ballet staged by Diaghilev in Paris in 1910 to massive public acclaim, was important for several reasons. In a certain sense, it marked the launch in the West of Diaghilev and separately, Pavlova. Although Pavlova had performed in Diaghilev's 1909 Paris productions, which met with some success, and was scheduled to dance the lead in *The Firebird*, she declined to dance in the revolutionary production after listening to Igor Stravinsky's score. She judged it inharmonious. Despite Diaghilev's efforts to lure her back, she would never again appear in his productions. Instead, Pavlova launched her own company, appearing sometimes in music halls with popular acts, but acquiring her own company and worldwide reputation by the magic of her dance.

The Firebird was the talk of Paris and the entire world. It solidified Diaghilev's reputation as the most famous producer in the world, whose productions were awaited with anticipation by dancers, artists, and designers eager to be associated with the Ballet Russes and its packed houses. *The Firebird*, based upon two ancient Russian fairy tales, is the story of a prince who happens upon a magic garden maintained by an evil wizard full of imprisoned, transformed women. The prince finds his love with one and also captures a magic firebird who delivers a future promise in exchange for her freedom. Later when the evil wizard appears, the firebird delivers on her promise.

The score by Igor Stravinsky was revolutionary, a clear departure from the largely harmonious music of Russia. Many great composers received it coldly. The sets and costumes were opulent and spectacular to a degree never before seen in ballet. They were paired with wonderful choreography by the great Mikhail Fokine, who danced the male lead and who had also done Pavlova's *Dying Swan*. It was the *Phantom of the Opera* of its day: a vast multi-art show of beautiful paintings; wonderful costumes; a large, diversified orchestra; brilliant music; and splendid dance never before seen. Although Russian critics believed it a "horrifying poverty of melodic invention," others like Rachmaninoff believed it "a work of genius," and "true Russia."[10] Like *Phantom*, it has been recreated and replayed many times. *The Firebird* was foundational for Diaghilev. From its production until his death, he would remain the most discussed and most important ballet producer and art director in the world. Additionally, *The Firebird* assured that Pavlova would leave the comfortable nest of the Ballet Russes and begin a flight that would eventually take her all over the world as her own boss.

Perhaps because they no longer had a true homeland with Russia, the slave state, ballet itself became the homeland of Pavlova and Diaghilev. To many it was pure magic—from *The Dying Swan* to *The Rite of Spring*. But it was not so in Russia for Stalin.

The Rite of Spring (1913)

If *The Firebird* and the 1910 Paris Ballet season made Diaghilev and his Ballet Russes famous by its vast, rich, multi-art approach, it was *The Rite of Spring* that, by its genius, made him and the Ballet Russes immortal. Art at this time, particularly in Paris, had moved from extraordinarily epic and realistic depictions by artists like Delacroix to the great Impressionists whose depiction of light and color was to them at least as important as subject and form. Still undiscovered Vincent Van Gogh was depicting the thoughts of the subconscious mind on canvas. Picasso was pioneering contemporary abstract art with *Les Demoiselles d'Avignon* and cubism, not tied to either the forms or colors of nature by 1907. And on May 29, 1913, ballet exploded into the new world of abstract artistic expression often called "Modernism" with the revolutionary *The Rite of Spring* performed in Paris at the Théâtre des Champs-Elysées.

The score by Igor Stravinsky, which opened with strangled bassoons and other strange sounds never before heard from any orchestra, was intentionally and brutally jarring, but brilliantly conceived. Minutes into the show, the audience split into factions. One was cheering while others were booing the orchestra and pelting them with programs. Fights broke out, mock duels were fought, canes and hats flew. Stravinsky fled the theater within five minutes.

The stage designs and costumes by the great Russian artist Nicholas Roerich were among the strangest ever seen in a ballet. The other-worldly stage set was disorienting to many. They have since appeared in several science-fiction works and productions. The costumes were mostly exotic takes on primitive Russian designs.

The lead male dancer and *Rite's* choreographer was twenty-four-year-old Vaslav Nijinsky, a strikingly handsome and brilliant male Adonis, who was the love of Diaghilev's life until other loves and then insanity consumed Nijinsky. He was the most acclaimed male ballet star of the early twentieth century (and perhaps of all time) and *The Rite of Spring* was possibly his greatest performance. He fought for weeks with Stravinsky over the meshing of his choreography with Stravinsky's score. *Rite* was at complete war with traditional ballet, with Nijinsky, in the words of one critic, "tromping around the stage." From the contrived and calculated chaos, something amazing and wonderful emerged—arguably the most influential and creative ballet and music of the twentieth century.

Diaghilev, recognizing that controversy is fame's father, was elated at the near riot of the audience, telling friends that opening night went exactly as he had planned. The Parisian papers were full of stories about *Rite's* opening—some critical and some adoring.[11] Of course, everyone, not only in the world of art but also the larger world, wished to see, hear, and experience it for themselves. Diaghilev would produce sixteen more years of new or recreated ballets (many quite innovative), but neither he, nor anyone else, would have another night like the opening of *Rite*. He truly became the father of a new age of ballet and art.

Parade (1917)

Sometimes a work of art is good in itself, but noteworthy because of the circumstances when it appears. So it was with *Parade*. In early 1917, World War I had already raged for three terrible years, killing three million French soldiers, two million British, three million Russians, and perhaps four and a half million Germans and Austrians. By the spring of 1917, it appeared the Allied powers, including France, would surely lose the war. Russia had overthrown the tsar and descended into chaos. The French Army revolted after the catastrophic failure of an ill-conceived offensive. England moved towards starvation because of effective German unrestricted submarine warfare.

In the midst of this heartache, chaos, and likely defeat came Diaghilev's *Parade*—the story of circus performers—on May 18, 1917, to a suffering city soon to be the subject of the last great German offensive of World War One. It was among the lightest and most fun of all the Ballet Russes' ballets. The scenario and plot were conceived by poet Jean Cocteau (dubbed the Frivolous Prince), who would return from his grisly work as an ambulance driver to work on *Parade*. The libretto was by the badly wounded poet Guillaume Apollinaire, who worked on the ballet with terrible battle scars and bandages. The music was by Erik Satie—at fifty-two-years-old too old to fight but still adept at the piano. His style is notable for the crispness and energy of his compositions. The production featured confetti, bells, fronds, and perhaps ballet's most unusual costumes, even by the standards of *Firebird*. Both the costumes and the sets were again the imaginative works of Pablo Picasso, the twentieth century's leading artist, whose sets inspired by murals at a marionette theater were bright, happy, vivid, and innovative.[12] Many of the Cubist-style costumes and sets are still the subject of study and controversy.

Critics were often unkind to *Parade*, but Diaghilev himself (perhaps because of the dark times in which it appeared) claimed, "*Parade* is my best bottle of wine. I do not like to open it too often."[13] Many mark it as the beginning of surrealism in art.[14] And it was surely a candle inspiring Paris at a dark and terrible time.

After these ballets and many others, the Ballet Russes continued for twelve more years, its creations in the 1920s forming the center of the world of ballet and art. Arguably, although usually brilliant, it would never again quite reach the heights of the earlier ballets. Nor would anyone else. Diaghilev had anticipated and helped to begin two great ages of art. He brought light and hope back to the City of Lights at one of its darkest moments.

CHAPTER FIVE

Années Folles, "The Crazy Years"

A fter the losses of World War One and the even more deadly 1918–19 Spanish Flu epidemic, the Western World (with the exception of Russia where war and then executions still raged), moved for a time towards peace and relative prosperity. The automobile became common. Radio brought the entire world together. By train and coal-powered steamship, the time taken for international travel was reduced from months to weeks and days. Mass production ushered in a more prosperous era.

And in Paris, the true center of the world for Diaghilev and Pavlova, these were the *Années Folles*, the "Crazy Years" as they were called in Paris. Paris in the twenties was the center of ferment and creation in art, theater, and music. In literature, these were the days of the famous "Lost Generations," a café society of writers like Ernest Hemingway and Gertrude Stein. It was an age of wonderful painters as the great impressionists like Matisse slowly yielded to abstractionists like Picasso and surrealists like Salvador

Dali. In music, Cole Porter, Claude Debussy, and Sergei Prokofiev composed their most celebrated work. Terrible pain and disillusionment remained from the carnage of the war and its aftermath. The street painter of Paris, Éduard Cortès (terribly wounded himself in the war) painted street scenes of the city. In each piece until the end of his life, he included in the Parisian crowds an image of his wife who had died in the flu epidemic and sometimes of French soldiers he served with who had died on the Western Front. But for most, life in Paris became frenetic activity centered around cultural events, jazz or Cole Porter in cafes, the Paris Exposition of 1925, and the latest productions of the Ballet Russes. The old limits and rules died. Josephine Baker, spurned in a racist America, with her *Danse Sauvage,* became the toast of Paris. There were no longer the old boundaries on art or conduct.

Diaghilev and the Ballet Russes

Sergei Diaghilev and Anna Pavlova remained at the center of the Parisian cultural maelstrom for years. As Pavlova clung to the Russian Orthodox religion and the classic ballet style of the Mariinsky, Diaghilev looked elsewhere for inspiration, turning to the Russian poet Alexander Pushkin, whose poems, operas, and other works had inspired generations of Russians. Pushkin, jailed and exiled for his "Ode to Liberty" wrote some of his greatest poems in jail. A contemporary of the great English poets Keats, Byron, and Shelley, Pushkin shared with them a belief that the purpose of life was the creation of great art, free from restraint, and not for wealth or fame, but as a good in itself. Pushkin died young and in poverty and scandal after a duel.

On the evening when *The Rite of Spring* opened with a near riot and opinion divided over whether Diaghilev was a lunatic or a genius, the producer sat quietly repeating Pushkin's poetry as he did on many other occasions. His life and death would mirror Pushkin's: free from restraint, consumed by a burning desire to create great art for art's sake. Unlike Pushkin, Diaghilev was often impoverished but never suffered poverty.

The 1920 season in Paris for the Ballet Russes occurred after a two-and-a-half-year break following the 1917 season, most of which Diaghilev spent in London. The season opened with *The Nightingale*, with sets and costumes by Henri Matisse, the famous male lead dancer Léonid Massine, and a score by Stravinsky. It featured other brilliant sets by André Derain and then Pablo Picasso with an assemblage of great composers, choreographers, and dancers. The season of 1920 was a fitting kickoff to the Crazy Years of the twenties and its bohemian writers, artists, and mentors.

Diaghilev's fortunes always hung by a thin financial thread. The love of danger which partially motivated his long string of often scandalous affairs with male ballet dancers, also controlled the business affairs of the Ballet Russes. Without any state support, each of its immensely expensive productions was dependent on a patron to provide the capital, and on its own success to sell tickets.

In 1922, Diaghilev's genius failed him, and his luck ran out. Unlike most of his innovative productions, he proposed to recreate in London Petipa's 1899 production at the Mariinsky of *Sleeping Beauty*, renamed *The Sleeping Princess*. The costs were staggering, and given Diaghilev's business plan of investing every penny (and then some) into the most sought-after artists, dancers, composers, and the like, the Ballet Russes's future was mortgaged to the success of *The Sleeping Princess*. It proved to be a moderate artistic success and a box office dud. *The Sleeping Princess* broke the producer's finances. Diaghilev fled from England with many angry creditors and the risk of imprisonment behind him. He had no assets other than his genius and his friends.

It appeared to be the end, but new patrons appeared and a sponsorship from the tiny city-state of Monaco. Back in business, the Ballet Russes was reborn in the South of France and reopened new, successful productions in Paris, always with every available franc and then some invested in artists like Pablo Picasso, Léon Bakst, Georges Braque, as well as Coco Chanel for costume designs and George Balanchine in choreography. As Stalin enclosed Russia with an iron curtain, the supply of new Russian talent dried up, and the Ballet Russes became in its last years an artistic Tower of Babel.

And then in 1925, Diaghilev was contacted by Stalin's close associate, Anatoly Lunacharsky, Soviet minister of enlightenment, with an "invitation" delivered personally over breakfast in Paris. He was politely asked to return to Russia.

Pavlova

In contrast to Diaghilev, the crazy twenties for Anna Pavlova were a decade of trains, ships, and hotels, evangelizing ballet around the world. It has been estimated that her great tours in the 1920s covered more than 400,000 miles, a staggering total in the days before air travel. She began the decade in her home in London. In 1922, she began the first of two tours of Japan, China, the Philippines, and India—first exposing those countries to ballet. After other trips, it was on to Australia, New Zealand, and Africa; then North and South America; Asia again; the Middle East and Europe. There were photos that appeared worldwide of her always elegantly dressed in train stations greeted with flowers, with camels and elephants, with Charlie Chaplin and her close friends John Barrymore and Mary Pickford and Isadora Duncan. Her fame snowballed. She was one of the first truly international stars. She matured from a beautiful ballerina to an international legend.

Both the dance of her small company and the art she loved were vastly different from Diaghilev and the Ballet Russes. She largely danced extracts from *Giselle*, *Swan Lake*, and the other classic ballets with interspersed short pieces (often solo) like *The Dragonfly*, *Autumn Leaves*, and *The Dying Swan*. In the *Swan*, the spotlight would remain upon her alone as she danced solo en pointe until the end, dancing in crazy turns seeking to avoid the death which was pressing in upon her and would surely find her, marked by a crimson blood-red brooch against the white costume. She would finally and gently succumb to death in a famous posture of surrender later captured in the porcelain dancer next to her ashes.

In contrast to Diaghilev, Pavlova was never in need. She had been financially prudent and acquired substantial wealth through her endorsements of everything from shoes to cosmetics to pianos. Other than Diaghilev's criticism of her for dancing outside of conventional venues and the difficulty of working for a perfectionist, there was nothing to criticize about her. To the papers and co-workers, she was ephemeral, "a cloud" floating through the world, "a flame."[1]

In 1920, Pavlova started and wholly funded a school for orphans in Paris. At her English home, she tutored for little pay a number of young ballerinas to enrich the world when she was gone. As she entered into her forties in the 1920s, she slowed a bit but remained near the top of her form.

The art Pavlova loved most was that of the earlier Renaissance and later Old Russia. She saw herself and her ballets as children of that age and of the bygone world of old Marius Petipa. And always, she dreamed of someday returning to the Mariinsky and Russia—an impossible dream.

In 1924–25, Pavlova's mother, lost for seven years in the chaos of Russia, suddenly and magically appeared in Odessa with papers permitting her to leave Russia to visit Pavlova in London. These clearly required approval at the highest levels of the Russian government. Her return coincided with a Soviet Secret Police operation called "Operation Trust," whose purpose was to lure émigrés back to Russia who would then be exploited or eliminated. It was a cruel invitation that couldn't be refused. When Pavlova refused to go home and was unable to convince her mother to stay, her mother returned to Russia, never again to appear in the West. Had Pavlova actually been lured back to Stalinist Russia, it is hard to imagine she could have performed the dreary industrial and tractor motifs of the Bolsheviks. It is easy to imagine she would have been a very disobedient prisoner in their Gulag and have died quickly and in obscurity. She would have ended like the ghost she played in *Giselle*.

In 1927, Pavlova visited the now-ancient Romanov Dowager Empress in Sweden. Two years later, both she and the Ballet Russes separately performed in France at the birthday of the last great Romanov pretender to the throne, shortly before the pretender's death. Stalin, through many agents, learned of these private performances.

Diaghilev and Pavlova had spent much of the 1920s reaping the harvest of their great fame gained in earlier years—for Diaghilev, *The Firebird*, *The Rite of Spring*, and *Parade*, and for Pavlova and her own dance company, *The Dying Swan*. Now Stalin's "invitation" refused, they would reap a whirlwind from which not even a swan could fly far or fast enough to escape.

CHAPTER SIX

The Devil

"The greatest trick the Devil ever pulled was convincing the world that he didn't exist."[1]

—Charles Baudelaire

"The second greatest trick the Devil ever pulled was convincing the world he is the good guy."[2]

—Ken Ammi

M any, including the famous Vatican exorcist Father Gabriele Amorth and the great Polish philosopher and writer Leszek Kolakowski, have come around to the belief that Josef Stalin was the Devil or at least demon-possessed.[3] One does not have to indulge the supernatural, however, to believe that the evil Stalin wrought and the delight he took in the agony of his victims, many once his comrades and friends, meets any definition of the demonic. But Stalin was not always the maniacal butcher history remembers him as. In fact, he once had ambitions of being a priest.

The master of Russia was born a Georgian, Ioseb Besarionis dze Jughashvili.[4] The future Joseph Stalin was born three years before Pavlova in 1878 in strikingly similar circumstances. Like Pavlova, he was born into poverty, although not nearly so poor as Pavlova. Also like Pavlova, he was an only child with a deeply devoted mother. Pavlova was born out

41

of wedlock; Stalin's mother was married to a shoemaker. Pavlova and her mother dreamed that she would somehow become a ballerina. Stalin's mother, nicknamed "Keke," dreamed that her son would become an Orthodox priest. Stalin's father, perhaps because he believed his wife had strayed and his son was not his own, became a violent drunk, beating up both his wife and his child and eventually (having lost his job) disappearing for years at a time. Young Stalin showed a flair for creativity, loving music, painting, and poetry. But his shows of sensitivity triggered terrible beatings by his father.[5]

Despite his family's poverty, Stalin's mother was able with the help of a priest to place her son in parochial schools and then, after some time, in an Orthodox seminary. Initially, Stalin did well in his studies and was known as the best singer in the choir. But by 1897, after four years at the seminary, Stalin found a new religion: Marxism.[6]

Stalin and his new creed made for a good match. As an abused and beaten child, he had learned to operate in stealth, a characteristic useful for a revolutionary. In 1898, Stalin planted revolutionary literature in the rooms of seminary students who had rejected his Marxist views, and then turned them in to school authorities.[7] It was the first of many secret actions showing his genius at "*liternoye*" (secret) crimes, untraceable to himself, in which his silence, stealth, and ruthlessness would become the mark of a master liquidator.[8] As Pavlova labored at the Imperial Ballet School, initially the subject of ridicule, Stalin was booted from the seminary and taken home by his mother. He became a criminal. For a time he saw himself as a romantic rebel in the Georgian bandit tradition, an idealistic revolutionary and a Georgian nationalist. He wrote poems that are still highly regarded and included in major anthologies of Georgian poetry. In 1934, Stalin visited his mother, who was close to death. He told her, with pride, that he had become the tsar. His mother told him—to his ever-lasting disappointment—it would have been far better for him if he had become a priest.[9]

As Pavlova slowly abandoned attempts to imitate the much stronger gymnastic ballerinas at the Imperial Ballet School and followed the great dance master Marius Petipa's advice to let her natural fragility and spirituality be her strength, Stalin absorbed a very different lesson. He had become a master at accumulating and using power ruthlessly and without pity. He planned murders and armed robberies, though he rarely partook in the crimes himself. When he was finally apprehended by the Tsarist police in 1903, he became a police informer, seeking protection and favors. He had begun to master *liternoye*, at once informing the police of some rival comrades and falsely suggesting his fellow revolutionaries as informers.[10]

In 1906, he married an extraordinarily beautiful and devoutly religious woman, Ekaterine Svanidze, nicknamed, like his mother, "Keke." Although he deeply loved his young wife, she was frustrated by his inability to reform himself. She died of typhus in 1907. At her funeral (for which Stalin had been released from jail) he told acquaintances, "with her passing goes my last feelings of any kind for mankind."[11] When, despite her final wishes, Ekaterine was not buried in a consecrated Orthodox cemetery, Stalin's hatred of Christianity no doubt increased. Keke and Ekaterine were Stalin's last real emotional ties to humanity. By the time Winston Churchill had come to know the dictator as an ally, the prime minister would privately observe that Stalin was "an unnatural man." Following Keke's death, Stalin continued the same pattern of alternating between low-grade criminal planning with disposable proxies and turning them into the police.

The critical turn in Stalin's fortunes came when he lobbied for and obtained a position as Lenin's indispensable criminal planner and later assistant. From his first casual meeting with Lenin in late 1905, Stalin sought to ingratiate himself and stay close to the great man, like a pilot fish to a whale. By 1912–13, Stalin had built the false legend of himself as a brave revolutionary and dropped the undignified name of "Koba," or even less dignified nickname of "Pock Face" or "Pockmarked," for the self-anointed title of "Stalin"—Man of Steel.[12]

Rise to Power

World War One and the Revolution gave Stalin his best chance to ingratiate himself with Lenin. Scarcely ever on the front lines, Stalin held various jobs and then became the editor of the Communist Party mouthpiece, *Pravda*. Stalin's rise was strongly opposed by Yakov Sverdlov, who served as Lenin's chief of staff. In 1919, Sverdlov suddenly died as a result of his lungs' inexplicably filling with fluid.[13] The way was now clear for Stalin who became, in effect, Lenin's secretary. By 1922 he had risen to the post of general secretary of the Communist Party. Some naively thought this just another low-level functionary position. In Stalin's hands, this secretariat became the greatest lever of power in Russia, allowing him to control all appointments, set the agenda for meetings, and assume greater control when Lenin was shot and recovered from a would-be assassin. Stalin put himself at the nexus of control of all power under the aegis of Boss Lenin. A truly heartless and evil man now controlled Russia, a master of deception and an expert hunter of human beings using *liternoye* liquidation techniques in which the fact of a death, the cause of a death (often arranged to appear natural), and the identity of those carrying out the murder were all disguised or concealed.[14]

As his power grew absolute, Stalin's appetite for cruelty became insatiable. He especially took joy in the suffering and agony of those who had been his friends or artists he had admired.[15] He became an expert at inflicting agony. Vsevolod Meyerhold, one of the greatest of modern theater directors, was arrested at Stalin's instruction. Shortly thereafter, his wife was tortured to death in their apartment, her eyes cut out before Stalin's agents stabbed her seventeen times.[16] Meyerhold was then tortured, his bones broken, and then secretly executed.[17] Another famous director, Solomon Mikhoels, was killed at Stalin's orders in a *liternoye* liquidation staged as an auto accident. For authenticity, Mikhoels' body was run over several times with a heavy truck.[18] At a birthday party, Stalin was amused by skits of the executions of weeping, pleading men who once had been his friends.

By the mid-1920s, as Pavlova danced all over the world, the romantic Georgian who had loved his mother and his young wife was a scheming, demonic man who took joy in agony and in using political illusion to hide his crimes. Stalin continued to develop the tools needed for his particular craft and strange tastes.

CHAPTER SEVEN

Stalin's "Special" Weapons Are Born

"It happened like this when only the dead
Were smiling, glad of their release."[1]
—Anna Akhmatova
Requiem

A short walk from the Bolshoi Theater (now the center of Russian ballet) lies the building known to all Russians as "the Lubyanka." For most of the past century, it was the headquarters of the dreaded secret police of the Soviet and Russian states. The police themselves—both civil and military—reconstituted over and over have had an alphabet soup of names. Some of the best known are the OGPU, NKVD, SMERSH, the KGB, and today, the FSB.

Plans and directions from inside the Lubyanka have killed more human beings than those devised in any other structure ever built by man, making possible exception for the 1942 Wannsee Complex near Berlin where the Nazis' so-called "Final Solution" was planned. Many thousands of direct executions occurred in the Lubyanka and its adjoining prison itself. The Gulag camps of the Soviet Union, Stalin's infamous White Sea–Baltic Canal project that consumed tens or hundreds of thousands of lives, the slaughter of the Kulaks and famine in

47

Ukraine, and the Great Terror of 1935–1939 were all planned in the Lubyanka.[2] The use of poison gas in 1920 at Tambov, which killed 15,000 of its own citizens, was planned there.[3] Plans for the slaughter of the old nobility and tsarist officials, the execution of many thousands of Polish officers in the Katyn Forest in 1941, and the slaughter of hundreds of thousands of Russian émigrés returned against their will from Europe in 1945 were likewise planned in the Lubyanka. The most prolific single executioner in history—Major General Vasily Blokhin, a thug personally selected by Stalin to execute as many as three hundred people a night—officed there.[4] If somehow the remains of its victims could be gathered, the pile of bones would far exceed the size of even the vast Lubyanka.

For a visitor, the building of the Lubyanka has a sinister feel, as if the spirits and agonies of its tortured prisoners linger there. It has the same sort of haunted, morose feeling as the Rivergate at the Tower of London, through which hundreds passed on their way to their beheadings. Muscovites quip that it is the tallest building in Moscow though it stands only a few stories high, because prisoners could see heaven or Siberia from its basement. Vasily Blokhin, who oversaw and participated in the massacre of seven thousand Polish officers at the Katyn Forest and who personally dispatched tens of thousands of others, had a special soundproofed room with a large drain and a hose designed for the Lubyanka. If the condemned had any doubts as to their fate, seeing Blokhin waiting for them in his butcher's apron and holding a German Walther pistol removed any question. Other parts of the building were also notorious killing spaces, for example, the building's courtyard. None of these spaces are open to the public.

But in the Lubyanka, indeed in all of Russia, there was no place as fearsome and notorious as the nearby facility called, "Laboratory One" or "Da Kamera." In Stalin's time, it was connected by a secret tunnel to the Lubyanka. In later times, most of its poisoning activity would be moved to a location outside of Moscow (and branches in many remote locations).[5]

This poison lab and its descendants may be the source of many of the greatest mysteries in modern history.[6] From the time of Stalin and

Pavlova to that of Putin, the lab has been an unseen fulcrum of Russian and world history. With the creation of the toxin Novichok, it remains in the twenty-first century a barbaric tool of Russian leadership.[7]

Dr. Death and Lab One

If Stalin was right that the deaths of millions were just a statistic, then Stalin collected statistics from Ukraine to the Arctic.[8] But he needed special tools to deal with individual assassinations that would have amounted to individual tragedies—and scandals—if their causes were known. Those tools for carrying out secret murders were Laboratory One and the Special Tasks Group.[9]

Laboratory One may have been authorized by Lenin and Stalin as early as 1921.[10] Upon assuming power and until his death, Stalin kept close control of this poison lab. The lab, which changed names many times, was originally called the Special Cabinet, but eventually changed to Laboratory One. Stalin's personal doctor, named Ignatii Kazakov (who treated him and others in positions of power with unusual remedies for psoriasis, impotence, and the like) became the early head of Laboratory One, acquiring the nickname, "Doctor Death." Before long, a pharmacist and chemist, Genrikh Yagoda, took direct control of the Lab. A sinister-looking apparatchik from central casting, Yagoda was so successful in his poisoning activity that he was promoted to head of the entire NKVD. His experience overseeing the White Sea–Baltic Canal was ample preparation for operations that relied on the ruthless exploitation of human life and suffering. The laboratory was physically established in a nondescript building off Red Square in Moscow, but close to the Lubyanka Prison for special prisoners and interrogations. With a short walk, Dr. Death, Yagoda, and his associates could select prisoners to be given poisons, as opposed to the more conventional bullet in the head in a courtyard at the Lubyanka. The poisons, usually administered while assuring the prisoners that they were simply medicine, were used to create later deniability for the death of completely innocent prisoners, those not even accused of phony crimes.[11] Thus it could be claimed that these victims died of heart failure or lung problems while being interrogated.[12]

The proximity to the prison was convenient for a second reason. Prisoners, referred to by lab personnel as "birdies," were often moved from the Lubyanka to Lab One to be used as human test subjects by Dr. Death and other lab technicians.[13] This inhumane conduct (paralleling the activities of the Nazis such as Dr. Josef Mengele and others at Auschwitz) was done with the goal of developing more effective poisons and poison delivery systems.[14] Indeed, following World War II, Nazi scientists, who had conducted human experiments in the concentration camps and elsewhere, were brought to Russia for debriefing at Lab One so the Soviets could learn the results of their tests of gases and bacteriological weapons upon Jews and others.[15] After divulging the information, the German scientists were with a dark but fitting irony themselves used as human test subjects.

The lab's early experiments revealed that it was hard to calibrate poison and bioweapons dosages using animal subjects. Because humans react differently than animals, the shift to human beings as test subjects by Lab One was inevitable.[16] The subjects were injected with "medicines" or fed meals with chemical or biological poisons. They were then observed through small windows in agony and usually death. If they survived, they were then again injected with or fed poison.[17] The report of one of the earliest poisonings describes a man in great agony as blood poured from his eyes while he tried to pull out his own tongue.

When correct dosages were reached, the bodies were sent without identification for autopsy at Moscow's public hospital. If the verdict was "natural causes," the Lab One team celebrated. They had succeeded and would be rewarded for their work, often in the form of state decorations.

From its modest beginnings in 1921–22, Lab One would become a highly sophisticated center of both poison and biowar—expert both in developing poisons that mimicked natural diseases and in bioweapons capable of dealing death wholesale through a variety of viral and bacterial diseases. It began to resemble a perverse Mass General set up to deal death instead of save lives. As the institution grew, it became the mothership of spreading satellite locations both for "special operations" like Paris and for long-term secret horrifying research in Kiev, the Aral Sea, and Yekaterinburg in the Ural Mountains. And as time passed, the laboratory birthed other poison and bioweapons labs in other Stalinist nations like the People's Republic of China and North Korea. To those who embraced Stalinist ideology, viewing man as simply a property of the state, poison and bioweapon labs were irresistible tools promising a godlike ability to mete out life or death to individual targets, classes, or nations. And Marxism, which promised equality yet delivered slavery and tyranny, desperately required anonymous death to eliminate wrong thinkers and cover up murders.

The Poison Dwarf

From its inception, Laboratory One was considered critical to the KGB and the Soviet Union. By November 1930, Nikolay Yezhov, known as "The Poison Dwarf" because of his four-foot-eleven stature and his special skill with poisons, was placed in charge of the "Special Department."[18] Later by 1937, Yezhov's successes were great enough that he too was promoted to head of the entire Soviet security apparatus. Even among thugs famous as a group for their cruelty, the Poison Dwarf was legendary for his joy in inflicting pain, conducting many tortures himself as a form of recreation and relaxation.

Nikolay Bukharin (a friend of Stalin, later executed by him[19]) wrote of the Poison Dwarf:

> In the whole of my [long] life, I had to meet few people who by their nature were as repellant as Yezhov. Watching him, I am frequently reminded of those evil boys . . . whose favorite form of entertainment was to light a piece of paper tied to the

tail of a cat drenched with kerosene and relish in watching the cat scamper down the street in maddening horror unable to rid itself of the flames that get closer and closer. I have no doubt that Yezhov utilized this type of entertainment in childhood and he continues to do that in a different form in a different field at present.[20]

In the 1920s and 1930s, with Yagoda's expertise and the Poison Dwarf's sadistic joy and ruthlessness, Laboratory One was fully staffed with accomplished and experienced murderers who were kept busy, night and day.

Purge of Lab One

In the late 1930s, as he would again in the early 1950s, Stalin determined to bury his crimes by sealing the lips of his accomplices. He liquidated virtually the entire top echelon of the security organs and Lab One in 1938, moving in new executioners and scientists to run the lab. Only at the 1938 show trials of top KGB officials did the first information of any kind on the ultra-secret poison lab become known.[21] KGB officials were accused of using poisons—a charge which was certainly true—but they were not allowed to testify that it was at Stalin's direction.[22] They were then condemned to death. Not only were the defendants like Yagoda (and later the Poison Dwarf) executed, but their wives, parents, brothers, sisters, and in-laws also went to their deaths, just in case something might have been shared with them. The execution of the executioners wiped out the only witnesses to hundreds of poisonings.

Not satisfied with simply executing the Lab One poisoners and their families down to the most remote relatives, Stalin directed their removal from history itself. Thus, many photographs were airbrushed to remove images of meetings with Stalin, award ceremonies, conferences, and the like. They became ghosts of history. A famous example is a photograph of Stalin, Vyacheslav Molotov, and the Poison Dwarf walking alongside the White Sea–Baltic Canal; the Dwarf was later erased from the picture, and his silhouette filled in with the water of the canal where so many had perished.[23]

Lab One Testing

After the liquidations, Grigory Mairanovsky was among the new crew of poisoners secretly brought in to staff the lab and other Soviet experimental facilities. He was a chemist who had survived the 1938 purge, and he remained in charge of the lab until 1952 when he was arrested by Nikita Khrushchev, probably to testify against others. After serving a prison sentence following Stalin's death, Mairanovsky (who directly mixed and delivered poisons for various executions) petitioned for the return of his pension and medals for rendering meritorious, if secret, service to his country by following orders to poison "many dozens of sworn enemies, including nationalists of all types (including Jewish)."[24] Even his subordinates were shocked at his "bestial sadistic treatment" of the birdies.[25] His notes of experiments, which mention approvingly that one prisoner was unable to shout or move while dying in "excruciating pain," could only have been written by someone devoid of any natural human empathy.[26]

Until the death of Stalin, the activities of Lab One and its associated facilities were almost totally unknown to the West. By the late 1920s, Laboratory One and a related bacteriological poison lab operated in the Urals were the most sophisticated poison facilities of their day. They devised poisons such as ricin, which mimicks respiratory diseases; warfarin which kills through anti-coagulation, causing an internal bleed-out; potassium, causing heart failure; and a variety of other poisons causing or mimicking natural conditions, as well as various infections. As a secret 1964 CIA report notes, the KGB had secretly used a large variety of poisons and infections to cause what they called "staged natural deaths."[27]

The Executioners—Sharks Eating Sharks

The secrecy required for the poisonings and infections required the formation of a special unit for the actual delivery and field use of poisons called "Special Tasks." This unit was in operation in Moscow by the early 1920s with two objectives: the elimination of people within Russia in cases that required secrecy, and the elimination outside Russia of "White Russian Émigrés" and others whose existence was inconvenient or troublesome to Stalin.[28] Immediately after their seizure of power, the Communists, like the Nazis, were at first content to allow many opponents to flee into exile.[29] As competence slowly vanished, borders were closed by 1925, and émigrés who did not return after 1927 were treated as traitors, subject to execution wherever located.

As with the first leaders of Lab One, virtually all of Special Tasks would be executed by Stalin in the late 1930s to forever distance the dear leader and Soviet leadership from their crimes. The effect of these executions, and their intent, was to hide forever the particulars of the massive poisonings and infections of the 1920s and 1930s.

Activities of the late 1930s and thereafter are not so well protected. There were survivors like Pavel Sudoplatov, a key planner of the ice pick murder of Trotsky, as well as a variety of murders in Western Europe in the late 1930s.[30] Sudoplatov survived long imprisonment to write a 1994 tell-all book in his old age which broke the KGB veil of secrecy, disclosing Laboratory One and some of the poisonings they facilitated.[31] Additionally, during the brief period of Russian freedom, scholars like Vadim Birstein (with the help of Russian refuseniks) gained access to documents quickly sealed once Putin gained control.[32]

CHAPTER EIGHT

Strange Deaths at Home and Abroad

The Mysterious Death of Lenin

Vladimir Lenin, the undisputed leader of Russia, revered with Karl Marx by Communists everywhere as the fathers of their new religion, went from Stalin's indispensable patron to an inconvenient obstacle to absolute power. On August 30, 1918, Lenin was shot twice—once in the shoulder and once in the chest, allegedly by a fellow leftist named Fanny Kaplan. Although the bullets in Lenin did not match Kaplan's gun, she quickly confessed to the shooting under terrible torture and likewise confessed she had unnamed accomplices. However, even under brutal torture, she supposedly refused to name them. Inexplicably, instead of interrogating Kaplan further to learn the names of her coconspirators (as the Bolsheviks did many times skillfully using exhaustion and torture), four days later the Communists changed their "law" reinstating capital punishment and dispatched Fanny Kaplan with the customary bullet in the back of the head, followed quickly by cremation at an unknown site.

It was out of character for the regime to fail to extract the names of either her actual co-conspirators or at least a falsified confession incriminating someone. Instead, Soviet leadership blamed French and British "agents" for the assassination attempt, immediately executing more than eight hundred political opponents. Many thousands of such "agents" would go on to suffer the same fate.

The wounds seriously disabled Lenin and nearly ended his life. To recover, he moved to a large dacha about six miles outside of Moscow. The dacha had been formerly owned by a high-level tsarist police general. It would later be the place of other strange deaths including that of writer Maxim Gorky. Since the mysterious death of Yakov Sverdlov, Stalin had become Lenin's right hand, controlling all access to the leader. He officed directly in Lenin's dacha.[1] Stalin used his control of communication with the weakened Lenin to build a powerful political machine of alliances to himself. Lenin's wife, Nadezhda Krupskaya, was the only person other than Stalin who could boast of unfettered access to Lenin. She was a tall, thin woman who shared not only Lenin's bed, but also his imprisonment and exile. Lenin and communism were her two great loves.

Lenin's rehabilitation was slow; he had to learn to substitute his left arm and hand for writing and other tasks that his useless right arm could no longer perform. As Lenin improved, he became very concerned with Stalin's accretion of power. Initially, Lenin had prized Stalin for his ruthlessness, calling him in 1921 "our nutcracker."[2] By 1922, however, Lenin realized he was in a cage with a lion and secretly dictated to his wife Krupskaya a last testament now called "Lenin's Testament" to the Communist Party. In it he warned the party and Russia of Stalin's ruthless power-grab and asked that Stalin be removed from all positions of power.[3] Lenin intended to present the testament when his condition improved either to an All-Union Congress of Soviets to be held in January 1924, or later at the Communist Party's meeting scheduled for June 1924. Stalin somehow learned of the testament and ensured it remained secret. After dictating the testament to his wife, Lenin had the third of three strokes that would leave him unable to speak for a time. But as 1923 rolled forward, Lenin again began to recover. Stalin reported to his cohorts on the Presidium that Lenin had asked Stalin to poison him, but that he had refused Lenin's request.[4]

By December 1923, Lenin was well enough to go hunting. Over the next two months, it was clear that it was not only animals that Lenin was stalking, but Stalin himself. Lenin was reaching around Stalin to reinvigorate his leadership. He showed those he came into contact with that he was able to talk and smile, and let it be known that he looked forward to returning to his duties.

On January 21, 1924, Lenin appeared in Gorki, near Moscow, where the next day he was to address the All-Union Congress and read his testament condemning Stalin. Before that could happen, Lenin suffered a set of violent convulsions. He collapsed and quit breathing. No effort at resuscitation could revive him.[5] Lenin was dead at fifty-three. While Lenin had serious, ongoing health problems—including hardening of the arteries in his brain and treated syphilis—none of these would cause seizures or convulsions, nor account for his strange death. In a matter of hours, Lenin went from talking and laughing to dying from lung failure and seizures. Lenin did not smoke; he was only an occasional, social drinker; and he often exercised. Forensic analysis by contemporary medical science affirms that strokes are not preceded by seizures.[6]

Lenin's death was announced one day later to the Congress, accompanied by much wailing, particularly by an apparently grief-stricken Stalin. He proposed, in effect, deification of Lenin, having his body quickly embalmed and preserved in a mausoleum, and erecting statues of Lenin in all Russian cities. This, of course, anticipated Stalin's later campaign to deify himself while still alive. Lenin's widow, Krupskaya, spoke powerfully in opposition to Stalin's deification campaign, arguing it violated everything Lenin believed in. She wanted the funds used for schools and hospitals, not statues. Krupskaya said that as a true revolutionary, Lenin often expressed his wishes to be buried in his family's simple plot without an exaggerated ceremony. She would ultimately pay a price for that speech. Krupskaya was massively out-voted, and the

Stalin era was launched with Lenin's promotion to divinity, along with his fellow living deity, Stalin. Stalin delivered Lenin's eulogy, which was followed by a series of, "We promise you Lenin" on each "command [from the late leader]," with an emphasis on the imperial "we." After the massive funeral in freezing weather during which Stalin both delivered the principal eulogy and acted as lead pallbearer, Lenin's embalmed body was placed on display in a mausoleum on Red Square. It was upon that mausoleum that Stalin would later review Red Square parades—literally over the body of the man who sought to oust "the nutcracker." And for a time many years later, Stalin's own embalmed body would be placed next to that of Lenin in a strange Soviet Valhalla.

Lenin's testament was largely suppressed in Russia until 1956, when Khrushchev read it to the Twentieth Party Congress. In May 1925, Krupskaya managed to deliver copies of it to the Presidium of Russia's leaders and to the West. The Presidium arranged that it be read secretly and then hidden. Verbatim texts of the testament appeared in the *New York Times* in 1925–26 but were denounced as forgeries.[7] In the 1930s, when Stalin had completely seized power in Russia, all those still alive and familiar with Lenin's final days and his testament suddenly and largely inexplicably died—Lenin's wife, brother, and sister—with Krupskaya, ever the brave revolutionary, claiming before her death that she too would be poisoned by Stalin. As would later happen to Stalin's poisoners themselves, the inconvenient conveniently died.

A symposium on the cause of Lenin's death was held in 2012 with doctors and Russian historians at the University of Maryland.[8] The conclusion was that Lenin's death could not be explained by his physical ailments. Physicians tried in the 1938 Purge testified that they had intentionally, but secretly, maltreated Lenin to cause his death—all concealed from Stalin in the adjoining room. The rapid embalming of Lenin's body at Stalin's direction would destroy all possible evidence, making it impossible to know with certainty whether Lenin was poisoned by Stalin, but the scholars at the University of Maryland concluded that it was a likely possibility.[9] Trotsky certainly believed that

Lenin was poisoned at Stalin's direction.[10] While Lenin's rapid mummification precluded further study, Lenin's brain amazingly has been preserved in Room 19 of the Moscow Brain Institute. To this day, Russia will not permit toxicology tests.[11]

Though hardly proof of foul play, it would be a remarkable coincidence if Lenin had died of an unknown cause on the night before he was set to present his testament denouncing Stalin. In the years ahead, Stalin's systematic efforts to poison his enemies, real and perceived, would come into full operation.[12] And a famous ballerina on her way to open a tour prohibited by Stalin would also suffer a convenient and inexplicable death.

Much of this lives on in Russia today as lore, "something everyone knows." In pre-Putin days in the Red Square's Alexander Garden, actors portrayed Lenin and Stalin in a strange resurrection.[13] For a few rubles or U.S. dollars, they would pose for a picture with tourists. The Lenin figure freely expressed his hatred of Stalin, but when asked whether he was poisoned by Stalin, he replied only with a knowing smile.

The "Natural" Deaths

The ongoing questions surrounding Lenin's death show why poisoning was such an effective way to kill. In his 1994 book, *Special Tasks*, Pavel Sudoplatov, a Russian KGB agent, discusses at length his participation in four "staged" natural deaths using poisons and infections from Laboratory One in the 1930s and 1940s.[14] A Soviet KGB defector, Walter Krivitsky, remarked that "any idiot can commit a murder, but it takes a true artist to stage a natural death."[15] Krivitsky, who predicted his murder by the KGB, was found dead shortly thereafter with a bullet in his temple and a suicide note, no doubt dictated by the KGB.[16] A secret study in 1963 by the CIA for the Warren Commission, only declassified and released in 1993, concluded that there were many apparently natural deaths staged by the KGB in Western Europe, particularly of targeted Russian émigrés.[17]

The staged natural deaths often resulted from poisons or infections, although they appeared to be heart failure or respiratory disease. They were often erroneously ruled natural deaths by medical examiners. Only later, defectors, who themselves committed the murders, revealed they were poisonings or other murders disguised as natural deaths.[18] Cleverly, the staged deaths were often specifically tailored to mimic existing, truly natural ailments already existing in the victims. For those with a coronary condition, potassium or curare made a fatal heart attack seem natural. For those who suffered from respiratory illness, anthrax mimicked respiratory death. There were poisons that also mimicked deaths of those with diabetes or tuberculosis. In the crude forensic pathology of the 1920s and 1930s, it was virtually impossible to discern such poisonings—if poison was looked for at all.[19]

One of the most spectacular and effective "natural death" deceptions would be that of a bishop in one of the Soviet Union's captive nations. As a vast war began on religion, an important obstacle was the Patriarch Tikhon who was difficult to eliminate because he was deeply beloved and a protected U.S. citizen. He died suddenly and inexplicably of heart failure in 1925 after international pressure caused his death sentence to be lifted.[20] By 1927, the bulwark gone, over 75,000 priests were executed.

Another obstacle to Stalin was "Iron Felix." The brutal founder of the KGB, Felix Dzerzhinsky, bitterly attacked Stalin in 1926. Shortly afterwards, both Iron Felix (and his taster) died suddenly of heart attacks with no prior symptoms.[21] Stalin was both a pallbearer and a eulogist, later erecting Iron Felix statues in many places.

Had the West been paying attention, details of the poison lab were revealed in the 1938 "Trial of the Twenty-One," where three doctors involved in the poison lab were accused of conspiring to poison high-level Communists. Some had actually poisoned Soviet leaders at Stalin's direction, but under pressure presented these crimes in the trial as rogue operations.[22] Like snake charmers who release a cobra only to be bitten, the executioners were executed.

The Black Baron and the White Russian Generals

By the late 1920s, the wave of convenient but inexplicable "natural" deaths spread into Western Europe and even the United States. Among the most famous victims was General Pyotr Wrangel, famously known as the Black Baron. Named for the black uniform he usually wore, Wrangel was among Russia's greatest heroes in World War One, winning Russia's few victories against the Austrians while commanding Cossack units. Leading his units against Austrian machine guns, the Black Baron won history's last cavalry charge victories against well-armed opponents—reminiscent of the last stand of the samurai, sword against gun, at Shiroyama in 1877. As cavalry men throughout history were apt to do, the Black Baron combined courage with panache to concoct a romantic legend.

In the Revolution, Wrangel joined the Whites—but only after the Reds had sought to kill his family. He was arguably the most successful and loved of all the White commanders and might have prevailed over the Bolsheviks had he been installed earlier. His fame was ensured when he became the last White Russian to leave Russia, refusing to embark until all his men were rescued and on board. The grudging respect the Reds held for him was commemorated in the marching anthem of the Red Army celebrating their victory over the Black Baron, "White Army, Black Baron."[23] It remains a favorite song of the Russian Army today.

After the defeat of the Whites, many of those who escaped gathered in Paris expecting that the Red regime would collapse in a few months. The Black Baron did the same. Wrangel was clearly the leading expatriate target for Stalin, not just for what he represented but for his effective leadership of the resistance abroad. Wrangel and his family narrowly avoided being on his yacht when it was rammed by an Italian steamer on a journey that had originated from a Soviet port. Unable to kill the Black Baron in an accident, Stalin turned to the secret Soviet tools of Laboratory One. Wrangel predicted his death in his autobiography, writing that the KGB would soon poison him in a disguised "natural" death.[24] And true to form, a stranger posing as a Russian refugee eventually came and stayed with the Wrangel family as a butler at their home in Brussels. Not long after, the Black Baron, previously in robust health, developed severe respiratory problems that swiftly took his life. The "butler" quickly disappeared; all efforts to validate the background of this phantom failed. The Wrangels and most observers were certain the Black Baron was murdered in a staged natural death. There would be no final charge across the steppes. He would live only in the Red Army's song celebrating victory over him, which failed to mention that Wrangel was not felled by a bullet or sword, but by poison.

Wrangel's successor in Paris was General Alexander Kutepov, until he suddenly disappeared on January 26, 1930.[25] He remained a missing person of uncertain fate for more than sixty years until information of his secret poisoning by the KGB during a botched kidnapping finally surfaced.[26] The next putative head of the White Russians was General Yevgeny Miller, who likewise disappeared in Paris in 1937. He was a missing person for sixty years until the 1990s when Soviet records revealed that he had been drugged and secretly brought to the Lubyanka, where he was tortured and executed.[27] There are few sadder documents than the undelivered letters held for sixty years in Miller's secret file, written by Miller to his wife and children, which his jailers falsely promised to deliver.

Murder in Paris was not always with poisons simulating a natural death. On occasion, it was important to make a murder a learning experience for opponents of the regime. Thus on May 25, 1926, Symon Petliura, first president of Democratic Ukraine, was gunned down on a Paris street as a flagrant warning.[28] Many attacks followed in Paris, sometimes open and sometimes secret. Shortly before Pavlova's final return to Paris, on December 7, 1930, the first president of Democratic Georgia, Noe Ramishvili, was murdered at the specific direction of Stalin.[29] Like Petliura, he was gunned down in a gruesome killing in daylight on a large Paris boulevard. It was a lesson that did not intimidate Anna Pavlova, who continued with her plans for a 1931 tour in Eastern Europe, despite Soviet efforts to discourage and even prevent it.

Any study of the records of the Russian émigré community would contain one story after another of similar mysterious deaths and disappearances. Émigrés like Pavlova and Diaghilev saw their friends drop dead at an alarming rate, and many shared Pavlova's belief that a "Sword of Damocles" hung over her head.[30] In Russia and the West, Stalin's mass murder campaign accelerated from the 1920s up until the outbreak of World War II, with the dictator dealing death to people in Russia and Europe almost at random. His victims were as diverse as Yevgeny Zamyatin, one of the greatest early science-fiction writers; Nikolai Koltsov, biologist and zoologist; Boris Savinkov, politician; and Andreas Pavley, ballet director, who leapt or was thrown out of a sixteenth-story hotel window in Chicago.[31] Prince Vasilchikov, Alexander Guchkov, and many others experienced quick, inexplicable, and convenient deaths, particularly in Paris in the late 1920s to late 1930s.[32]

A secret CIA study on Soviet assassinations written in 1964 was finally released in 1993.[33] The study had been prepared and secretly delivered to the Warren Commission in 1964 and remained sealed for thirty years. The CIA concluded that a "long list" of Russian émigrés (some not yet known) perceived as potential threats had been assassinated with Russian involvement, concealed, and usually recorded wrongly as natural deaths. After efforts to lure the targets back to Russia or otherwise neutralize them failed, they would be eliminated, many by poison designed to conceal the true cause of their deaths and to mimic natural deaths caused by prior diseases. According to the CIA, the devil's brew of poisons included arsenic, potassium, cyanide, warfarin, scopolamine, thallium, chloral hydrate, paraldehyde, and barbiturates.

Unlike Nero, Genghis Khan, or Robespierre, who openly gloried in the public infliction of death, Stalin, like Hitler, killed largely out of sight, except when an object lesson was deemed valuable.[34] Stalin increasingly turned to secret assassinations with poison to eliminate his victims, especially when dealing with enemies abroad.

CHAPTER NINE

Stalin, Music, and Ballet

Controlling All Songs

Stalin held a great interest in music from his early days. Evidence of his interest in and striving for control of all music can be found in his treatment of the Kobzars in Ukraine in 1930. Marx and Lenin were materialists who concerned themselves with the control of the means of production and the levers of power. Stalin's doctrine of cultural hegemony (often identified today with Antonio Gramsci, who popularized cultural Marxism for the world) goes much further than class warfare and control.[1] Stalin realized that to have the ultimate power, it was necessary to utilize all aspects of culture. Even words themselves had to be enlisted to serve the state. Thus, disapproved words like "God" or historical events that did not serve Communist aims were to disappear from the human mind. A Soviet-period joke relates "the future is certain, but the past is unpredictable." Art for art's sake or its own beauty must be brought under the yoke of the state or be eliminated. Forms of art which glorified the old world must eventually be destroyed. Along with religion, the notion of poets like Keats that truth is beauty and beauty is truth was seen as simply chaining man to capitalistic slavery. It was as important to control the songs, dance, and films as it was to make the laws. In this way, the party and the state (and Stalin) would gain total control of all aspects of life—even the mind of man.

In common with brother megalomaniacs such as Nero (a musician) and Hitler (a painter), Stalin was a frustrated artist of somewhat limited talent. He had an enthusiastic singing voice and a gift for poetry. For this reason, as well as his belief in cultural hegemony, he was consumed with both subjects. Stalin frequently attended the ballet and opera and was a prolific reader of fiction and poetry. He was also the modern period's greatest murderer of poets, writers, and those involved in music. Few of these survived who did not consent to becoming cowardly sycophants—and even debasement did not guarantee survival.[2] To be defiant or even insufficiently worshipful meant certain death. The only question was whether the writer, poet, or musician (and sometimes his entire family) would disappear, have his suicide staged, or be executed.[3]

The gifted poet Sergei Yesenin, after being denounced by the Soviets in 1925, was found hanged with a suicide note. Strangely, his face appeared beaten.[4] Vladimir Mayakovsky, whom Stalin would later rehabilitate five years after his death as the "greatest poet of our times," supposedly shot himself after he was denounced and his poetry barred.[5] However, two shots were heard, and the bullets used did not match the poet's gun. Likewise, the greatest poets of Georgia—Stalin's homeland—were executed or forced to commit suicide.[6] Beginning in 1930, about one-third of all Georgian musicians and writers were killed. Likewise, in 1930, the slaughter of writers and musicians began in Ukraine. By 1938, over 83 percent of these artists had been killed.[7] The slaughter beginning in 1930 in Belarus was so profound that October 29 is annually commemorated as the "Night of the Executed Poets" through poetry readings of the deceased poets throughout the night.[8]

The murder of those involved in music continues to be a psychic scar for the people of Ukraine. In that country, the folk music of Ukraine was largely performed by itinerant traveling performers called Kobzars, many blind, who for generations sang folk songs while playing an instrument called a kobza or bandurka, somewhat like a mandola or guitar. The wooden, stringed instruments had been carried on the steppes of Ukraine by the Kobzars for hundreds of years. This music, much like American country music, incorporated the history of Ukraine, from religious songs to the heroic adventures of the Don Cossacks. In their songs, the defiant hero Yermak still explored Siberia and the anthems of Cossacks still echoed across the vast steppes. These singers of the steppes carried on a wandering minstrel tradition of telling epic stories of great loves and tragic wars.

In late 1930 at Stalin's direction, these bards were summoned to a Congress ostensibly to form a workers' union and incorporate their songs into the revolution. They were to be fêted by the Soviet leadership. Three hundred fifty Kobzars came. There was no Congress, no meeting. They were taken instead to a killing field and massacred by Soviet agents.[9] To maintain secrecy, the remains of the three hundred fifty singers were thrown in a common trench. The Bolsheviks then denied any knowledge of their whereabouts. Thereafter, on pain of death, Kobzars, their songs, and even their musical instruments were prohibited.[10]

With a single stroke, Stalin wiped out centuries of a rich storytelling musical culture, their ancient songs no longer echoing on the windy steppes of Ukraine. Stalin continued to act on the belief that poetry and song are supremely effective methods of communication and inspiration. If there was any doubt as to Stalin's determination to control the culture and music of Russia and his ruthlessness in doing so, it surely lies buried with the bones, instruments, and ancient songs of the Kobzars in a secret mass grave in Ukraine.

Controlling All Dance

From the revolution on, Stalin's interest in the political possibilities of the ballet also grew as propaganda grew. When Lenin proposed abolishing ballet in Soviet Russia in 1921 as a decadent pursuit of the rich, it was Stalin's voice that proved decisive in saving it, although in a much degraded form.[11] This reflected both Stalin's inherent love of music and his deep belief that ballet, like music or altered history, properly yoked, could be used as a weapon for the Communist state. Stalin maintained a box overlooking the stage at the Bolshoi in Moscow, often sent roses to performers, and sometimes directly intervened in performances.[12] The ballerina Olga Lepeshinskaya and several others were rumored to be Stalin's mistresses. Olga was as notable for her fierce communism and official contacts as for her more limited talent. As Stalin's favorite, she was cast in a sequence of leading roles. This caused the great Soviet ballerina Maya Plisetskaya (often compared to the earlier Pavlova, yet described as being similar in her dance style to "a bomb going off") to confirm how deeply Olga and the NKVD were feared in the Stalinist ballet world where so many victims went missing.[13] Olga later married the chief interrogator of the MGB counterintelligence agency, with Stalin's permission, and then later divorced him as an enemy of the people when he was purged by Stalin. In post-Stalin tours of the West, Olga would be left behind in Moscow.

In 1924, Alexander Gorsky finished producing at the Bolshoi politically incorrect revivals of the Petipa ballets like *Swan Lake*. He was dispatched to an insane asylum where he died of unknown causes. Later in 1948, Leonty, a director of the Bolshoi, prepared a ballet commemorating the 1918 Revolution, which angered Stalin. Leonty died two days later of the unlikely, but familiar, "heart attack." Adrian Piotrovsky was among the most talented Soviet ballet writers and adaptors. He famously helped to create Prokofiev's *Romeo and Juliet*, but after his work fell into disfavor, he was shot in the Lubyanka on Stalin's orders in 1937. The torture and murder of Vsevolod Meyerhold, who helped shape modern theater, was a commonplace finale in Moscow music, theater, and ballet. Successive waves of irrational persecution for such crimes as "formalism" and "lack of meaning" made it difficult or impossible to craft inspiring ballet. Work on *Romeo and Juliet* could result in a quick death sentence by Stalin, who sat in a box at the Bolshoi and could deal death like an emperor with a thumbs down to disfavored performers or directors.

Although Soviet ballet would eventually produce gifted performers like Maya Plisetskaya, Mikhail Baryshnikov, Rudolf Nureyev, and composers like Sergei Prokofiev, who heeded Stalin's invitation to return, from 1920–1931 it was clearly far cruder than the performances staged by Diaghilev at the Ballet Russes and by Anna Pavlova. The world continued to look to them, rather than to the Bolshoi, as the heart of ballet.

Being sidelined as an inferior producer did not sit well with a dictator who recognized the great power of culture over the minds of men. To Stalin, as we've seen, control over the means of production advocated by Marx and Engel was not nearly enough. To control thought, it was necessary to control language, music, art, history and culture. Art for art's sake, for Stalin, was a sacrilege and a threat to his crude vision of the arts as simply a horse-team leading humanity to state allegiance. Diaghilev and Anna Pavlova, with no material power or armies, were nonetheless the sort of troublemakers who could stimulate minds and stir hearts. The images of Diaghilev and Pavlova flying free and celebrated throughout the world were infuriating to Stalin, a living insult—and therefore a threat—to his slave empire.

Stalin not only saw ballet as a tool of Soviet power. He likely felt that association with ballet might add a certain artistic patina to his crude exterior. In the twenties, before the full extent of his butchery was known, Stalin was often thought of as the clownish tin pot dictator portrayed by the Marx Brothers in the 1933 movie *Duck Soup*. Something of the early poet still lived in Stalin. Perhaps a flicker of artistic spirit still existed in his cruel, dead heart. His association with art would convey a certain panache. However, classical ballet romanticized the Old Russia that Stalin sought to destroy. There was no room in the new Russia for *The Nutcracker* or *Prince Charming* or the other Christian or traditional symbols. Like the destruction of old statues and symbols, the destruction of the old ballet and its replacement with Marxist ballet was a logical step toward erasing the Old Russia from memory.

Until the death of Lenin in 1924, the Soviets generally allowed travel to the West. Many great composers, such as Igor Stravinsky, and choreographers, such as Mikhail Fokine, made one-way trips. With the death of Lenin and the ascension of Stalin, what Churchill later famously called "the Iron Curtain" descended, and escape was difficult. By 1927, Stalin made it a capital offense to leave Russia without permission or to fail to return when summoned.[14]

The Missing Ballerina

One of the most famous early incidents of the Iron Curtain's closing involved the legendary "Gone Girl" of ballet, Lidia Ivanova, a remarkably talented young ballerina scheduled to tour Europe with four others, including George Balanchine, in early July 1924.[15] They did not intend to return. On June 14, 1924, Lidia went on a boating outing at the invitation of four Communist soldiers. She was never seen again. They claimed she was lost in a boating accident, but her body was never found. The story was believed by practically no one. The incident occurred after Stalin's succession and marked the beginning of what would become a slaughter of Russian artists, poets, and musical performers. It demonstrated that even a young dancer was not immune to the thugs of the state.[16] Staged deaths occurred even to ballerinas.

Ivanova was much beloved by George Balanchine, the legendary choreographer who planned to leave Russia with her and who left after her death. After working with the Ballet Russes in Paris, he co-founded the New York City Ballet, won the Presidential Medal of Freedom, and became one of the most important figures in ballet. Although much jaded by time and events, Ivanova's death haunted him, and he was still deeply saddened more than fifty years later while recalling the story of her death in 1979.[17] He commemorated her in the most appropriate of ways. At the conclusion of his much beloved *Serenade*, the dancers gather to lift up a ballerina, who arches her back up as if rising to heaven.[18]

Meanwhile, Stalin looked West at Diaghilev and Pavlova. Sjeng Scheijen's biography *Diaghilev* chronicles the Soviet efforts led by Soviet Minister of Culture Lunacharsky to lure Diaghilev back to Russia and then to pressure him to return. He recounts Diaghilev's unsuccessful efforts to placate Stalin by staging in the West a pro-Soviet ballet with crude Communist-inspired librettos of love in a factory with hammers sounding the score.[19] After a series of unsuccessful meetings in Paris with Diaghilev in 1925–26, Lunancharsky returned to Russia empty-handed and wrote an article condemning Diaghilev as an elitist catering to the wealthy and a class enemy of the Soviet people.[20]

There was never any real chance of Diaghilev's returning to a Stalinist Russia. Word had arrived in Paris of the enslavement of the Mariinsky to Bolshevik idealogy. Diaghilev, the freest of free spirits, who embraced over and over the different and unconventional, would never willingly have entered the vast Stalinist slave camp which Russia had become. To paraphrase his idol Pushkin, Diaghilev was not born to amuse Stalin.

With the article, certainly written with the advance approval of Stalin, the screws began to turn on both Diaghilev and Pavlova. Diaghilev's brothers, Valentin and Yuri, disappeared in Russia, their fates unknown for many years.[21] In response to inquiries from the French government, the Soviet foreign minister falsely reported that Russia had no record of any arrest, nor any idea at all of the whereabouts of the missing Diaghilevs. In fact, Valentin, who had actually fought as a member of the Red Army for the Bolsheviks, was imprisoned in Solovki Prison Camp. His 1927 booking picture there, which surfaced after sixty years as a missing person, reflects a particularly poignant, quizzical expression.

Pavlova's mother, missing for a decade, suddenly reappeared in London in 1924. She was unable to secure Pavlova's return to Russia and was unwilling to stay in England. After her 1926 return to Russia without Pavlova in tow, she was never again seen in the West.[22] Her fate is still unknown.

Pavlova had tried to maintain some connection to her homeland. She created a foundation in Russia to aid needy ballerinas. In 1929 she learned from newspaper accounts while on tour in Australia that her foundation had been seized and its funds given to the Red Army since she had been declared an enemy of the Soviet people by the Soviet government.[23] The beloved ballerina was a most unequal and unlikely enemy for a large totalitarian nation-state. The action of the Soviets was condemned by newspapers and public figures all over the world. It became clear to the Soviets that the next actions against the popular Pavlova must be taken in secret so as to avoid the public condemnation they had already received. And the Soviets would surely move against Pavlova for outshining Stalin's crude ballet, consorting with the Romanovs, and refusing Stalin's "invitation" to return.[24]

CHAPTER TEN

Into the Storm

After 1927, Diaghilev and Pavlova each faced a critical decision—to become whimpering sycophants glorifying Stalin (as so many others did) and flee his rage, or to stand against him to preserve the integrity of their art and their belief in human freedom. One artist was flamboyant and fond of spectacle and surrealism. The other was orthodox but impassioned with a mission to evangelize the world with her art.

Despite their differences, they shared a courage and a sincere devotion to artistic freedom. Such courage was second-nature to Diaghilev, who spent a lifetime defying the crowd: he was an openly gay man in a homophobic world, rejecting conventional morality and limits on art. Pavlova was always the courageous ballerina devoted to ideals drawn from Christianity, classical art, and Old Russia, whether calling a strike of the Imperial Ballet for justice, performing Petipa's great creations, or dancing in a bullring in the middle of a violent revolution.

La Chatte

After Lunacharsky's failed efforts in 1926 to woo Diaghilev back to Russia with various promises, Stalin had the impresario declared a class enemy in Russia. Diaghilev, even with his family members' lives in the balance, did not change anything at all to placate Stalin or curry his favor. There was no ballet of "The Great Leader" or even symbolic red-flower dancers defeating white-flower dancers. By the time the strange deaths of Pyotr Wrangel and others became conspicuous in 1928, Diaghilev was continuing to produce exactly the ballets Stalin had hated, such as the epic *La Chatte*. This was the story of a cat who became a woman and then a cat again, anticipating somewhat the poetry of T. S. Eliot converted into the play *Cats* by Andrew Lloyd Webber many years later. It featured revolutionary art, designs, costumes, and choreography by a largely new group of gathered geniuses. But it did nothing to advance Stalin's objectives. It was art for art's sake with a dollop of bourgeois spectacle—purely antithetical to Stalin's Russia.

Diaghilev's season in Paris in 1928, followed by a successful London season, may have been the high point of his fame. His work in this period did not match the earlier epic ballets, but he achieved the height of recognition for the twenty-year-life of his Ballet Russes, along with artists such as Chanel, Balanchine, Chirico, Prokofiev, and Stravinsky and legendary dancers participating in the productions. In 1928, Diaghilev also committed Pavlova's ultimate sin by presenting a performance at the birthday party of Stalin's greatest enemy, the last real Romanov pretender. As he had so often done to conventional moralists with his lifestyle, and to the critics with his unconventional ballets, he was directly challenging Stalin's right to restrict his artistic freedom. It was a challenge that tempted an answer on behalf of Stalin by the Yasha Gang.

Pavlova in Peril

After the 1929 seizure of her foundation in Saint Petersburg for poor ballerinas and her condemnation in Russia, it was surely clear to Pavlova that she faced a major decision. She could return to a tour of performances in Europe where Stalin clearly did not want her or she could stay in the United States where she was much loved by the public and her friends like Mary Pickford, Douglas Fairbanks, and Charlie Chaplin. At Pickford's request, she even made a short test film, likely for the many offers from Hollywood she received. She could again tour South America, where she was loved from Buenos Aires to Bogotá. But instead, she returned to Europe where Stalin tried to prevent her 1930 tour through Soviet Ambassador Kollontai and others—word of which surely came to Pavlova. In the fall of 1930, she again had to decide whether to tour safer places with a U.S., South American, or even Far East tour, or to defy Stalin with another European tour.

She chose to defy Stalin in his backyard.

For the ballerina who laid the funeral wreath for artistic freedom in 1906 and defied death threats to dance before 32,000 in the Plaza de Toros in Mexico City, there was really no choice at all. Her 1931 tour would again be in Europe, but this time it would go to the very border of Stalin's slave empire. She would dance in Poland and other formerly Russian territories.[1] Prince Charming would kiss Sleeping Beauty, and the White Swan and her lover would dance as close to the Mariinsky as possible. With millions being murdered in Russia and death being freely dealt by the Yasha Gang in Paris, she realized the danger this tour schedule involved, but went ahead disregarding danger as she always did.

On her last night in Cannes on January 11, 1931, she stopped at the grave of her friend, the last Romanov pretender, before beginning her final trip to Paris. We do not know what prayers she uttered or what words she actually said over the grave. She certainly remembered that long-ago night in 1914 at the Mariinsky when she promised Nicholas to return there and dance *The Dying Swan*. Perhaps, among whatever prayers she said, she whispered her intention to redeem that promise as nearly as she could by going as close to Saint Petersburg as possible. Perhaps she sensed that this trip would be the last flight of the Dying Swan.

Bend, Hide, or Die

Beginning in 1928, Russia entered a more violent period, which Marxist historians characterize as the Cultural Revolution of 1928–31.[2] Much like the Great Cultural Revolution of 1966–71 in China, which mimicked it and itself killed tens of millions, the ostensible purpose in Russia was to ensure the absolute hegemony and command of the proletariat and its increasingly deified representative. Stalin strove to preside over all aspects of art history and culture. Every feature of life would either bend to Stalin's view of the needs of the proletarian revolution or be destroyed. As in China, Russia's cultural revolution occurred with both mass executions or disappearances of some, and the shameful surrender and obsequence of others. The "Revolution" logically involved eliminating anyone antithetical to the revolution and represented Russia abroad. Bend, hide, or die.

CHAPTER ELEVEN

Death of the Ballet Russes

"A thing of beauty is a joy forever:
Its loveliness increases; it will never
Pass into nothingness, but will still keep...."[1]
—John Keats, *Endymion*

The first to fall was Sergei Diaghilev. Diaghilev's nephews were arrested and executed, though their fate was unknown for many years. Sergei's brother Yari was exiled to a remote camp in Asia, his exact fate still unknown. Valentin, for whom Diaghilev had great affection, was arrested in 1927. By 1928, both of his brothers (and their wives) had been secretly arrested, apparently for being related to an enemy of the state, and Diaghilev himself publicly denounced by Soviet Minister Lunacharsky on behalf of the Soviet state. Inquiries as to the whereabouts of Valentin Diaghilev, Yari, and their wives were futile. The Soviet Foreign Minister said there was "no record" of them or their arrests. They had become non-persons.

While the Ballet Russes hit the height of recognition in the 1928–29 season, Diaghilev struggled emotionally with the disappearance of his family. In late March, he gave a charity gala for a Romanov heir—Grand Duke Mikhail Mikhailovich, who would die soon after from a sudden and convenient "flu." Pavlova also attended and danced at the duke's birthday party. This was dangerous conduct, given Stalin's hatred for the Romanov heir. The 1929 season through the early summer in London was among the most successful of the Ballet Russes.

The last great ballet of the Ballet Russes was *The Prodigal Son*, scored by Sergei Prokofiev, that brilliant composer first made famous by his association with the Ballet Russes after his discovery by Diaghilev. The Christian theme was hardly endearing to Stalin, particularly coming from Diaghilev, himself a prodigal son who refused to return home. In the strange symmetry, Prokofiev would later return to the Soviet Union and die on the same day as Stalin, March 5, 1953. Diaghilev's death was far more imminent.

Following a trip to Paris, Diaghilev went to Venice with friends. There he experienced raging fever over a five-day period and died. The great impresario's death was officially attributed to "blood poisoning" from recurrent boils on his stomach that didn't heal because of his diabetes.[2] With his family missing and seized by the Soviets and Diaghilev condemned in Russia as a class enemy, a coincidental, sudden, and convenient blood poisoning may have killed him.[3] This has been the generally accepted verdict on his death.

Stalin later tried unsuccessfully to torture and perhaps eliminate Russia's greatest woman poet, Anna Akhmatova, by similarly imprisoning or executing those whom she loved—her son, ex-husband, husband, fellow poets, and friends. This only resulted in Akhmatova's writing greater poems of Gulag witness and sadness such as *Requiem*. In Diaghilev's case, the loss of his entire Russian family, including the disappearance of his beloved brother, and wholesale condemnation in his own land as an enemy of Russia, might have hastened his death, given his other ailments.

But there is a great deal of evidence that Diaghilev did not die of natural causes. After condemning Diaghilev as an enemy of the people, Stalin had a motive to arrange for his death. With the Uncle Yasha Ring in Paris and the sophisticated poisons of Laboratory One, Stalin had assembled the means to carry out the murder secretly and without a trace. Many of the bioweapons then in the Soviet arsenal—like tularemia—would have produced or closely mimicked Diaghilev's symptoms. Hosting a birthday party for the Romanov heir was a direct challenge to Stalin. And by 1929, Stalin had murdered many émigrés in Western Europe, many of whom the aforementioned CIA report noted were wrongly attributed to natural causes. The death of Diaghilev is strikingly similar to the 1978 ricin killing of Georgi Markov in London and many contemporaneous, convenient, and inexplicable deaths of Russian émigrés. These deaths, including that of Anna Pavlova, were often attributed to unknown "infections" but were later revealed to be murders.[4] Diaghilev's death fits the pattern described secretly in the 1964 CIA analysis—a rejected offer (order) to return, condemnation, and a "natural" death designed to mimic natural symptoms, but actually produced by organic or inorganic poisons.

The murderers in Yasha's Group took their secrets to the grave after their own executions. If Diaghilev was murdered, Sergey Spigelglas—master of liternoye killings—and Nahum Eitingon are the most likely suspects.

After Diaghilev's condemnation as a traitor and capitalist lackey in Russia in 1927 and his rejection of Stalin's invitation to return delivered by Lunacharsky, the impresario (as well as Pavlova) was clearly high on the KGB target list, along with the remaining White Russian generals and Romanov survivors. Diaghilev and Pavlova were in particular peril because Stalin, who saw threats to his rule and survival at every turn, feared they would engender a cultural sympathy that would lead White Russians to return with English and French military backing. Moreover, the specific attention Stalin paid them in extending "invitations" home and in interfering in their work, barring, for example, Diaghilev's planned "Art of the World" exhibition in Moscow in 1927, demonstrates the importance Stalin assigned to these great artists. Could the death of an artist already so targeted simply have been a convenient coincidence? Perhaps, but a ghost's gallery of poisoned or infected victims who appeared to have died natural deaths, and the team of liternoye murderers assembled with Yasha in Paris, suggest that the sudden, convenient death of a wanted man in the prime of his life and career was a homicide. There was motive, means, threats, and considerable circumstantial evidence of execution. On almost the same day as Diaghilev's actual death, the Soviets moved on Anna Pavlova, seizing a charity in Russia she had founded for poor ballerinas and with great fanfare declaring her an enemy of the Soviet people—an offense punishable by death. The coincidence suggested coordinated action, although Pavlova was then safely far from Europe on an Australian tour.

Additional important evidence of the high-level coordination of the killing occurred within Russia itself a few days after Sergei Diaghilev's death. His brother Valentin, a Red Army veteran, was executed at the faraway Solovki Labor Camp instead of being worked and starved to death.[5] In 1928, this particular camp had become notorious for its use of prisoners as human test subjects for poisons and infections. Valentin's fate was concealed for many years. It requires considerable belief in coincidences to think both Diaghilev brothers were not killed on Stalin's orders. The symptoms of melioidosis, weaponized at the camp when Valentin was there, closely matched his brother Sergei's death symptoms in Venice—abscesses, boils and fever.[6]

The Funeral

Diaghilev loved Venice and had spent several summers there. Many times he expressed his wish to die there like Richard Wagner and Robert Browning. As Diaghilev's condition worsened, many of his closest friends rushed to be with him. Similar to his idol, Pushkin (whose original letters he had bought and carried to Venice), Diaghilev would die penniless. His friends Coco Chanel and Misia Sert (the salon queen of Paris) paid for his funeral and burial. Like everything about Diaghilev, the procession was expertly staged. A photo from the funeral shows a large black gondola with twelve boatmen dressed in black surrounding his coffin and heading through the canals of Venice to the Island of San Michele, the historic cemetery where he would be buried. The scene resembles Charon, the ferryman of the River Styx, conveying a Grecian hero to Hades. Behind the large dark funeral gondola were a string of other black gondolas full of mourners, including Chanel, Sert, the great dancer and choreographer Serge Lifar, and many other composers, dancers, and friends. In the hands of his friends, Diaghilev's funeral was a tribute meant to serve as his last and greatest production. Although he certainly would have missed Stravinsky and others who could not attend because of time and distance, Diaghilev died like his idol Pushkin: broke, beloved, and unshackled by the world.

After Diaghilev was buried in the Greek Orthodox section of the ancient cemetery, an unusual, almost surreal nine-foot monument with a tunnel in it designed by Lifar and Chanel was added over his grave by his friends. Even now this is almost always full of flowers, ballet shoes, programs and pictures. In addition to Diaghilev's name and a Russian cross, the monument has engraved on it (at Lifar's instruction) a phrase of Diaghilev in French: *"Venice eternal inspiration of all that brings peace."*[7]

From time to time in later decades, Chanel, Lifar, and other friends, themselves then aging, gathered at his grave to remember him.[8] In 1971, more than forty years after Diaghilev's death, the great Igor Stravinsky died. He was then an old man for whom the Crazy Years of Paris were a long-ago memory. His *Rite of Spring* was now regarded as perhaps the greatest ballet and score of the twentieth century. Stravinsky's last wish was to be buried next to Diaghilev.[9] In accordance with his wishes, Stravinsky rests today a few graves down from Diaghilev at San Michelle. Flowers, ballet slippers, and photographs may often be found on his grave as well. And from time to time, in violation of the quiet, ancient cemetery's rules, but in a way Diaghilev and Stravinsky would likely approve, one can hear visitors play on their cell phones a bit of *Rite* or *Petrushka* or *Firebird*.

In his life, Diaghilev was famous for an impudent explanation of his job to King Alfonso of Spain. The king asked, since he didn't dance or compose, what did Diaghilev do? He answered, "Your Majesty, I am like you. I do not work. I do nothing, but I am indispensable."[10] In the impresario's case, it was true. After the death of Diaghilev, the Ballet Russes had fitful but failed efforts at revival in Monte Carlo, Monaco, and Paris. Diaghilev once said he devoted his life to art because it offered immortality and in this, like much else, he was right. As with Pavlova's ballet, Ballet Russes would reseed itself far and wide. Out of its death came George Balanchine in New York, Bronislava Nijinska in London and Los Angeles, and Mikhail Fokine in too many places to recount. To commemorate Fokine upon his death, around the world seventeen different ballet companies who had been influenced by him performed simultaneously the very first Ballet Russes production, *Les Sylphides*.[11] *The Firebird* still flies, and *The Rite of Spring* still comes almost every spring. While it is easy to kill a wildflower, it is quite hard to destroy all of its seeds.

While the art world mourned Diaghilev on the front pages of virtually every newspaper, in Stalinist Russia, the sole notice of any kind was a few lines on a back page in an obscure publication. With the death of Diaghilev and the Ballet Russes, the sole pillar of Russian ballet in the West was Anna Pavlova and her smaller, but brave company.

> *"Even so, one step from my grave, I believe that cruelty, spite,*
> *The powers of darkness will in time,*
> *Be crushed by the spirit of light."*
> Boris Pasternak
> *Selected Poems*[12]

CHAPTER TWELVE

Swan Song

"It seems to me you lived your life like a candle in the wind....
And I would have liked to have known you,
But I was just a kid,
Your candle burned out long before
Your legend ever did."[1]
—Elton John
Candle in the Wind, 1973

Tyrants, from Ramses confronting Moses, to Pontius Pilate interrogating Jesus, to the Afrikaners trying to bury Mandela, have always recognized the symbolic threat of a single unbroken free soul. In 1929–31, there was no greater symbol that contrasted the great legacies of Russian culture and Western freedom with Stalin's imprisoned nation than the little ballerina, Anna Pavlova.

If the Ballet Russes was fading away, the Swan herself still flew free, her photos on front pages throughout the world a daily challenge to Stalin's slave empire. She arrived in Australia in 1929, shortly before Diaghilev's unexpected death. It was then that word arrived that the Russian government had confiscated her Saint Petersburg foundation for poor ballet students, giving all its funds to the Red Army. The announced justification was that she was a tool of the rich classes and an enemy of the people. Pavlova, her husband, and the world were shocked by this bit of thuggery, as were the reporters who mobbed them on their arrival.

Notwithstanding losses occasioned by the U.S. stock market collapse of October 1929 and the onset of the Great Depression, Pavlova laid off none of the members of her company. She personally absorbed all losses.

Like Princess Diana and Marilyn Monroe after her, Pavlova became in the public mind a larger than life celebrity. She became a symbol of grace, style, and nobility of character. And ultimately, like them, of tragedy and death.

A very different kind of celebrity was Alexandra Kollontai, a hardline Bolshevik radical, close friend and likely consort of Stalin, famous for her view that all children should be shared as communal creatures owned by the state. Kollontai, who served as the Soviet ambassador to Norway as well as coordinating with the KGB on assassinations, noted in her private diary in 1930 that she had been instructed to stop Pavlova's performances in Norway. When she attempted to secure the help of the Norwegian government to do this, the Norwegians laughed, treating it as a joke.[2] She later complained in her diary about the exhaustion and grief of executions.[3]

The selection of Kollontai to enforce the boycott against Pavlova's company and its performances illustrates how Pavlova was targeted by Stalin and how important blocking her was considered. Kollontai was among the most important Soviet diplomats in the world, a Soviet delegate to the League of Nations, and close to Stalin. In 1942–43, he would select her to attempt to open secret peace negotiations with Hitler.[4]

By the late 1920s, Pavlova was the most famous Russian identified with Imperial Russia in the world, which was ironic since she had risked her career daring to embarrass the tsar's regime by supporting the strike of imperial dancers after Bloody Sunday. That was not nearly enough. Her fame, her generosity to the numerous Russian émigrés in Paris, her friendship with the dowager empress and remaining Romanov relatives, and her love of classical ballet written in Imperial times, marked her as the "darling of the aristocrats," the Soviets' deadly enemy.[5] As a symbol, she was inadvertently the last great rallying point for the dying age of Old Russia. Just as the Soviets had killed Imperial Russia and the

Romanov children, it was necessary to kill the memory of Imperial Russia, even in ballet.

After branding Pavlova an enemy of the people yet failing to stop her 1930 tour with diplomatic and other pressure, the Soviets' remaining available solution was the one used on dozens of pesky Russian émigrés like Wrangel, Kutepov, Diaghilev, and others.

The Uncle Yasha Ring centered in Paris had used a variety of poisons.[6] Indeed, in June 2017 in a speech commemorating the founding of the Russian foreign intelligence service, Vladimir Putin began by recognizing Uncle Yasha and his Paris group of poisoners and assassins. Perhaps Putin also celebrated Yasha's "Operation Trust," that program that deeply infiltrated White Russian circles in Paris, convincing many to return to Russia where they were executed after being compelled to dispatch letters to Paris portraying how wonderful their return had been to lure others back. And Putin may have had in mind those who did not return and died by heart attack or lung failure.[7]

In 1929, Uncle Yasha's capabilities were augmented with the addition of the Paris poison lab. Yasha's group added some of the most skilled Soviet operatives in the world, such as Vasily and Elizabeth Zubilin (disguised as Czech citizens, both famous for setting up a drug trade to China), and most importantly the notorious Sergey Spigelglas, a specialist in liternoye operations and liquidations in which secrecy was paramount.[8] We will never know how many people Spigelglas murdered and disguised as having died naturally or by suicide. He left a trail of blood in Paris and across Europe, revealed only by the occasional public mistake. His cover as a worker at a fish market near the Montematre left him free to kill much bigger fish.

Pavlova spent much of the last few weeks of her life in London at her beloved Ivy House near Golders Green with her husband, Victor D'André. Leading up to Christmas she danced before packed houses at the Golders Green Hippodrome. Shortly before Christmas, she closed the final public performance of her life before a sold-out crowd, concluding with *The Dying Swan* and *Autumn Leaves* in which she portrayed a beautiful flower killed by the North Wind.

Often in history, those who are the subject to persecution, from Julius Caesar, to Abraham Lincoln, to Martin Luther King Jr., have premonitions of their deaths. And so it was with Pavlova. Although she could not have known any particulars of Uncle Yasha's Group, in the fall of 1930, she told Nina Kirsanova, "Go to a Russian Orthodox church and pray for me...I feel in the shadow of a heavy dark cloud. I feel the Sword of Damocles over my head."[9] She knew of the slew of Russian émigré deaths and her condemnation by Stalinist Russia as a traitor. Pavlova also knew of the numerous strange deaths among the Russians in Paris. She surely believed her 1931 tour very dangerous. The Sword of Damocles would fall just before she could defy Stalin by beginning her 1931 tour.

After touring European capitals and before traveling to the United States, Pavlova's 1931 tour was scheduled to take her to former Russian territories in Poland, near the border of the Soviet Union itself. On Friday, January 19, packing for her departure she had the hotel deliver lunch to her room.[10] The Yasha Ring clearly knew her plans through secret informers planted throughout the Russian art community (including her dear friend, famous singer and Soviet double-agent, the singer Nadezhda Plevitskaya). A short time after lunch at the hotel, Pavlova boarded the train from Paris to The Hague. Within a few minutes on the train, and for the first time in her life, she fell seriously ill.[11] From the beginning, she told the doctors she immediately saw in The Hague, "Just imagine, *I must have been poisoned* by something I ate in Paris."[12] The doctors ignored her self-diagnosis and instead treated her only for her symptom of pleurisy as her suddenly inflamed lungs filled up with water. The treatments that should have worked, particularly for a great athlete like Pavlova, all inexplicably failed. She likewise insisted to her husband that she must have been poisoned in Paris.

The existence of the Yasha Group or Lab One would not be widely known for another sixty-plus years. So no one—her doctors, her husband, nor her numerous later biographers—had any reason to know of Spigelglas, Yasha, or the many Paris murders in progress. After all, what type of monster would intentionally murder a ballerina loved by the whole world?

The doctors were unable to stop the inexplicable deterioration of Pavlova's lungs and the weakening of her heart. Within a few days, she died. Some believed pneumonia caused her death, and others blood poisoning from incisions made to drain her lungs.[13] Recently, Russia claimed she had merely exercised "in a chilly room," wholly ignoring her actual words.[14] Many simply could not understand it at all. The definite cause of her symptoms was unknown—another convenient and inexplicable death. How could such a healthy athlete's body fail so suddenly and inexorably? Her death was so suspicious that the Amsterdam police even investigated her husband before concluding he bore no responsibility for her death since he was absent when she first became ill. Pavlova's death is a virtual exact duplicate of various later confessed murders by respiratory inflammation using Laboratory One poisons, as we will see in the deaths of writer Maxim Gorky and his son, as well as earlier murders like that of the Black Baron.

Anna Pavlova's final actions when she briefly regained consciousness were to make the sign of the cross and tell her beloved maid to bring her swan costume in which she had performed *The Dying Swan* so many times.[15] Gathering her company by her deathbed, she swore them to go forward with the show in The Hague in her absence, defying her death.[16] Like the Dying Swan of legend, did she feel both sadness at parting and the joy of a great life well spent? Stalin's poison and thugs did what his threats and ambassadors could not do. They stopped Pavlova's dance.

The front pages of newspapers all over the world, including *The New York Times*, expressed sadness and shock—except in Soviet Russia.[17] As in Tennyson's great poem *The Dying Swan,* Anna Pavlova filled the world with sorrow and joy at her death—sorrow at its prematureness, and joy that such a person had ever lived.[18] For many in 1931, it was the first day the music died.[19]

Many thousands came to the Russian Orthodox Church in London to view her memorial services and coffin. Services were held in Orthodox churches all over Europe.[20] At the last instant before her cremation at Golders Green so close to her beloved Ivy House, a worn Russian imperial flag was placed over her before she was committed to the flames. Like the hidden massacre of the Romanovs marking the end of the Empire, her death truly marked the end of the great Imperial Ballet of Saint Petersburg. Stalin, no doubt, believed he had completed the murder of an age by murdering its great symbols—the Romanovs, Diaghilev, Pavlova, Tikhon, the Black Baron, and the great Moscow Cathedral of Christ the Saviour.

Stalin proved as disingenuous in Pavlova's demise as he had in Lenin's. After feigning sadness over Lenin's death, he stood for decades on poisoned Lenin's tomb to review parades. In Pavlova's case, the Soviet government at Stalin's direction filed claims against Pavlova's estate, claiming to be her sole heir either directly through escheat or indirectly through her aged mother whose property belonged to the state.[21] They denied Pavlova had ever legally married Victor D'André, with whom she had lived for more than twenty years.[22] They sought the immediate liquidation of everything—Ivy House, her company, the costumes and sets assembled over a lifetime. They sought the dissolution of her ballet company with the discharge of its ballerinas, choreographers, set designers, and the others involved in her shows.

Her Deepest Secret

Who was Victor D'André? He was a French-Russian businessman who managed her troupe and financial affairs. He took care of her and her business. He was her shield from the press of fans and reporters. From Pavlova's earliest ballet days, he was also her almost constant companion and lover. By 1911, they told people they married in a private ceremony. D'André lived in the Ivy House with Pavlova. He accompanied her all over the world sharing both the triumphs and the danger of places like Mexico City. She often introduced him to reporters and to many others as her husband.[23] She discussed him as her husband in print. And no one who read his great biography of her, *Anna Pavlova in Life and Art*, could doubt his deep love for Madame, as he called her. When Pavlova was asked on occasion about her marriage, she replied that her art was public, but her marriage with Victor D'André was private, her own possession.[24]

But along with everything else, Stalin's agents knew Pavlova's greatest secret. She and Victor D'André were never formally married. And so following her death, ostensibly on behalf of Pavlova's ancient mother, they publicly filed a suit in court claiming her entire large estate, contesting D'André's claim as Pavlova's husband, claiming they had lived together illegally for twenty-plus years, and seeking the immediate liquidation of her assets. Any proceeds would, of course, go to the Soviet state. D'André, in fact, apparently could produce no written evidence that he and Pavlova were formally married. The Russian claim was clearly calculated to destroy Pavlova's reputation and end her ballet company as it had taken her life. Stalin failed in this because, like Princess Diana, Pavlova was so well loved and deeply mourned that the attempted scandal was largely ignored.

They did, however, succeed in gaining by settlement a substantial portion of her estate. The suits settled with the estate split. At the insistence of the Soviets, everything was in fact quickly liquidated. The great Ivy House was sold. The ballet school was closed. The dancers and artists were discharged. On June 21, 1931, at what was surely among the saddest of all auctions, the contents of Ivy House and the costumes, slippers, and stagings of the company from thousands of performances all over the world were sold. Jack the Swan disappeared. Most physical things commemorating her were dispersed and apparently gone. The Golders Green Hippodrome where Pavlova danced was purchased to house an Islamic center, but became instead a Christian church when residents objected. After his death, D'André's ashes were placed below Pavlova's at Golders Green, along with her slippers.

The Soviet State had one final step for preserving the secret of its murder. In the case of the Romanov children, each of their executioners was in turn executed in Stalin's secret prison called "Special Facility 110," or "Sukhanovka," also known as the "Torture Dacha."[25] Likewise, Sergey Spigelglas, Genrikh Yagoda, the Poison Dwarf, Theodore Maly, and all the others were executed in the late 1930s—except for Yasha himself, who was beaten to death in the Lubyanka after Stalin and his protector Lavrentiy Beria were both killed.

To all appearances, Stalin had destroyed not only the Swan, but the estate and things that reminded people of her. But had they destroyed her memory?

Pavlova

Following the condemnation in Lunacharsky's 1927 article, the seizure of Pavlova's Russian charity, the reaction to that brutal 1929 conduct, and Stalin's unsuccessful orders to Ambassador Kollontai and others to stop Pavlova's 1930 tour, it must surely have been clear that the only way to stop the brave ballerina Anna Pavlova was to kill her. Yet any leak or inkling of this would be deeply destructive to Russia's charm offensive to rejoin the family of nations and to "Uncle Joe's" benevolent, avuncular image.

It is for this reason that Sergey Spigelglas, the greatest of all Russian secret killers, was brought to Paris to join Yasha's gang. Poisoning Pavlova's food as it was taken to her room as she left Paris was likely the means. It was both simple and brilliant. It meant that Pavlova became sick and died, not at the place of the crime or anywhere near her liquidators, but on a train to another country, in The Hague, the Netherlands. This stroke of genius completely removed the investigation from the locus of the crime itself, leaving the Dutch police little chance of locating the witnesses or forensic evidence back in France necessary to unlock the nearly perfect crime. The timing of the poisoning is also notable—at exactly the last moment to stop her 1931 tour.

From the beginning Pavlova was insistent that she became very sick upon boarding the train because she had been "poisoned by the food in Paris."[26] As her condition spiraled, no one believed her. And so they blindly treated symptoms, not knowing the cause. When she swore her company to go forward with the opening performance of the 1931 season, even if she was dead, it was hard to believe that this was not her parting answer on earth to Stalin's efforts in 1927, 1929, and 1930 to stop her dance and that of her company. Despite the brutality, threats, and conduct of the butcher, her scheduled performance did go on. So an empty spotlight replaced the irreplaceable Swan in front of a grieving crowd.

Still, if Stalin thought destruction of Pavlova's person and possessions would write an end to her he was sadly mistaken. She lives as a growing inspiration to almost every lover of ballet and to almost every aspiring ballerina.[27] A famous 1911 painting by Sir John Laverty depicts a young girl putting on a ballet slipper while looking into a mirror and seeing herself transformed into Anna Pavlova. Even today there are girls all over the world putting on their ballet shoes and dreaming that someday they will dance as a swan in front of thousands like Pavlova did, and ballerinas mimic Pavlova's *Dying Swan* in London, Paris, Melbourne, and even Moscow. A statute of Pavlova sits atop London's Palace Theater and in many other places. From time to time, flowers are placed at the feet of her statues by ballerinas, dancers, and aging matrons who remember and love her.

Frederick Ashton's student and friend, the great ballerina Margot Fonteyn, perhaps the most recognized of the modern non-Russian ballerinas, wrote only one book. It was a magnificent biography dedicated to Ashton and entitled *Pavlova*—one of thirty-seven biographies, each one inspired by the life of this divine creature. Pavlova is still remembered on lists of history's greatest dancers ahead of Michael Jackson, Mikhail Baryshnikov: gone, but a legend of grace and still the most famous dancer of all time nearly a century after her death.

So, Anna Pavlova left an obvious legacy in the great cities of ballet—Paris, Saint Petersburg, New York, and London. But because she traveled the entire globe as a self-described seeder of ballet, her legacy was also sown person by person and city by city. Ray Bradbury wrote of the disappearance of a single butterfly affecting all of subsequent history in *A Sound of Thunder*: the so-called "Butterfly Effect." Pavlova, who often danced *The Butterfly*, is depicted with wings as if about to take flight. She would prove to be Bradbury's Butterfly. Stalin could and did kill the butterfly, but he could not kill all those inspired by her, nor eliminate the numerous places she fertilized with dance.

Echoes of the trauma of Pavlova's death rippled in media and the arts. In the year following her death, *Grand Hotel*, starring John Barrymore, Pavlova's close friend, and Greta Garbo, who played a tragic Russian émigré ballerina loosely patterned on Anna Pavlova, won the 1932 Academy Award for Best Picture. It was Hollywood's farewell to someone who had visited several times, leaving behind many friends and an enduring impression. In the film, the ballerina's fate is uncertain, as the cause of Pavlova's death was to her friends.

Long after Pavlova's passing, the photo of a Soviet woman named Maria Limanskaya directing traffic in 1945 after the fall of Berlin at the Brandenburg Gate became one of the most famous images of World War Two.[28] Maria looked stunningly like Anna Pavlova. Since Soviet media and the Soviet people had been deprived of the censored news of Pavlova's murder, the photo was identified over and over in the Soviet press as Anna Pavlova directing traffic, showing that Pavlova lived and still lives in the hearts of the Russian people.

And to millions of girls in North America and Europe, Pavlova remains the ballerina on top of the jewelry box. She is the stuff of magic and dreams even for matrons remembering long-ago childhoods when everything seemed possible.[29]

With the real Anna Pavlova dead and the great golden dome of the Cathedral of Christ the Saviour destroyed, Stalin had reason to believe he had utterly eradicated the last symbols of Old Russia and Christian faith. Like Nero's planned *Domus Aurea* after the great fire of Rome, Stalin planned to build a great Palace of the Soviets with immense statues of Soviet leaders, most prominently of himself. There was also to be a gallery of his hidden victims like Lenin and Iron Felix, replacing Christ and the saints, who had been honored on the site in its cathedral days. It never happened. Sand formations made construction impossible and the location remained empty for many years. Stalin's never-completed project became the subject of many jokes. Eventually in the 1960s, the Soviets built an open-air swimming pool, an odd choice for a city with such a short summer. Soon, even that would be replaced. The Soviets wanton destruction of the church was no more permanent than their effort to eradicate Diaghilev's Ballet Russes or the ballets and memory of Pavlova. In the 1990s, the great cathedral of Christ the Saviour was completely rebuilt.

Atop the Palace Theater in London, amid skyscrapers near Victoria Station, a golden statue of Anna Pavlova looks up *en pointe*, seeming to take flight to a better, kinder place—still unbowed and unbroken by the cruelties of this world. Anna Akhmatova suggests in her poem *Rosary* a line designed for another yet applicable to brave Pavlova: for brave Pavlova, "let love become the gravestone that lies upon" her life.[30]

CHAPTER THIRTEEN

Stalin's Legacy

The almost certain murders of Pavlova, Diaghilev, and so many others were but a prelude to accelerated Marxist stealth murders and executions. These crimes were templates for others, mass and individual, that would continue to be carried out by Stalin and later by his Stalinist successors, using the very same killing techniques. While many victims under Stalin simply disappeared or starved to death in Ukraine or labor camps, there were always some too prominent to disappear or, like Pavlova, too far away to seize. A few stories of the most well-known of these victims follow. These are a template for the monstrous legacy programs still used by Stalin's heirs. They were, as we shall see, way stations on the road to the great pandemic of our times.

In Lab One, Stalin had created a unique and indispensable machinery of death for the Soviet state. As the years rolled on, it would mature in Russia into a vast bioweapons program designed to break out of the nuclear stalemate. After Stalin's death, the bioweapons program would be duplicated in Stalinist countries like North Korea and Xi's China. It would mature from its early focus on retail chemical poisons like curare and warfarin to mass killers like the smallpox virus and the coronavirus. Long after it's creator's death, it would bring the world to its knees. But that was decades in the future and far away. In the 1930's, Lab One and "Special Tasks" remained Stalin's most closely held secrets.

After Anna Pavlova's murder was carried out, the activity of Stalin, the Special Tasks Group, and Laboratory One intensified. For example, on August 26, 1935, Henri Barbusse, the author of a Stalin biography that offended the dictator and which he suppressed, became ill immediately after eating dinner. Within four days, almost identically to Pavlova, Barbusse was dead of "pneumonia" and pleurisy.[1] His files of unpublished material on Stalin for a second biography of the dictator were destroyed.

Stalin moved from liquidation of the Orthodox Church to his campaign against the peasants or "kulaks." The direct murder of kulaks and famine in Ukraine killed between four and six million. It was during this period that Stalin's wife, Nadezhda, shot herself in shame at her husband's butchery and personal abuse.[2] By 1935, Stalin used the suspicious murder of friend and potential rival, Sergei Kirov, to launch a bloody purge of the government, the party, the army and finally, ironically, Soviet intelligence and its executioners. Because of the millions killed, this came to be known as the Great Purge. A brave Welsh reporter, Gareth Jones, broke the story of the Ukrainian slaughter, which was denied by Walter Duranty, Stalin's *New York Times* shill. Duranty received the 1932 Pulitzer Prize for his stories denying the vast famine then underway. Gareth Jones was rewarded for his truthful story with a bullet in his head in 1935 after he was captured by Chinese Communists.

Gaslighting

In the 1940's play and movie titled *Gaslight*, starring Ingrid Bergman and Charles Boyer, a husband keeps slowly dimming the gaslights but denies it, telling his wife she is hallucinating in order to convince her she is insane. Thus the term "gaslighting" describes the creation of misleading illusions. History's greatest gaslighters are Stalin and his Communist successors. When Robert Conquest published his estimate that six million people had been killed by Stalin in Ukraine, Mikhail Gorbachev and his *perestroika* (restructuring) government, certain that the estimate was wildly inflated, initiated a study of the records. Gorbachev was shocked to learn that Conquest's estimate was much too low. The great slaughter had been hidden by Stalin and the KGB for more than fifty years by operatives like Duranty and murders like that of Gareth Jones.

Perhaps the most famous of the secret poison murders of Laboratory One and Stalin were of the Gorkys, which displayed not only Stalin's ruthlessness, but the black humor that led him to stand upon Lenin's tomb as a reviewing platform for thirty years. Like the mob bosses of Chicago and New York who sent wreaths to the funerals of those they had killed, it was Stalin's habit to deliver crying eulogies for those he had secretly murdered, erecting statutes and even naming cities for his victims.

Maxim Gorky was among the most read authors in the world in the early twentieth century. Like Dickens, his novels were populated with common folk—often poor—around whom he wove fantastic tales, generally glorifying the downtrodden and assailing the rich and the powerful. He was a strong supporter of the Bolsheviks, both financially and with his writings, as well as a close friend of Lenin. He participated openly and actively in the 1917 Revolution, and his somewhat mentally challenged son, Maxim Peshkov, became an officer in the Soviet secret police by 1918. Following the Revolution, Gorky split with Lenin, criticizing both Lenin's terrorism and his autocratic rule. In October 1921, Gorky and his son left Russia not to return during Lenin's life.

After Lenin's death and about the same time Diaghilev and Pavlova received and turned down the very same invitation, Stalin invited Gorky and his family to return to Russia. After negotiations, Gorky returned on a visit in 1928, receiving adulation from large crowds and special events all arranged by Stalin. Unlike Diaghilev and Pavlova, Gorky unwisely returned permanently to Russia in 1932 with his family. That decision would cost both himself and his son their lives.

Gorky, once a brave voice fighting for liberty against the tsar, became an aged, captive shill, writing articles praising the White Sea–Baltic Canal (where many thousands of slave laborers died) as well as the campaign against the kulaks.[3] By 1934, with the slaughter of the kulaks well underway, even Gorky had apparently had enough. In a secret diary discovered after his death and then seized by the Soviet government, Gorky rather accurately compared Stalin to a flea under a microscope who had become a fearsome monster only because of magnification.[4] Following hints of disaffection and perhaps high-level conversations by his son about overthrowing Stalin, son Maxim contracted the now familiar pneumonia and pleurisy after a meal.[5] Shortly after falling ill on May 4, 1934, Maxim, a young man in perfect condition and health like Pavlova and so many others, died, to the surprise of doctors who could not understand why their treatments had not worked. The senior Gorky himself was now made a house prisoner with tightly controlled access.[6] He was used by Stalin from time to time for carefully controlled propaganda events. Maxim Gorky had gone from a great writer to a dictator's prop. By June 9, 1936, Gorky himself became conveniently ill with the now familiar disease of lung inflammation causing pleurisy.[7] With gallows humor, Stalin ordered Gorky placed in the very same room at the same villa on the same bed where Lenin had earlier been poisoned and died. After Gorky seemed to rally a few days later, he had a second sudden attack of pneumonia and pleurisy and died.[8]

True to form, Stalin served as Gorky's leading pallbearer. He delivered a stirring eulogy at his crowded funeral. The city of his birth, the historic Russian city of Novograd, was renamed for Gorky, as was a large park in Moscow and a car factory. Gorky's ashes were entombed in the obligatory Kremlin wall. In death, Maxim Gorky had become a saint of the Revolution.

The Purge Trials, 1936–1938

But for a curious set of events, the "natural deaths" of the Gorkys and others would have remained only suspicious circumstances—not confirmed murders. In 1935 (using as a pretext the murder of a rival, Kirov, which Stalin may have himself arranged), Stalin began the so-called "Great Purge" in which the target became the Bolsheviks themselves. In three large sets of trials and a parallel secret army trial of the Soviet Army's leadership, Stalin caused the execution of most of the Soviet leadership, including virtually all of the actual survivors of battles in the 1918–21 Revolution. Initially, the trials were supervised by Yagoda—head of the NKVD and a chemist deeply involved in the creation and use of Lab One. In addition to the major trials, Yagoda supervised summary proceedings and executions of hundreds of thousands of political cadres, army officers, and government officials. Having served his role, Yagoda was removed from the directorship of the NKVD. He was replaced with Nikolay Yezhov, the "Poison Dwarf," and, along with the entire leadership of Labratory One, tried for poisoning the Gorkys, Lenin, and others (supposedly with a varying cast of German or British spies and Trotskyites). This was a charge that was certainly true—at least as far as poisoning of the Gorkys—but the mastermind himself was never mentioned in the trial.

Nevertheless, after beatings, torture, arrests of families, and macabre rehearsals, the staged Trial of the Twenty-One commenced in March 1938. Those on trial, in addition to Stalin's earliest comrades, were Kremlin doctors Levin, Pletnyov, Kazakov, and of course, Yagoda. In the trial, Levin (a distinguished doctor who may have regretted his involvement with Stalin, Yagoda, and Lab One) and each defendant delivered carefully choreographed confessions of their use of poisons to create fatal lung conditions mimicking as closely as possible actual lung diseases to kill the Gorkys and others. When one of the defendants sought in court to recant his confession, the court was adjourned. Returning to court in obvious great pain, the defendant quickly offered his confession. The defendants also confessed to the highly likely poisoning of Lenin and others. Gullible Communists in the West supported these confessions as complete and genuine. Since Yagoda was a pharmacist intimately involved with both Russian Intelligence and Lab One, his confession rang true. Stalin, whose name continued to be kept out of the proceedings, watched the trials from a hidden room. He publicly posed as a bereaved victim whose life had been threatened and friends stripped from him by the poisoners. The hideous Poison Dwarf, Yezhov, planned the final trials and continued the massacres of the Great Purge. He took delight in personally torturing Yagoda and the other defendants.[9] As the Great Purge neared an end, the Poison Dwarf realized his own days were numbered. After his wife, a chronic alcoholic, committed suicide, Yezhov was secretly tried as a German agent based on a most unlikely confession and executed while weeping, professing his love for Stalin to his last breath.

The Purge Trials provided the first hint to the West of the prevalence and sophistication of poisoning in Stalin's Russia and elsewhere, but the West did not investigate. Like the death of the Romanovs (and then their executioners), the Trial of the Twenty-One and the Poison Dwarf's demise followed Stalin's pattern of horrific secret acts now followed by Putin and Xi. These atrocious murders were predictably concealed, and the executioners executed for "rogue acts" that Uncle Joe would never have approved. Past photos of Stalin with the poisoners were altered so that the poisoners were literally eliminated from history—soulless phantoms who had never existed at all.

In order to wipe all memory of the actual source of the poisonings, and consistent with Stalin's view of people as simply state-owned human material, the entire leadership of Laboratory One and almost all of the Special Tasks Group in the Great Purge were executed, mostly in the Lubyanka.[10] Yagoda, however, was killed in a nearby building with a basement designed by Yagoda himself with a sloping floor so that the blood of thousands could be easily washed away.[11]

The 1938 trial was the first warning to the West that poison and infections were secretly being used on a large scale by the Russians. Typically, Stalin presented the poisonings and infections as rogue operations conducted without his knowledge and in violation of his wishes. While the chemists, doctors, intelligence officials, and Special Tasks operatives knew differently, it didn't matter, for they were soon executed. Both Laboratory One (and its biological poison branch in the Urals) and Special Tasks were secretly restaffed by Stalin with new personnel. Only a few knowledgeable members of the staff were retained and promoted.

The 1938 Purge Trials were not the end of Stalin's poison and bio-labs, nor even the beginning of the end. They were to Stalin a reaffirmation of his ruthless ideology and techniques of death. Like a fickle god, he wanted with a mere word or flick of a pen to continue to kill secretly. The long road to biowar disasters such as the "biological Chernobyl" at Yekaterinburg in 1979, and in Wuhan, China, in 2019, had been paved. Soon enough, Stalin's ideological children, Putin and Xi, would take joy in being armed with the godlike power to strike down their enemies.

The 1939 Biowar Leak from Saratov

On the banks of the wide and lovely Volga River is one of Russia's most beautiful cities—Saratov. It was the historical capital of the Volga Germans, who had graced the region with their industriousness since the reign of Catherine the Great. Beginning in the 1920s and accelerating after Hitler turned on the Soviet Union, Stalin had had most of these Russian citizens of German descent executed or sent to Siberia. They left behind the Nikitin Brothers Circus—Russia's oldest permanent large circus—and a magnificent conservatory, as well as other wonderful landmarks of a once-thriving but now vanished people.

And it was here in the late 1920s in Saratov, among the ghosts and echoes of the deceased Volga Germans, that Stalin began a vastly different project: huge bioweapons development and the erection of manufacturing facilities for a range of terrible diseases from smallpox to pneumonic plague, as well as a range of delivery systems from poisoned apples, to artillery shells, to aerial bombs. The concealed but massive secret facilities at Saratov have been updated from time to time and are still in use today by Putin. At Saratov, Russia has been manufacturing the means for inflicting mass hideous death for nearly a century. The U.S. government recently embargoed drugs from these facilities for this reason.

Hints of Wuhan and the world's present pandemic were apparent as early as 1939, when Abram L. Berlin, a biochemist and prominent local official from Saratov, was summoned to meet with very high officials at the Kremlin.[12] These meetings were likely to include the Poison Dwarf Yezhov and Beria, as well as Stalin himself. Arriving in Moscow and staying at the Hotel National—Moscow's most glamorous hotel—before the planned meeting at the Kremlin, Berlin became gravely ill. A brilliant Moscow physician, Dr. Simon Gorelik, determined that the illness was pneumonic plague (then an untreatable death sentence) which Berlin was weaponizing through vaccine research in Saratov.[13]

Perhaps realizing the Soviet leader had just barely missed getting infected himself, the meeting was, of course, cancelled. Berlin died shortly of the plague. Others were soon stricken, including Dr. Gorelik, who also died. Moscow's grandest hotel was cleared on a pretext and disinfected. All word of the leak was sealed with secrecy. A time would come when the Marxist creation of bioweapons would infect not just a hotel, but the entire world.

CHAPTER FOURTEEN

The Murder of a Saint

"Faith of our Fathers, Holy Faith;
We will be true to thee till death."[1]
—Frederick William Faber
"Faith of our Fathers"

After the brief rule of the intervening monster named Nikolay Yezhov, who was himself executed, Stalin turned over the NKVD to a fellow Georgian, Lavrentiy Beria, a man regarded by his colleagues as notably evil, a real distinction in that rogues' gallery of mass murderers.[2] Beria was reviled for his rape of hundreds of women, many young girls, over a fifteen-year period. But Beria was effective. He quickly reinvigorated intelligence operations in the West and Laboratory One and grew facilities elsewhere for poison and biowarfare. The Lab was placed under the direct guidance of Grigory Mairanovsky, a highly competent chemist most known for his brutal and heartless treatment of human beings used as his test animals. It was he who dehumanized his test subjects by calling them "birdies." He was a worthy successor to the executed Dr. Death and Yezhov. Elaborate biolabs were constructed and established in the Urals and at Kiev.

During this period an underground tunnel was built between Lab One and the Lubyanka to allow secret transfers of the prisoners and poisons. Mairanovsky conducted extensive human poison experimentation paralleling that of Nazis like Josef Mengele at Auschwitz.[3] It was under Mairanovsky that Nazi scientists involved in human poison experiments were themselves sent to Laboratory One at the conclusion of World War II so they could be debriefed and their results adapted.[4] Although Spiegelglas and most Special Tasks Operatives were shot to silence them after defections began to reveal the existence of Special Tasks, Beria rescued Uncle Yasha—the Paris "baker" who murdered so many—for a time while he was awaiting execution. Beria restored him as a trusted executioner.

A very partial list of the known murders inside Russia and throughout Europe by Laboratory One/Special Tasks was compiled in an appendix to *The KGB's Poison Factory* by former Soviet military intelligence operative Boris Volodarsky. In Russia's brief freedom between the end of Communist rule and Putin's dictatorship, many documents were retrieved from secret KGB archives. These are summarized in *The Perversion of Knowledge* by the brave Soviet refusenik and scientist, Vadim J. Birstein, once a member of the Russian Academy of Science.

Among the many murders (many dozens according to Laboratory One head Mairanovsky's testimony during his trial in 1955), one in particular stands out as a good illustration of the secret wave of killings: the secret murder of Ruthenian Catholic saint and martyr, Theodore Romzha.

A well-documented graphic illustration of the Lab One poisoning techniques used on Pavlova, Tikhon, and so many others occurred in 1947 in Ruthenia. Located on the borders of Eastern Slovakia, Poland, Hungary, and Ukraine near the Carpathian Mountains, Ruthenia was one of history's footballs, seized and traded between the Mongols, Russians, Austrians, Lithuanians, and other great powers for centuries. By the twentieth century, even the Ruthenian language was largely extinct. After brutal occupation by the Nazis in 1944–45, it was occupied in turn by the Soviets. Of the 600,000 or so estimated Ruthenians, perhaps 200,000 were killed by the Nazis or the Soviets. And by 1945, the survivors' country was in ruins.[5]

What the Ruthenians did have was their belief in the small, but historic Ruthenian Catholic Church. When the great schism in Christianity occurred between the pope in Rome and the patriarch in Constantinople in 1054, the Ruthenians (although following most Greek Orthodox rituals), retained their allegiance to the Roman pope. The small church in its Catholic enclave stubbornly retained their faith despite efforts by the Muslims, Protestants, and Russian Orthodox Church to smother it.

As the Soviets liberated Ruthenia from Nazi occupation, thirty-two-year-old Theodore Romzha, a priest, youth minister, and professor, received the most dangerous of promotions. He was named the bishop and leader of the Ruthenian Catholic Church. Like the popes of the early church, Romzha, the youngest bishop in the Christian world, had received a great title with limited prospects for a long tenure.

In 1945, the Soviets annexed little Ruthenia into Ukraine. They demanded that Romzha pledge allegiance to their state-controlled Orthodox Church rather than the pope in Rome. Romzha, backed by the clergy and congregations of the Ruthenian Church, refused. The Soviets then seized all Ruthenian churches, institutions, and buildings; appointed new bishops and clergy loyal to Moscow; and fired Romzha and all Ruthenian clergy. They even seized Romzha's car to ensure he could not minister to the various congregations.

Romzha visited his flock in a horse-drawn cart instead. The Soviets had made a miscalculation: they believed that the Church was a building. But they would shortly learn the Ruthenian Church, which had survived so much, was built upon human hearts and faith.

In the late summer of 1947, at Romzha's call, more than 80,000 Ruthenians gathered around an outdoor altar in the small city of Mukachevo to celebrate Christ's mother, Mary, and to profess their belief.[6] This was the largest gathering of Ruthenians in many years, terrifying the Soviets who had assumed the ancient church would simply fade away. A nearby celebration of "reconciliation" with Moscow by the official "Bishop" Nestor Sydoriuk drew virtually no one. The Soviets were humiliated. As they would conclude with Pope John Paul II in 1981, a priest who could summon such an outpouring of faith was dangerous and needed to be eliminated.

On October 27, 1947, Romzha's horse-cart was struck by a large Soviet military truck.[7] The soldiers got out and began beating the six passengers with clubs. After several had died, traffic gathered. The soldiers left Romzha horribly beaten, all teeth knocked out, jaw broken, numerous fractures, and in critical condition and apparently dying. Romzha was taken to a nearby Catholic hospital where under the care of the nuns, he began to recover. On the night of October 31, 1947, a Doctor Bergman, accompanied by a large muscular nurse named Masha, appeared at the hospital explaining they were taking charge of Romzha's care. After the nuns were ordered home and against Romzha's wishes, Masha gave Romzha a shot to "help him sleep." Masha and the doctor then disappeared, never again to be seen in Ruthenia. Bishop Romzha, of course, never opened his eyes again. The Soviets denied any knowledge of his death, which they listed like so many others as the result of an "auto accident." The Ruthenian Catholics proclaimed him a saint and martyr. But like Tikhon, Pavlova, the Gorkys and so many others, the murder retained for a time plausible deniability.

As with the Romanov murders, the regime's deniability slowly vanished. In the 1954–55 purge trial of Lab One (following Stalin's poisoning), one of the four sample poisonings which the head of Lab One confessed to was the faraway murder of Romzha in Ruthenia. Mairanovsky confessed that he and an agent had been the fake "Doctor Bergman" and "Nurse Masha" who had poisoned the bishop in the hospital. He detailed in his confession how they had brought fatal doses of curare, an almost undetectable poison that paralyzes the heart, from Lab One to Ruthenia and killed Bishop Romzha with an injection.

Mairanovsky was not then asked or allowed to testify at whose direction he had performed the murder.

After his release from prison in 1961, Mairanovsky sought his pension and honors back, pleading on account of his "great heroic" service to his country in killing hundreds "including Jews." He stated that the Romzha poisoning had been specifically ordered by Nikita Khrushchev, then the Soviet leader, upon Stalin's instruction. Within a short time, Mairanovsky, with no prior history of coronary disease, himself died of a Soviet "heart attack."[8] Later refuseniks, during the brief period of Russian freedom, actually located Khrushchev's written order to Mairanovsky to murder Bishop Romzha, sealing Bishop Romzha's fate.

If Stalin still believed after the experience of the murders of Tikhon or Pavlova that the murder of Bishop Romzha would end the stubborn Ruthenian Catholic Church, he had once again seriously miscalculated. Long ago, the Roman historian and philosopher Tertullian in 197 A.D., during the surprising early growth of Christianity in the midst of fierce Roman persecution, noted that "the blood of martyrs is the seed of the church."[9] And so it would be with the Ruthenian Catholic Church. Still alive and much loved in little Ruthenia, the tiny Church has created a fascination in the secular West with its rituals and evident sincerity. In the United States alone, there are now twenty-three Ruthenian Catholic churches from Houston to a new church in Alaska named after Romzha.[10] In a period of decline for most churches, the Ruthenians boast 472,000 members. And on each October 31, Romzha's feast day, prayers are directed to the martyr saint throughout the world. Stalin survives in Ruthenia only as a nightmare. But his elimination of Romzha set a classic pattern for Putin and Xi murders of today.

As he finished overseeing the Romzha murder, Mairanovsky was busy with Laboratory One's most famous visitor.

CHAPTER FIFTEEN

The Missing Man, Prisoner Number Seven—1947

"Stone walls do not a prison make
Nor iron bars a cage....
If I have freedom in my love,
And in my soul am free,
Angels alone, that soar above,
Enjoy such liberty."[1]

—Richard Lovelace
"To Althea, from Prison"

Prisoners, both real and imagined, play an outsized role in history and our moral imagination. Thus, the *Man in the Iron Mask* and *The Count of Monte Cristo* are joined in real life by Alfred Dreyfus, Henri Charrière (a.k.a. Papillon), and Nelson Mandela. And among the Soviet Union's most famous prisoners was Raoul Wallenberg, the missing man of the second half of the twentieth century. There was nothing in Wallenberg's background to suggest what he would become in 1944–45. Like Oskar Schindler, the Nazi atrocities so disgusted this bureaucrat that he became, in just a few months, one of history's greatest heroes.

In the last years of the war, Wallenberg participated in the protection of many thousands of Jews in Hungary. Adolf Eichmann was deporting nearly 12,000 Hungarian Jews a day, mostly to the death camp at Auschwitz. Wallenberg, a Swedish diplomat, began issuing without authority thousands of Swedish passports to Hungarian Jews, identifying them as Swedish subjects. He also rented thirty-two different buildings in Budapest purportedly as Swedish sovereign territory with Swedish flags. One was called "The Swedish Library." These buildings were safe houses that protected more than 10,000 Jewish men, women, and children. He saved many dozens of Jews departing for Auschwitz by climbing on the cars and handing out passports. In all these activities, Wallenberg took hideous risks with his life. But it would not be the Nazis who killed him.

On January 17, 1945, in the midst of bitter fighting in Budapest between the Soviets and the retreating Nazis, Wallenberg was summoned to Soviet headquarters and detained. A few days later, the Soviets informed the Swedish government that Wallenberg was under their protection. And that was the last definitive word on Wallenberg's whereabouts for half a century.

In February 1945, Soviet radio reported that Wallenberg had been killed by the Gestapo. In reality, as Budapest fell, at the request of the Soviets, Wallenberg had gone to their military headquarters and was taken into custody on January 13, 1945. Wallenberg was then transferred by train under KGB escort to Moscow where he was not placed in a hotel or on a train to Sweden, but to the Lubyanka Prison.[2]

At that point the Soviet story changed. A Soviet diplomatic note said the Soviets had protective custody of him. The notorious Alexandra Kollontai, who had served as the Soviet Union's ambassador to Sweden and had worked feverishly to block Anna Pavlova's performances, met directly with Wallenberg's family and assured them that he was safe in Soviet custody. He would soon be home. Then came Soviet silence and denial. At a 1946 meeting, Stalin denied knowledge of Wallenberg and said he would ask about him. In August 1947, the Soviet Union denied any knowledge of Wallenberg at all. A Soviet periodical claimed once again that the Germans had killed him.[3]

The fact of his death was questioned when many other witnesses over the next fifty years claimed to have been cellmates of Wallenberg or prisoners with him in portions of the Gulag in Siberia, in the Lubyanka, or in the European Artic. His family desperately sought word. His mother, relatives, and friends lived their lives and then died without ever knowing his exact fate. There were a variety of conflicting Soviet official statements ranging from a claim of no knowledge to an official 1957 statement by the Soviet Government that he had had a fatal heart attack in 1947 while a prisoner in the Lubyanka.[4]

By 1957, under increasing pressure from Sweden and the case's own notoriety with Stalin gone, the Soviets finally felt pressured to break their silence. Soviet documents show that Soviet officials, after first considering an alibi of Wallenberg's death from the familiar "pneumonia" fatal to so many victims, settled instead upon a "heart attack" in the Lubyanka in 1947.[5] The newly created documents supporting this were childish fakes, and there was no explanation for why his body was cremated in the Soviet Union rather than returned home.

Finally in 1991 during the brief pre-Putin period of Russian freedom, an investigation by the Russian government concluded that Raoul Wallenberg died in 1947 in the Lubyanka while being used as a test subject by Mairanovsky for a new poison called "C-2."[6] This poison causes a human being to actually shrink and grow shorter and then die in terrible pain in about fifteen minutes. A profound and terrible end for such a man. This manner of death would explain his cremation, since his remains would have shown traces of poisoning.

The mystery was compounded when documents surfaced in 1991 showing a secret "Prisoner No. 7," likely Wallenberg, was interrogated after the reported use of C-2.[7] Promises by the Russian government to cooperate by turning over documents to the remaining living members of the Wallenberg family have proven false and a Moscow court recently dismissed their suit seeking the actual documents surrounding his death.[8] As with so many others, the Putin regime continues to hide details of Wallenberg's murder from his family, even now, almost eighty years after his disappearance.

Mairanovsky was famous even among his Labratory One colleagues for barbaric and bestial treatment of his human test animal "birdies," sometimes injecting them over and over, or burning them repeatedly, while noting with clinical indifference in his notebook their suffering and anguish.[9] It is likely that the Russia of Putin, indifferent even now to the horrible uncertainty of Wallenberg's ninety-six-year-old brother, nieces, and friends is simply too cowardly to allow the world to see the actual records of the tortured death of brave Wallenberg in the poison lab. These would include the records of his interrogations and Mairanovsky's observations on the manner of his death.

In Budapest, two statues tell Wallenberg's story. The first is a monument "thanking" the Soviet Union for its "help" to Hungary. By treaty, the Hungarians are unable to remove or alter this hideous statue. In a typically Hungarian solution, Hungarians have surrounded the large statue with trees and bushes, making it largely invisible. Nearby is a statute dedicated to Wallenberg that prominently features a heroic, classical figure throttling and clubbing a snake. Statues of Wallenberg can be found in London, Buenos Aires, Israel, and many other cities. Even in Moscow itself, a statue commemorates his life near where he was tortured to death as a lab animal in Laboratory One. The Russian government today remains dedicated to concealing documents reflecting his imprisonment, torture, and death as a birdie in Lab One.

CHAPTER SIXTEEN

The Poet—"A Former Person"

"*So many stones are thrown at me, they no longer scare.*"[1]
—Anna Akhmatova
"Loneliness"

Stalin did not always kill just by poison or a bullet. Perhaps the most unusual survivor of his rage was Anna Akhmatova. She was Russia's greatest woman poet, increasingly recognized as one of the most gifted poets of the twentieth century. Akhmatova became famous for her poems of romance. For many young Russians and others, she was the poet of love. The vivid images of her poetry and their clear, dramatic statements survive even the loss of meter and rhyme often produced by translation. Like John Keats, she is wonderful even when translated.

Daringly for the period, she became the lover of the young and then unknown Italian painter Amedeo Modigliani, who painted her a number of times. When civil war came and Stalin's Iron Curtain descended, she would not leave Russia yet continued to openly oppose Stalin. In the Stalinist period, Anna Akhmatova stands alone as a surviving outspoken opposition poet from a period when the choice for an artist was submission or death.

Deeply religious, passionate, eloquent as a poet, and committed to human freedom, she uniquely combined everything the Bolsheviks and Stalin as dialectic materialists hated. They described her as "half harlot and half nun," and from 1924 targeted her by kicking her out of the Writers Union—the normal prelude to a bullet in the head in the dark days of Stalin. But the bullet never came.

Instead, Stalin conceived of and directed an even crueler punishment than death, used by the Roman Emperor to silence Ovid, the first great poet of love. In 8 A.D. Ovid's poetry, offending the prudish Emperor Augustus, got Ovid exiled for life to a frontier town. In his new home, no one spoke his language, understood his poetry, or could even talk to him. It was effectively death by ostracism and loneliness.

For Akhmatova, her death was supposed to come about from grief, despair at the denial of publication, and her reduction to utter poverty. Akhmatova's ex-husband, lover, and son were all executed or shipped to faraway labor camps. Anyone who assisted her or became close to her likewise disappeared. The poetry she wrote was rarely published, and because of regular searches, she had to have the memory of Homer to pass on her works orally. Her earlier poetry volumes were systematically destroyed. She was silenced year after year with almost no money. As far as Stalin was concerned, she was a breathing corpse.

But Anna Akhmatova remembered. And in terrible desolation, she conceived of and ultimately wrote the greatest Refusenik poetry of the Soviet era. In one of her greatest poems, *Requiem*, she describes standing freezing for hours with a crowd in the prison yard of Kresty Prison, hoping to pass packets of food to a beloved and praying with a rosary for the inmates. When recognized as a great poet by the crowd also waiting to say farewell to prisoners, a woman asked whether she would someday tell people about the horror. When Akhmatova said yes, they faintly smiled. She also wrote passionately of lighting candles to remember those who had disappeared into the Stalinist night never to return.

In her haunting poem *1913*, written in 1940 during the siege of Leningrad, she wrote of an imagined New Year's Eve party in 1913 to which the dead of World War I and the gulag returned to attend the party as ghosts. After Stalin's death as her poems and her story slowly spread, Leningrad officials asked her in old age in 1966 if they could erect a statue of her. She repeated her promise in her 1935 poem *Requiem* that she would only give her permission to a (then politically impossible) statue of her in the prison yard at Kresty Prison, where she spent so many waiting hours. This was so that as the snow fell on the eyes of her statue, they could shed tears for the missing of the prison.[2] Long after her death, when her statue had been built staring at Kresty Prison on the Neva River, it became a major tourist site at Saint Petersburg, often covered with flowers. Putin, embarrassed at the attention directed to his own brutal gulag, closed Kresty Prison at a cost of many millions to avoid the cold stare of Akhmatova's statue, its tears, and the power of her words. Like Stalin, Putin is strangely afraid of even Akhmatova's statue. Refuseniks often meet there free of Putin's thugs, protected only by Akhmatova's rosary and gaze.

In Russia, although Akhmatova was the only prominent surviving unbroken Refusenik poet in Stalinist times, there were many like her called "former persons" by the KGB, whom Akhmatova described together with the certainty of better times for Russia.[3] She would prove a great prophet of hope, as well as a great poet.

In Xi's China and Putin's Russia today, brave non-persons like China's greatest actresses and Russia's writers are also isolated through fear and intimidated into becoming non-persons and phantoms. But like Akhmatova, brave souls like Alexei Navalny; the late writer, Nobel laureate Liu Xiaobo; and Jimmy Lai accept imprisonment rather than subjugation.

CHAPTER SEVENTEEN

Poison Makers, Stalin's Himmler, and Yasha's Gang

W e have seen how Stalin executed his executioners, from Yagoda to Yezhov, the Poison Dwarf. Their fall from positions of trust was dramatic: going from being tasked with some of the most sensitive and secret operations, to being condemned traitors killed with the customary bullet in the back of the head, a fatal beating, or sometimes an experimental toxin, followed by burial with their executed family and friends, often in the mass graves of their own victims. With Stalin's typically dark humor, the mass grave at Kommunarka in Southwest Moscow was the site where Yagoda with his family in happier times had a forest dacha. It is now where their bodies and many thousands of victims are buried.[1] Yagoda and the Prison Dwarf were intensely political Bolsheviks who had a zest for playing the deadly game of intrigue. Why did the others—technicians, engineers, chemists, biologists, and doctors—participate in the design and creation of such horrific and inhuman poisons and bioweapons? What motivates those who currently participate in the Russian and Chinese bioweapons programs? Here is a deeper look at a few of these past killers—some we've already come across, some new—examining their life stories to try to understand how they could serve such a regime by offering every last shred of humanity and their own lives.

Lev Levin, the Twisted Doctor

Lev Levin, a highly respected doctor in tsarist times, was one of the first co-heads of Laboratory One. Prior to World War One, Levin trained both in Moscow's best hospital and in Berlin and became a distinguished doctor in Moscow. Levin attended to Stalin by 1920 and through that connection became head of the Kremlin's medical facilities and physician to Lenin, Iron Felix, the Gorkys, and most high-level Communist officials. As a respected and trusted confidant of Stalin, he became "Doctor Doom," so nicknamed for his creation of Laboratory One. Dr. Levin attended to many Soviet officials who suffered sudden, inexplicable, but convenient deaths. By all accounts, he was both a capable doctor and loved his family. He was also a doctor who wrote prescriptions for murder.

The most prominent photograph of him shows Dr. Levin in a wool suit, grandson on his knee, with a kindly face framed by glasses. At the time of this loving photograph, Levin was preparing poisons for untold numbers of people, from the Gorkys to quite possibly Pavlova and Diaghilev. It was also the same time that labs he supervised with his co-defendant, Dr. Ilya Ivanovich Ivanov, were seeking unsuccessfully to create "humanzees"—part human, part orangutan—through fertilizing women "volunteers."[2]

On December 3, 1937, Levin and two doctors working with him were suddenly arrested. The Poison Dwarf charged them along with eighteen other defendants with belonging to a ring that sought to kill Stalin, Lenin, Iron Felix, the Gorkys, and others with poison or poor care. At his trial, and after considerable torture from the Poison Dwarf, he "confessed" to poisoning or killing the Gorkys, Iron Felix, Lenin, and others with intentionally negligent care or poisons designed to mimic and worsen their pre-existing diseases. Levin claimed he had done so only after being frightened by colleagues who were tried with him, concealing Stalin's involvement. Why would a distinguished doctor participate in murders and the design of terrible poisons? Status and wealth, coupled with fear for his children, were his answers.

Levin and his fellow doctors were apparently last-minute additions to the 1938 trial, perhaps to make the conspiracy story more plausible. Since the charges against them of poisoning and biowar activities disclosed the existence of the Poison Lab for the first time, the decision must have been made without officials' thinking through the degree of public exposure it would give that institution. Documents show that all sentences had been set before the trial. Although a few were given prison sentences, all the prisoners were actually executed shortly after their trial. In Levin's picture from the trial days, the smiling grandfather is gone, replaced by a man with the gaunt look of fear. His colleagues and friends of many years—the medical establishment of Moscow—all testified against him to avoid joining him in the Kommunarka grave. Stalin's prosecutor, Andrei Vyshinsky, described Levin as a monster for participating in the poisonings. It was a truthful testimony, but it missed the true mastermind who watched from behind a screen like the producer of a truly grim play.

The drama did not end with Levin's execution. His wife, Maria, disappeared, and his son, Vladimir, a lawyer and law professor, was subsequently shot for involvement in the "plot." His son, Georgy and daughter-in-law, Eva, both nutritionists, were imprisoned in 1949-54 for involvement in Stalin's new wholly invented Doctors' Plot. His daughters were not charged and had exceptional grandchildren. Stalin's attainder of blood, at least for invented crimes, didn't always extend to all of the women in the family.

Grigory Mairanovsky, the Moscow Mengele

Grigory Mairanovsky, Georgia-born like Stalin, was a brilliant biochemist whose early work at the Bach Institute of Biochemistry in Moscow was brilliant but conventional. In the 1920s, he married Mirra Rabinovich and in 1926 had a son named Shal. In 1932, Mirra died from unknown causes. It was a period of both starvation and murder, but the records are silent as to how she died. As with Stalin after the death of his wife, Mirra's death at the age of thirty-two apparently deadened Mairanovsky to any remaining human empathy. By the mid-1930s, he was involved with the NKVD's complete operational takeover of Laboratory One.

The description of Mairanovksy by Pavel Sudoplatov and others portray him as an inhuman monster like the earlier Poison Dwarf. And his few surviving pictures show cold, dead, furtive features—more of a rat than a tiger. In order to complete his secret 1940 thesis for a doctorate in biochemistry, he conducted secret experiments on living human beings with mustard gas, causing agonizing blistering of the skin, eyes, and lungs. Using men, women, and children as his "birdies," he conducted massive experimentation on humans with both poisons and diseases. He kept clinical notes on the excruciating deaths from his experiments. Unlike most chemists, he delighted in personally administering poisons after creating them, as described in the murder cases he confessed to, including that of Bishop Romzha. When he was arrested and imprisoned, he couldn't understand the reasoning as he had only poisoned many "enemies (including Jews)." According to testimony at his 1954 trial, he and his co-workers played loud music on the radio to drown out the screams of pain and death that they found tiresome and annoying.[3] When finally released in 1961, he applied for the return of his medals for his poisoning activities. Like Mengele at Auschwitz, Mairanovsky was a sociopath who justified the murder of his victims with the conviction that "they would have died anyway."

Surprisingly, Mairanovsky's son, Shal, survived, not sharing either his father's misfortunes, nor his evil deeds. Perhaps he had Mirra's heart. Shal was reputed to be a great and inspiring professor who taught electroanalytic chemistry to adoring students for many years. He died in 1991 at the age of sixty-five, probably not fully aware of his father's heartless crimes.

Lavrentiy Beria, the Rapist

Beria assumed control of the NKVD following the arrest of Yezhov, the Poison Dwarf. Mairanovsky of Laboratory One reported to him from the 1930s through the early 1950s. Eventually, Beria commanded the entire police apparatus of Stalinist Russia. He was the king of the gulags, the KGB, and the rest of the state security apparatus. His nickname, "Stalin's Himmler," comes from the 1945 Yalta Conference where Stalin introduced Beria to Franklin D. Roosevelt by that moniker. It was a black joke to flash in front of the ailing Roosevelt. The Allies were only then learning of the exact nature of Himmler's butchery of millions of people. But it was not an exaggeration. If anything, Beria would exceed Himmler in total number of murders.

Beria delighted in directly poisoning rivals, who would suffer a "natural death" at their dinners. Or instead he would stage their suicide in his office. Like Stalin, he liked to punctuate his crimes by publicly shedding crocodile tears. And like Stalin, Beria was a Georgian raised by a deeply religious Greek Orthodox mother. By age seventeen in 1917, Beria worked for the Islamist anti-Bolshevik Müsavat Party. After nearly being executed by the conquering Bolsheviks, Beria managed the feat of convincing the Communists to allow him to join them during the Revolution. Beria rose quickly in the ranks of the secret police. As he grew in power and authority, the number of executions carried out at his command rose from the tens to the hundreds, then thousands, and finally millions. On occasion he delighted in directly torturing his victims. If they were women, he often raped them. One of the most famous of his victims was the beautiful Russian actress Tatiana Okunevskaya. Beria picked her up, promising to free her father and elderly grandmother from a KGB prison if she submitted. After raping her at his dacha, he happily told her that her relatives had already been executed, and then sentenced her to ten years of solitary confinement in the Gulag.

Though suffering from syphilis, Beria raped hundreds of women, many children, and many randomly plucked off the street. Some were murdered and buried behind his beautiful pastel mansion on Kachalova Street, where the bones of the murdered children have been found.[4] Like the high-ranking SS officer Reinhard Heydrich in Czechoslovakia, Beria managed to morally disgust his fellow gang of murderers. From 1937 until shortly before Stalin's death in 1953, Beria was seen as Stalin's most powerful and loyal lieutenant. Then Stalin would learn that his fabled nose for conspiracy had failed him as Stalin himself experienced the power of Laboratory One. It is perhaps history's single greatest irony that Beria, among the most prolific murderers, likely averted Stalin's plan to incite nuclear war, saving tens of millions of lives by ending Stalin's rule and life, and with them, the dictator's plans for an eventual first nuclear strike. Beria did not long survive Stalin. His "comrades" scrambling for power soon arrested and sentenced him to the same bullet in the head and anonymous burial that he had delivered or ordered for so many others.

Beria, like Himmler, left a family who was ultimately freed and lived long lives. They sought to clear their father's well-documented reputation as a rapist, torturer, and butcher, claiming until their own natural deaths that they never heard the inhuman screams and cries coming from the basement and backyard of the pleasant pastel mansion where they lived that their neighbors heard and Soviet officials witnessed. The site now houses the Tunisian embassy, but is still avoided by passersby because of its reputation as a place of suffering and slaughter. Beria's children claimed both in print and in a speaking tour that Beria was a kind, jolly father who tried hard to ameliorate the worst of Stalin's brutality.[5]

Yasha's Gang

In 1925–30, Stalin created an all-star team of assassins in Paris. They were the greatest and most capable group of assassins ever to operate since the Nizari Ismaili killed at the direction of the Old Man of the

Mountain. In KGB circles they were commonly called "Yasha's Group," after their legendary founder Yakov Serebryansky, known as Yasha.

A Museum of Foreign Intelligence opened to the public briefly in Moscow under Yeltsin but closed as soon as Putin assumed control of Russia. According to those who visited it then, the museum was a KGB Hall of Fame for murderers and spies, much like the Baseball Hall of Fame in Cooperstown, New York, honors athletes. Instead of Babe Ruth's uniform or Jackie Robinson's number "42" jersey, artifacts and plaques told a sanitized portion of the hundred-year murderous history of Russian intelligence. At the front of the museum was a plaque listing the ten greatest agents in the long, dark history of the KGB. Among the ten names on the plaque are four agents from Yasha's group in Paris.[6] In June 2017, Vladimir Putin delivered a speech commemorating the hundredth anniversary of the founding of the KGB. In his speech, he provided a short list of the KGB's greatest agents. The first listed name was the prolific "Yasha," Yakov Serebryansky.

The most legendary of all KGB officers, Yasha was born in Minsk in 1891.[7] At an early age he began what would become a lifelong vocation of assassination and intimidation. He was arrested and imprisoned for involvement in the murder of a Russian prison official in 1909 at the age of seventeen, the first of his many murders. Indeed he spent much of his life thereafter in prison, sometimes in tsarist, but often Communist confinement. By the early 1920s, Yasha was recruited for the overseas arm of Soviet intelligence. Russian historians of the secret agencies have said Yasha was not assigned to Russian foreign intelligence. Instead he invented Russian foreign intelligence. With the help of money and intimidation, he first became well-known for organizing various spy rings among both Jewish Zionist refugees from Russia and Arab agents.

In the pictures of him that survive, Yasha has an angular face like a blade, reflecting the many beatings and wounds he endured and inflicted. He operated as a team with his rather inconspicuous wife,

Polina. At least twice, they were jailed at the same time. His son describes his parents as speaking softly and gently.[8] Yasha and Polina were nearly executed in 1940–41 as Stalin sealed the lips of those who could tell of his murders.

What forged such cold-blooded killers? What made killers able to poison or otherwise kill men and women whom they did not know and who were often non-political? The answer is that like some modern Jihadis, they were fanatic true believers in Marxism: badly deluded, irrational, but sincere. When Yasha was arrested for the final time, his son noted the inventory of possessions of this man who handled millions was one suit and one pair of shoes. Yasha and his wife were not motivated by greed or personal power, but made more ruthless by a fanatical belief in their cause.

According to his son, Anatoly, the Russian government has boxes of documents relating to Yasha and the Yasha Group. These are completely sealed with the highest security classification of Russia, never to be released. Yasha was the man picked by Joseph Stalin to organize a group of assassins in Paris for targeted killings or arranged "natural" deaths as directed by Stalin. Like each member of his group in Paris, Yasha had a cover identity—in his case a baker. He began in 1925 with a program named, with a twist of dark humor, "Operation Trust." Using double-agent informers, Yasha created a fake White Russian anti-Communist organization in Paris that recruited patriotic Russians from anti-Communist organizations to return to Russia to join a mythical resistance in Russia. Of course, after arriving and being compelled to send optimistic reports inviting members to join their efforts, they were shot.

In 1927–29, Yasha's Group was supplemented with several of Russia's deadliest assassins in preparation for additional killings. Almost all of Yasha's Group were liquidated by Stalin once their usefulness was done. One exception was Yasha himself. He was sentenced to be executed in 1938, but narrowly survived only to be imprisoned and beaten to death in the Lubyanka in 1956.

Nahum Eitingon, Stalin's Secret Sword

Shortly before the Diaghilev and Pavlova's deaths, Stalin dispatched to Paris yet another skilled murderer, Nahum Eitingon, later known in the KGB as "the Sword," or "Stalin's Secret Sword." Eitingon was renowned for his successful planning of numerous murders, including, along with Sudoplatov, that of Stalin's great enemy Trotsky, who was killed by an ice-pick-wielding infiltrator in Mexico City. The Sword was installed as number two in the Yasha Group. He was already famous for inducing the Japanese to kill twenty-two Russian émigrés as supposed double-agents, a masterpiece of deception. The émigrés actually loyally served the Japanese and provided them with good intelligence on the Communist regime in Moscow. The Sword was also famous for his women, whom he married sometimes as many as three at a time. One of his wives was the very famous Muse Malinowska, a strikingly beautiful blonde famous not only for her looks, but for executing and surviving the highest parachute jump without oxygen in history.

The Sword disguised his murderous objectives in Paris with a cover as a small factory owner. He and his women also worked together as a team. Eitingon detested working for anyone, but particularly hated Yasha. This would save his life in 1933 when he was transferred out of the Yasha Group, more than five years before Stalin purged the group and executed its members. The Sword, almost alone of the Yasha Group, would die in his bed in old age in 1981.

Sergey Spigelglas, the Liternoye Killer

As Walter Krivitsky of the KGB once noted, any fool could murder someone, but it took an artist to arrange a "natural death." Sergey Spigelglas, was dispatched to Paris by Stalin in 1929. He was an exceptional artist at causing the "natural" death or fake suicide of untold numbers inside and outside Russia. His cover identity in Paris was a fishmonger off the Boulevard Montmartre. He actually was a skilled fisherman, but he came to Paris to catch much larger prey.

Spigelglas, a quiet, nondescript man of intense but ordinary appearance, concealed great intelligence with silence (despite his ability as a polyglot). He was the key "hands on" murderer of the Yasha Group when a natural death (as opposed to a brutal death administered as a lesson) or an apparent suicide was desired. When the killings of Russian émigrés were largely over, he was summoned home to Moscow in 1938 ostensibly to be promoted to head of all foreign intelligence. In reality, the promotion was a fraud employed to make Spigelglas a Judas goat to lure the entire group home to Moscow for slaughter. Spigelglas was rewarded for his loyal service with a bullet in the back of the head, and his body was dumped with many of his own victims in that huge, hidden mass grave at the Kommunarka.[9] But as the executioners gathered in Paris in 1929, their own executions were still unforeseen and far in the future.

Rudolf Ivanovich Abel, the Undercover Agent

A young agent who looked up to Yasha as a hero and mentor was dispatched to Paris in 1929 to operate the secret coded radio communication of the Yasha Group with Moscow. This was necessary to coordinate activities and receive liquidation instructions. His name was Rudolf Ivanovich Abel, and he would later become the most famous of all KGB agents. Abel, portrayed in Tom Hanks's *Bridge of Spies*, was an undercover agent in the United States for many years much later, participating in the theft of U.S. military and atomic secrets. After he was traded for the U.S. U-2 pilot Francis Gary Powers, he described Yasha as his great mentor and teacher.

Others

Amidst the great gathering of undercover murderers in Paris in 1927–31, many others are worthy of note. For example, Theodore Maly was an Austrian priest captured by the Soviets in World War One. Maly lost his faith in the horrors of a Russian prison camp and adopted communism as his new religion. He was likewise dispatched to Paris, sometimes using priestly dress and duties to effect his disguise.

CHAPTER EIGHTEEN

Stalin's Last Day

The industrial-scale murders of Laboratory One, Special Tasks, Mairanovsky, and Stalin did not slow, but rather continued at a fast pace in the late 1940s. For example, in 1942 the Russians notified the United States government that they were holding American Isaiah Oggins and his wife in Russian custody.[1] In 1942 and 1943, Oggins met with U.S. embassy representatives, who were told he would be released upon the expiration of his sentence in 1946. However, perhaps because of his knowledge of the gulag and ability to explain the dimensions of the horror to the West, a decision was made in Russia in 1947 to kill him and to present his wife in New York with false documents attributing his death to an attack of tuberculosis of the spine.[2] The death certificate actually presented to his wife showed death from cancer, and Oggins was actually still alive at that time. In 1948, he was finally poisoned by Mairanovsky in Laboratory One.[3] Oggins was used as a birdie in a trial for the poison curare, soon to be used in actual KGB assassinations.

Injected with curare, it apparently took Oggins fifteen minutes to die, mute and paralyzed on a table.

In late 1951, Stalin initiated his last purge, of the so-called "Doctors' Plot."[4] The purported plot followed other anti-Semitic purges initiated by Stalin. Stalin's creative story for this purge was that there was a high-level plot by Jewish doctors to poison the Soviet leadership. In connection with the plot, Stalin ordered the arrest of Laboratory One head Mairanovsky; the head of KGB, Viktor Abakumov; and many others. He also ordered the arrest of his bodyguard and head of his security detail, Nikolai Vlasik, all on false charges of involvement in the Doctors' Plot. Vlasik prophetically said Stalin would not long survive his removal. Stalin's nose for nascent threats and paranoia, often prescient, led him fatally in the wrong direction.

Lavrentiy Beria had been Stalin's number two and head of the NKVD for almost fifteen years. Few of Stalin's confederates survived for so long at such a high level. In such a position, Beria had ultimate control below Stalin of Laboratory One, the biolabs, and the KGB. By 1949 under the direction of Beria, the Soviets had developed an atomic bomb, ending America's nuclear monopoly. And the Soviets were well on their way to developing a hydrogen bomb. They were also working on the intercontinental missiles that could carry them within the decade. There is considerable reason to believe that Beria had told his colleagues the truth, that Stalin was preparing for the unthinkable: a first nuclear strike in the late 1950s against the West.[5] It was Stalin's fanciful calculation that in a World War III, Russia would suffer no greater losses than her terrible losses in World War II. He believed that when the fallout cleared, the Soviets and communism would control the world. There is substantial evidence that Stalin's underlings—particularly Beria who had seen first-hand damage from atomic tests—did not agree.

In addition, it is clear that Stalin was using the Doctors' Plot purge simply as a prelude to a much larger purge he had planned, which, similar to 1935–39, would result in the execution of his underlings and their families, laying the foundation for the complete and unquestioned control he needed to wage nuclear war with the West. Stalin in particular targeted Beria's underlings, imprisoning the head of the KGB and Mairanovsky, both of whom reported to Beria. This followed Stalin's customary practice of severing the roots before cutting down the tree. Beria, Khrushchev, and Malenkov were the targeted trees as their underlings were forced to confess their guilt.

February 28–March 4, 1953, would mark Stalin's last days. The dictator had acquired as his own private property a series of country homes. These dachas ranged from the Crimea to areas close to Moscow. Several he seldom, if ever, visited, leaving full-time staffs for decades awaiting an arrival that never came.

His favorite dacha and virtually full-time residence in later years was at Kuntsevo, a country district south of Moscow, where other leaders had also built their dachas.[6] In 1933–34, Stalin ordered a young architect, Miron Merzhanov, to build him a dacha on the banks of the Moskva River. To Stalin's delight, Merzhanov's completion of the project did not prevent the architect's imprisonment along with his son, or the execution of his wife. Large trees, already decades old, were replanted around the estate to create an instant forest.[7] While Ukrainians starved in the 1930s, farmers were brought in to plant groves of lemon and apple trees. Grapes were planted and grown, together with large rose gardens.

A discreet moat with bridges was created to surround the large dacha itself.[8] Two large, camouflaged double fences, guarded by both antiaircraft guns and more than three hundred security personnel encircled the dacha at all times. The dacha had a second floor for Stalin's son and daughter. As Stalin grew older and directed his brutal conduct even at his own children, they very seldom visited, so the second floor became Stalin's hermitage. In later years, except when he convened his subordinates for late night drinking parties, Stalin, surrounded by servants and soldiers, was a deeply lonely man with few, if any, friends, and a family that feared him. It was there at Kuntsevo that Stalin summoned and met with his principal subordinates: Beria, Malenkov, Khrushchev, Molotov, and Bulganin, each of whom must have felt Stalin's breath on his neck.

Molotov's wife had already been arrested and imprisoned as a Jewish conspirator, with Molotov saying nothing in her defense. Beria's chief underlings, like Mairanovsky, had already been arrested and were undergoing interrogation and torture. In the dining room at Kuntsevo were portraits of each of these lieutenants. Stalin insisted that each sit under his portrait.[9] And from time to time as officials disappeared, so did their portraits, leaving a blank space on the wall.

On February 28, 1953, the group ate dinner and listened to Stalin's questions about the status of the "confessions" from the Doctors' Plot and other arrests. He complained about insufficient pursuit of the conspiracies against him. They apparently then watched a movie. At the dacha (and in the Kremlin), each portion of food or drink was first sampled for poison by a taster known as the Rabbit, then by the server.[10] Stalin and his cronies drank heavily until 4:00 or 5:00 a.m., following which Stalin retired to his bedroom and his minions were allowed to go home, no doubt sighing relief that they had lived to see the sun rise again. The following afternoon on March 1, at about 1:00, the maid and a guard tentatively entered Stalin's bedroom after knocking. They found Stalin on the floor, soaked in urine.[11] They changed his clothes, put him in bed with the assistance of guards, and contacted Beria. Ignoring Stalin's unconscious condition, Beria completely dismissed taking any action to aid the "Beloved Helmsman," instead claiming he was just recovering from heavy drinking.[12]

At 7:00 a.m. on March 2, after Stalin had been unconscious for perhaps a day and a half, Beria finally visited the dacha with doctors to care for him. Stalin's highly competent former doctors were by then all prisoners in the Lubyanka for their supposed participation in the made-up Doctors' Plot. The imprisoned physicians were nonetheless contacted to give medical advice by phone.

Very minimal medical care was provided to Stalin, who was diagnosed as having had a stroke, his blood pressure high at 190/110. Camphor was rubbed on his back to prevent bed sores and, as in Medieval Europe, leeches were applied to his neck to reduce blood pressure.[13] Stalin remained unconscious as his underlings arrived. As Stalin died slowly, only semi-conscious, Beria acted very strangely, treating Stalin with contempt and perhaps even spitting on him before dropping to his knees, weeping, and kissing Stalin's hands when Stalin stirred and seemed to recover.[14]

The end finally came on the evening of March 5. Stalin began vomiting blood, a detail concealed for many years.[15] According to his daughter, Svetlana Alliluyeva, his oxygen level slowly dropped, and his lips turned black.[16] He "opened his eyes with a terrible glance, insane or perhaps angry, full of the fear of death..." Then something happened "I will never forget," described his daughter, "He suddenly lifted his left hand as though he were pointing to something above and bringing down a curse on us all."[17]

Had the poisoner realized he had been poisoned? Or was he reacting to something even darker? Christians, Orthodox Jews, and Muslims, all with traditions about "dark angels," would conclude he had been dragged to Hell by demons. An American today might think of the horrible fate of the damned in the movie *Ghost*.[18] Perhaps Stalin was merely choking in his death rattle. In any event, death came for the dictator.

Stalin's death was a boon to humanity. It brought to an end his plan for a nuclear strike on the West, starting a war that would have killed millions and possibly destroyed civilization. It also prevented his latest planned purges in Russia that would have consumed the lives of hundreds of thousands. The doctors arrested in the mythical Doctors' Plot were freed, along with millions of innocent prisoners like the great writer Alexandr Solzhenitsyn.

The mysterious, but very convenient, death of Stalin would also unleash a torrent of discussion and speculation about the strange conduct of Beria at Stalin's deathbed, his obvious survival motive, and his later conduct. Stalin was protected at Kuntsevo by an army of loyal guards and tiers of tasters, designed to protect him from the same poison death he visited upon Tikhon, likely Pavlova and Diaghilev, and many others. How could any assassin, other than the Angel of Death, actually kill

Stalin? Both Khrushchev (in his 1970 autobiography secretly smuggled out of Russia)[19] and later Molotov (in conversations with Felix Chuev)[20] disclosed many years later that Beria had repeatedly claimed that he was responsible for Stalin's death.

As a mournful Stalin had reported Gorky's death, so Beria solemnly reported Stalin's death from a stroke. The funeral quickly followed. Without Stalin's genius for closing every avenue, Beria first allowed an autopsy of Stalin's remains. But he had the presence of mind to see to it that Stalin's actual autopsy report was massively altered and sections deleted when it was publicly released in 1953.[21] The public autopsy showed only a brain hemorrhage or bleeding. The actual report shortly after his death, kept secret for forty years, showed massive bleeding in other areas, particularly his stomach lining. This was almost certainly caused by large doses of an anticoagulant drug that prevented his blood from coagulating normally in his stomach lining. Since at least 1928, Laboratory One had worked on the most well-known and virtually undetectable of anti-coagulants—the drug warfarin that was then detectable only through the massive bleeding it caused.[22] The actual autopsy results strongly suggest poisoning with warfarin. It is telling that the Soviet leadership, including Beria, purposely edited out and concealed portions of the autopsy evidencing the use of warfarin. Like Stalin's altered photos, his own murder was to be concealed from history.

Warfarin, according to the 1964 CIA Report to the Warren Commission, was in use in the 1950s by the KGB as an assassination tool. Those with high blood pressure like Stalin and a history of strokes are particularly susceptible to uncontrolled bleeding from warfarin. It was largely unknown outside intelligence circles until 1948 when it was commercially used for rat poison. The anti-coagulant could be delivered both in a single lethal dose or in smaller doses. A taster Rabbit exposed to only a single dose was unlikely to be injured, but a target exposed to multiple doses would be killed. It was colorless and odorless: a perfect poison for a patient murderer. Neither an army of guards, nor a multitude of Rabbits, could protect against it.

Since warfarin used as a poison produces uncontrolled stomach bleeding, it is not painful, and the victim feels only some weakness and, in late stages, nausea. The victim has little way of knowing he has been poisoned until near the end as his blood slowly leaks away. It is a poison worthy of the evil genius of Mairanovsky and Beria, well-designed for Stalin's high blood pressure that multiplied its effect. An easy antidote to warfarin bleeding is Vitamin K, but that its only helpful if it is known that a victim has been poisoned with warfarin. The attending doctors had no reason to suspect warfarin until Stalin's autopsy. The leeches used to drain blood from Stalin who was bleeding to death were hardly a remedy. Armies of KGB agents, antiaircraft weapons, and poison tasters could not stop its fatal progress.

Following his death, Stalin was given the obligatory massive funeral attended by perhaps 300,000 with Beria (the poisoner) as pallbearer and one of the principal eulogists. One wonders how many of Beria's colleagues looked upon his weeping face with a mix of fear, amusement, and contempt.

On the very same day as Stalin's huge Moscow funeral, a tiny funeral was conducted in the same city for Sergei Prokofiev, a great composer of the twentieth century, perhaps second only to his friend Stravinsky.[23] Prokofiev, composer of *Peter and the Wolf* and many other famous works, had begun his career as a Diaghilev discovery long before in Paris with the Ballet Russes. He composed the score for its final ballet months before Diaghilev's likely murder. Unlike Diaghilev and Pavlova, he unwisely returned to Russia in 1936 at Stalin's invitation, and his health was broken by the murder of friends and family, his wife's confinement to a death camp, and his own political condemnation as a capitalist tool. Prokofiev's final work for the Ballet Russes was *The Prodigal Son,* and in sunshine and shadow deeply Christian, as he died in peace, Prokofiev believed he was returning home at his quiet death, quite unlike Stalin's terrible passing.

There were neither flowers nor musicians at the great composer Prokofiev's simple funeral: they had all been taken for Stalin's funeral.[24]

A story later claimed that when one of the weeping musicians at Stalin's funeral was asked about this, he said that while the musicians were at Stalin's funeral, their tears were for Prokofiev.[25]

Stalin was embalmed and placed for a time in Lenin's tomb next to Lenin. For a short time, Beria ruled Russia and ironically, like Stalin, reviewed parades standing atop the Lenin-Stalin mausoleum containing Stalin, whom he had poisoned, now alongside Lenin, whom Stalin had poisoned. The Stalin-Lenin tomb could have been a memorial to the poison of Labratory One. By mid-1953, Beria was overthrown and arrested by his former associates. At a quick and perfunctory trial, according to the autobiographies of both Molotov and Khrushchev, Beria pled for his life, crying on his knees, and allegedly claiming to have saved all their lives by killing Stalin.[26] Other accounts have him standing as he was executed. All agree that on December 23, 1953, Beria received the same mercy he had shown to millions and was executed with his closest associates by a bullet in the back of the head. His family was sent to a brutal Siberian labor camp.[27] Beria's body joined his victims in a mass grave.

The death of Beria cleared the way for Uncle Yasha—the Paris baker who likely supervised Pavlova's death by the Uncle Yasha Group in Paris in 1931—to be beaten to death in the Lubyanka in 1955. It is unknown whether Yasha actually aided Beria in the poisoning of Stalin. The poisoning of Stalin by Beria closed the book on poisonings Lab One personally directed, but by no means brought their poisonings to an end. They would shortly resume with new faces and new poisons. Lab One, Stalin's hideous legacy institution, had acquired a life of its own.

On the night of October 31, 1961, a day fittingly celebrated as Halloween in much of the world, Stalin's body was removed without ceremony and buried in an obscure spot in the nearby cemetery with only a small marker (larger, though, than millions of his victims enjoy). Many Russians continue to worship him as a strongman who reminds them of the days when their country was a super-power. Others remember him as a rat killed by rat poison.

When one considers the chain of events, it is tempting to believe that metaphysical justice occasionally occurs. Providence or serendipity repaid Stalin's joke on Lenin, the Gorkys, and many others by poisoning Stalin with poison from his own creation. His poisoners acted as his pallbearers. Later his body was even exiled from Soviet Valhalla and returned to the same dirt to which he had consigned so many millions. Stalin left a world he had not yet destroyed. The perverted science that he launched and often used would continue and grow after his death as a part of his evil legacy. His death stands as both a warning to his successors, Putin and Xi, and a promise to the world. Like Stalin, their suffering people should remember that the day of these tyrants will someday end and they will face a final judgment—before, we hope, they can destroy the world with their nuclear and biological weapons.

> *"For the Angel of Death spread his wings on the blast*
> *And breathed in the face of the foe as he passed…*
> *And the might of the Gentile, unsmote by the sword,*
> *Hath melted like snow in the glance of the Lord."*[28]
>
> "The Destruction of Sennacherib"
> Lord Byron (1815)

CHAPTER NINETEEN

Stalin's Shadows

The Road to COVID-19

Although Stalin was dead, his ideology of ruthless domination over all aspects of life and his perverse instruments of death were not buried with him. Stalin's ruthless ideology and bioweapons would dominate the next years of Russian history and later China. Although his monstrous acts were partly exposed and denounced by his successors, his poisons and bioweapons programs were concealed.

Stalinism is a cult based upon the total control of man, including his mind. For those who could not be coopted or cowed, poison and bioweapons are irresistible to any modern Stalinist. Through dealing untraceable anonymous death, they convey an unfettered power to mete out death secretly and without accountability. Such a level of godlike power a good Stalinist could never refuse.

While he was denounced for some of his crimes in Russia—principally killing other Communists, not the untold millions of non-Communists—

Stalin's ideology of total control would continue to rule in Russia, China, and North Korea. And like a virus, poison and bioweapons spread to North Korea, and most importantly, to Xi Jinping's China. So mankind unknowingly continued its march towards the dark world of COVID-19, accompanied by the seemingly immortal zombie ideology of Stalinism and its bioweapons.

Lab One Morphs

With the death of Stalin, Laboratory One's leadership was again cycled out, and a generation of new, less-colorful murderers took the helm. Like a malignant cancer, Laboratory One would grow in reach, power, and danger. Far from bringing the Soviet poisonings to an end, Russia entered a new birth of horror with a secret, massive increase in its poison facilities. Laboratory One—now variously called Laboratory X, Special Lab Number 11, and the Kamera—was expanded into new facilities a short distance south of Moscow and beyond.[1] Massive bioweapons labs opened in many locations. Like the viruses on which it worked, the Poison Lab, now expanded and serviced by tens of thousands of apparatchiks working on new nightmares, seemed itself to have a nearly independent and immortal life.

Following Stalin's death, the Soviets upgraded its programs to develop the most secret and gruesome poisons and bioweapons in human history. Although they continued to poison defectors and refuseniks like the great writer Aleksandr Solzhenitsyn (unsuccessfully using ricin in 1971) and defectors like Markov and Koskov, their focus shifted from the simple retail murders of the Stalin era to the production of wholesale poisons and bioweapons capable of killing millions.[2] Although the Soviets pursued chemical poisons like sarin gas, later used by terrorists in the 1995 Tokyo subway attack to injure nearly a thousand people, and mustard gas used by the Russian client states Syria and Iraq under Saddam Hussein to kill thousands of Kurds, the Russians concentrated on novel and powerful bioweapons. Although the Soviets agreed to the 1972 Biological Warfare

Convention ("BWC"), pledging never to possess or develop biological agents or weapons, they secretly spent billions in the development of such weapons in the 1970s, '80s, and '90s while fraudulently certifying on numerous occasions that they were not doing so.[3] This was an old pattern, seen in the 1938 claim repeated again in the 1950s that poisonings were simply a rogue operation now discontinued. Although the West suspended bioweapons development in 1972, for Russia the BWC was not a stop sign, but a starting gate for accelerated development to gain advantage over a naïve West.[4]

As the Soviet Union collapsed in 1991, the high-ranking Soviet scientist Ken Alibek, who spent twenty years in the bioweapons program, defected and in 1998 wrote the tell-all book *Biohazards*, exposing fully the Russians' horrific duplicity.[5] Building on human experiments in Lab One, as well as research captured from Nazi experiments in concentration camps and Japanese human experiments on Allied POWs in secret germ labs in Manchuria, the Russians had begun development of the most sophisticated biological weapons in history.[6] As the years rolled forward, Laboratory One had morphed into a vast, but wholly secret bioweapons project in many locations throughout the country, employing more than 30,000 technical personnel.

The faces changed from Mairanovsky and Uncle Yasha, but the callous cruelty remained the same. The aim was not simply to kill a ballerina, a writer, or helpless "birdies," but to weaponize the most dangerous diseases in the world after finding or developing incurable strains.[7] The Soviets sought to create previously unknown diseases. Like the movies *Andromeda Strain* and *Contagion*, the Soviets sought a perfect killer with no known cure. The aim of the program was not to kill one or two, but millions.

When the Soviet Union signed the 1972 BWC barring such developments, Russia simply grouped all biological weapons development under the civilian sounding name of *Biopreparat* and proceeded with the development of bioweapons at an accelerated pace.[8] Some of the diseases perfected as weapons were coded: L-1 Plague; L-2 Tularemia; L-3/4

Brucellosis and Anthrax; and L-5 Glanders. Some of the viruses being perfected were coded N-1 Smallpox; N-2 Ebola; N-3 Marburg; N-4 Marchupo or Bolivian hemorrhagic fever.[9] Less than a year after signing the 1972 treaty barring such activity, the Soviets had initiated their largest weapons project of the Cold War codenamed "Enzyme": the secret development of genetically altered pathogens turned into weapons for various delivery systems.[10]

They cleared an island in the faraway Aral Sea, which they jokingly called "Rebirth Island" and used it to test various biological weapons on animals, sometimes accidentally infecting fishermen, other civilians, and animals with the plague.[11] After all of the animals on the island died from the disease being tested, the island was "rebirthed" with new animals to be infected. The AIDS virus proved too unstable to be usable, greatly disappointing the researchers.

The first known inadvertent leak of bioweapons in Russia occurred in 1939 when Soviet microbiologist Abram Berlin was infected with pneumonic plague (at the time a death sentence).[12] He was working to weaponize the disease in the Saratov bioweapons facility when he was called to meet with top officials in Moscow. Immediately before meeting with Stalin, but after dining and staying at the National Hotel, he had unknowingly infected others with the disease. The hotel was disinfected at night, so as not to cause alarm, and those in contact with Berlin were quarantined. Only three people were reported to have died from the leak, but it came very close to wiping out the top Soviet leadership. The Soviet bioweapons facility at Saratov that leaked the deadly pneumonic plague was still a vast bioweapons facility in full and very dangerous operation in 2020, celebrating eighty-plus years of deadly research all denied by the Soviets and then Putin.[13]

On April 2, 1979, in the city of Sverdlovsk, now Yekaterinburg, careless filtering allowed weaponized anthrax to escape into the air, killing hundreds. Called "Anthrax 836," this strain had evolved from an earlier escape of anthrax into rats in the sanitary sewer system of Kirov, where it mutated into the deadliest known form of anthrax.[14] Hundreds of Russians died from the disease at Sverdlovsk, which the Soviets misrepresented to the world as infection from tainted meat sold by illegal private butchers, shades of the later Wuhan wet-market alibi. Local butchers were duly rounded up and falsely prosecuted for selling contaminated meat.

Thus the Soviets covered up this anthrax outbreak just as they tried to cover up the Chernobyl nuclear disaster. The site of the anthrax outbreak was particularly fitting given its location, at a place that's name had changed twice to try to escape its notoriety. In Sverdlovsk, then Yekaterinburg, on a July morning in 1918, the Romanov children, their parents, and nurses were slaughtered in a basement and their bodies dropped down a mine shaft. In 1979, unknown numbers died there from Anthrax 638. After the Soviet state collapsed, the name of the city reverted to Yekaterinburg. This incident is often remembered today as the biological weapons equivalent of Chernobyl. The meat-market cover story, however, was more effective than the lies about Chernobyl. A similar cover story would again be used by the Xi government to explain the COVID-19 leak at Wuhan.[15]

Marburg virus, closely related to Ebola, is among the deadliest of all natural viruses. The Soviets obtained samples of the virus ostensibly to develop vaccines, but instead weaponized it.[16] In 1988, a Soviet researcher named Ustinov working on weaponization became accidentally infected during efforts to weaponize Marburg. Much like Mairanovsky's clinical notes on the slow death of the poisoned "birdies" in the 1940s, Ustinov's co-workers (not ones to waste a good test human) slowly and clinically noted his horrible death over a fifteen-day period.[17]

When word of Project Enzyme leaked in the late 1980s as the Soviet Union collapsed, the Soviets discontinued for a time most or all of their germ and virus production lines (which could be easily restarted), but continued full speed with development and weaponization design.[18] While the world celebrated the elimination of smallpox in 1980, smallpox weaponization accelerated in the Russian labs. This was a strategic play, since vaccines were no longer available and the world had become defenseless. The development of mass killers was apparently code named,

"Operation Bonfire," weaponized through devices as small as an aerosol or as large as a ballistic missile.[19]

The program to kill troublesome individuals was code named "Operation Flute," and was used in 1978 to kill Georgi Markov, a dissident, in London with a ricin pellet injected by an umbrella gun.[20] The Soviet Union itself came to an end, but not these Russian practices. The chairman of the Russian Business Roundtable and his secretary were killed with a similar Operation Flute poison in their tea in 1995.[21] These weapons and many more assassinations were all developed at so-called Laboratory 12, the latest incarnation of Laboratory One.

Unexplained deaths continued in the post-Stalin years. For example, Giovanni Catelli recently assembled substantial evidence that Albert Camus' 1960 car crash death was a staged KGB "accident" in retaliation for the writer's anti-Soviet articles. Camus was a brilliant anti-Soviet author whom the Soviets hated, but like so many others, we will never know whether his death was another KGB murder or a genuine accident.[22]

Vlad the Poisoner

In the long years following Stalin's death, the dacha at Kuntsevo remained closed to the public, except for a brief period in the mid-1950s when a Stalin museum was considered. Although closed, the dacha remained fully staffed, a strange secret ghost of the past, as if waiting for Stalin's spirit to return. Finally, in July 2000, after nearly fifty years of non-use, Vladimir Putin, newly elected president of Russia, summoned the most powerful figures in Russia for a critically important first meeting following his election.[23] It was not at the customary Kremlin location, but in Stalin's dacha at Kuntsevo. It was the first official use of the notorious dacha in many decades. The location of the meeting was the message without any need for words.[24] Putin, unlike most Russians, knew the dacha well, at least from stories. His grandfather had been a cook and taster for Stalin, likely at the dacha during Stalin's death struggle.[25]

And Vladimir Putin sees himself as the return of Stalin: a man he saw not as evil, but simply a great leader who had some rough spots and excesses.[26]

As we will see, Putin has been directly implicated in several poisonings—most recently his primary political opponent, Alexei Navalny, who survived being poisoned with Novichok. Putin has refused to investigate the poisoning and even imprisoned Navalny, who was brave enough to return to Russia from a safe haven in Germany, ostensibly for failing to report for parole while critically ill in the hospital.

In 2001, President George W. Bush, after first meeting newly elected Russian president Vladimir Putin, famously said, "I looked the man in the eye. I found him to be very straightforward and trustworthy.... I was able to get a sense of his soul."[27] Perhaps Bush should have looked a bit deeper into Putin's eyes. Putin's mentor, Anatoly Sobchak, a strong Putin supporter, called him "the new Stalin" in 2000. This was shortly before Sobchak and his two bodyguards had three simultaneous heart attacks on a trip ordered by Putin, marking the first famous poisonings of the Putin era.[28] Sobchak died from his heart attack and was buried near the grave of Galina Starovoytova, a famous democratic reformer shot to death in 1998 in Saint Petersburg by various ex-KGB thugs organized by unknown ex-KGB personnel, whom many believe were acting for Vladimir Putin.

Sobchak noted many similarities between Putin and Stalin. During much of World War II, Putin's father served with a KGB extermination squad whose job was liquidating politically unreliable people. Even Putin's mother was apparently like Stalin's deeply religious mother, giving Putin an Orthodox cross he carries today.[29] In the pattern of Stalin and Beria, his mother's religiosity obviously has had little influence on him. From earliest childhood, Putin's lifelong ambition was to join the KGB. After law school he did so, but there was no evidence he ever served on any dangerous missions or heard a single bullet fired other, perhaps, than in a back-room execution. In the long terrible years of Russia's Afghan War and the deep involvement of the KGB in dangerous intrigues all over the world, Putin was warm, safe, and sound as a KGB official in East Germany. His bare-chested poses on horseback and as a man of strength and action are, like Stalin, self-anointed heroism.

With Putin's election in 2000, the young Russian democracy began slowly to die.[30] Combining elements from his former KGB and Communist associates with oligarchs and extreme right-wingers, Putin used his successful campaign against brutal Chechen terrorists to consolidate power. His United Russia Party is not united by a single ideology beyond a fierce shared hatred of the West and its values. With his accession, his opponents began to die or, like the imprisoned and later exiled oligarch Mikhail Khodorkovsky, were targeted for selective prosecution. Religious worship was permitted, but only in the approved churches that collaborated with United Russia. Worship outside these controlled locales was criminalized.[31] In effect the "approved" churches were viewed as a drunk tank or drug ward where religious addicts could be treated or reformed by state approved "ministers."[32]

At the center of religious life is the Russian Orthodox Church, with so many martyrs from Soviet times, now infiltrated at high levels with Russian intelligence agents. While many Russians and priests retain very deep Christian beliefs, Putin personally and through his agents pushes a hollow religion that, while following ancient rituals, teaches war against the degeneracy of the West, that Lenin should be recognized as a Christian saint, and that communism comes directly from the Bible.[33] Recently, Putin has outlawed churches outside those sanctioned and controlled by his government. For example, many small Baptist churches have been closed, and many Russian Baptists have fled to Germany. Rather than killing individual believers like Stalin did, Putin seeks to kill the church itself by making it meaningless under state control. In the world of Putin's cultural hegemony, there is a place for the church, but only as a servant to the state.[34]

Putin's attempt to rebuild the tarnished reputation of his predecessors, Lenin and Stalin, is a strange canonization for men who murdered thousands of priests, wrecked churches, and equated religion with necrosis. Lenin described "any religious idea, any idea of a God at all…the most inexpressible foulness."[35] Similarly, although Stalin's statue had been torn down with celebrations even in his own hometown, Putin lamented that the criticism of Stalin was "excessive" and that he was an effective manager.[36] Any attack on Stalin, he implied, was tantamount to an attack on Russia itself.

Putin has placed images of Stalin on the sides of buses and in front of parades.[37] The butcher of millions is converted in documentaries to a kindly Russian patriot, whose only failings were false claims by the dishonest West and executions by a few over-zealous henchmen.[38] Thus, poor Uncle Joe simply went a little too far in repression and was forced against his will to sign his 1939 alliance with Hitler because of the untrustworthiness of the West. And Putin's constant drumbeat to rehabilitate the monster Stalin is having a demonstrable effect.[39] As those with first-hand knowledge of this monster die, and opposition is silenced, Putin leads a steady drumbeat to convert the Stalin who supplied the Nazis and then hid for days at the onset of World War II into a heroic, brilliant military strategist. As a result of this rehabilitation campaign, 47 percent of Russians in a recent poll had no knowledge of any repression by Stalin. Some 70 percent (up from 8 percent) now approve of Stalin.[40] The rehabilitation of Stalin is crucial to Putin precisely because in policy and manner of governing, Putin is Stalin. Indeed, 38 percent of Russians now believe Stalin to be the greatest of all Russians. And in the West, Russian-funded propaganda and organizations like the risible Stalin Society push a constant theme that the massacres, purges, and poisonings never occurred or, if they did, Uncle Joe never knew of the zeal of a few officials. Like Stalin's photoshopping or Holocaust deniers, they seek to obliterate from history the millions of Stalin's victims.

Similar to Stalin's attachment like Gorky's "flea" on Lenin, Putin attached himself as the indispensable man first to Sobchak (who likely met Lenin's fate) and then to Boris Yeltsin.[41] Many believed Putin and his close KGB friends to be involved in the death of reformers like Galina Starovoytova in order to isolate a very sick Yeltsin, just as Lenin was isolated by

Stalin, from their influence. As Stalin placed his friends in key positions to consolidate power, so too, Putin placed his friends largely from the KGB or Soviet securities forces in positions of power throughout government, business, and the media. They are called the *siloviki*—an infinitely more powerful Russian mafia. And when Yeltsin's health finally compelled his departure, there was really only the indispensable man, Putin, to assume supreme power. The transfer of power was hastened by bombings of apartment buildings, which killed hundreds, creating a law-and-order atmosphere that discredited Yeltsin and propelled Putin upward. Blamed on Chechen terrorists, these bombings have never been fully explained. Putin's opponents in Russia, ranging from reporters, to activists, to business executives, to ex-military men and politicians, have had a truly remarkable run of accidents, deaths at an early age (often inexplicable), terrible beatings of themselves and their family in mystery attacks, and loss of their companies and property due to legal complaints and tax issues. Coincidental murders also occur quite frequently, but invariably are left unsolved despite the "very best" efforts of the state police. At least as much as Stalin, Putin is a builder of Potemkin villages—phony elections in which his opponents are disqualified, the superficial patina of a free media in which critical reporters encounter very bad luck, and a free enterprise system run by the siloviki, in which opposition or genuine competition means conviction and imprisonment.

Like Stalin and Xi, Putin loves collecting homes. He secretly built for himself a billion-dollar home nicknamed "Putin's Palace" on the Black Sea at Cape Idokopas, discretely hidden for years from the Russian people. Now, thanks to the social media posts of Alexei Navalny before his return to Russia, the world has seen drone footage surveying the vastness of Putin's Palace.

Unit 29155—Yasha's Group Rides Again

Like in the 1920s and 1930s, beginning around 2005 a series of mysterious deaths (some "natural" and some overt murders) began to be

Anna Pavlova as the Dying Swan. *Wikimedia Commons*

Anna Pavlova wearing a *kokoshka* at the last Imperial Ball in 1903. *Wikimedia Commons*

Anna Pavlova dancing with an elephant in Hamburg. *Richard P. Gibbs*

Sergei Diaghilev. *Saint Petersburg State Museum of Theater and Musical Art*

Ballet Russes costume designed by Pablo Picasso for *Parade*. *Maurice Raynal*

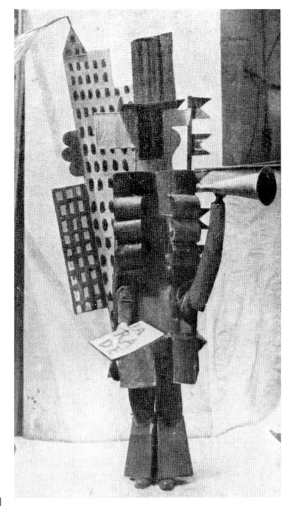

Statue of Anna Pavlova atop the Victoria Palace Theater in London. *Andreas Praefcke*

Twenty-three-year-old Joseph Stalin in 1901. *Archive of the Georgian Ministry of Internal Affairs*

Statue of Anna Akhmatova opposite Kresty Prison on the River Neva. *Angelius 1979*

The Lubyanka Prison. *A. Savin*

"The Poison Dwarf" Nikolai Yezhov walking with Stalin. *New Yorker*

The same photo retouched to exclude Yezhov after he fell from favor and was executed. *New Yorker*

Raoul Wallenberg, a Swedish architect who saved the lives of thousands of Jews during the Holocaust. After going missing during the Siege of Budapest, he was murdered in Lab One.
University of Michigan

The assassin Yakov Serebryansky, "Uncle Yasha," in 1941. *Russia Beyond*

Stalin with Lenin before Stalin's corpse was removed on Halloween, 1961. *Russian Life*

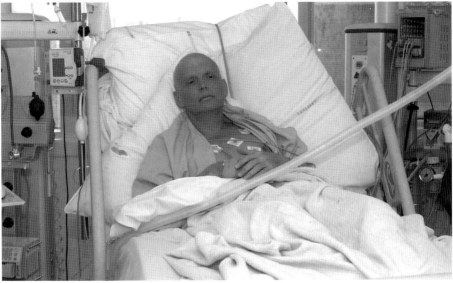

Former FSB officer Alexander Litvinenko on his deathbed after being poisoned in London. *Wikimedia Commons*

Nobel Peace Prize–winner Liu Xiaobo and his wife shortly before his death after years in prison. *The Guardian*

Chinese president Xi Jinping. *Todd Benson*

The Wuhan Institute of Virology. *Wikimedia Commons*

noticed once again in Europe. While the Russians and Putin were instant suspects, there were cases similar to those of Pavlova, Romzha, and others long before, with no physical evidence directly linking Putin to the crimes and no apprehended suspects. History does in fact sometimes repeat itself. And like ghosts of Stalin, Yasha, and Sergey Spigelglas, Putin has unleashed a new gang of killers on the world. They are just as heartless, though not nearly as competent as Yasha's Gang.

Recently, an incompetent series of mishaps exposed for the first time the existence of a previously unknown poisoning team in Russia called "Unit 29155."[42] Commanded by a general, media reports name its most important killer as Colonel Anatoliy Chepiga, a master of disguises, new occupations, and aliases. The unit includes a doctor and poison specialist.[43] Based on the eastern edge of Moscow, Unit 29155 casts a wide net of murder. Returning to its Yasha Gang roots, Unit 29155 for at least five years actually had its operational headquarters in France. In addition to an unknown number of "natural deaths," the unit has engaged in open "reprisal" murders in England, sloppy collateral murders of innocent civilians, attempted murders in Bulgaria by rubbing doors and steering wheels with lethal poisons previously unknown in the West, and the attempted murder of high officials as part of a coup in Montenegro. Chepiga uses a changing variety of names, disguises, and occupations— most recently appearing to be a sports nutrition salesman—much like Spigelglas's assumed identity as a fishmonger long ago. Chepiga's cold killer eyes remain the same in all the photos and videos of him, also very reminiscent of Sergey Spigelglas. The unit has traveled undercover to eighteen or more countries, but the full account of what they have done and who they have murdered or poisoned is unknown.

They have all received Russia's highest decorations from Putin, such as the "Hero of Russia" award. These heroes are poor descendants of the Yasha Gang and Sergey Spigelglas in Paris, who would be ashamed of their ineptitude and lack of tradecraft. They've botched easy killings and get-aways, childishly post videos together to social media, and brag on the internet about their military decorations. Russian records show the luxurious Western cars they drive and even their opulent homes.[44] They are pitiful compared to the true Russian heroes: the brave men and women who fought in World War II.

When confronted with evidence of murders, the Putin regime has deflected blame onto others and spread lies, responding, in the tradition of Stalin, through a mouthpiece. *Pravda* reports, "It's a pity it [the unit] doesn't exist," and (disclaiming any knowledge of the unit in an article with Chepiga's picture), claims their travels in Europe were just innocent fun.[45] *Pravda* continues, with shades of Stalin, that British Intelligence was responsible for the poisoning attacks. These are alibis even cruder than the childish fabrications of the 1938 purge trials. The activities of the unit show that Putin will murder anyone anywhere in the world whom he finds inconvenient. Like Stalin, he kills sometimes secretly in staged "natural deaths" and sometimes openly in gruesome reprisal killings—all loosely justified, as by Stalin before him, on the grounds that since Putin is Russia, his opponents are attacking Russia itself.

The Poison Lab/Bioweapons Project is critical to Putin's regime. Poison gives Putin, like Stalin, a means of removing without attribution dissenters, defectors, and opponents. But importantly, the bioweapons project gives Putin a potential ability to avoid the nuclear stalemate, which had tied up and contained the aggression of the Soviet Union. At least in his speeches and dreams, Putin someday intends to restore the contours of the Soviet Union, embracing Eastern Europe, Russia, Ukraine, and perhaps the former Soviet republics of Central Asia with the use of bioweapons. In Terry Hayes's best-selling novel, *I Am Pilgrim: A Thriller*, the author fantasizes about smallpox being systematically spread through mailed products.[46] Hayes's fantasy is well within the capability of Putin's government. Although Putin's Russia, unlike China, is as yet only a retail killer of selected individuals rather than the vast, murderous reach of COVID-19, its bioweapons program is the most sophisticated on earth. Stalin might have been proud of his heirs' being able to produce a human Armageddon. Putin's bioweapons program presents an existential threat to mankind. And like Stalin, Putin smiles and simply denies its existence.

According to *Russia Today*, the average Russian army recruit spends one day out of every five in a biohazard suit protecting him in the event of war using biological and chemical weapons.[47] With only Putin's Russia and Xi's China possessing bioweapons at such a scale and intensity, why is this necessary? The answer is quite ominous. They are anticipating the widespread use of their own biological and chemical weapons in future conflicts. In contrast, the United States and the entire West remain almost completely unprepared. Dramatically, the USS *Abraham Lincoln*, a critical part of the U.S. strategic and tactical arsenal, was forced offline and to port by a March 2020 outbreak of COVID-19.

CHAPTER TWENTY

North Korea's Poison Labs

S talin's shadow and the legacy of Laboratory One spread like a noxious weed to North Korea. Near the end of World War II, "Stalin's Himmler," Beria, interviewed various candidates to control Soviet-occupied North Korea. On Beria's recommendation, Stalin selected Kim Il-Sung, establishing the cruelest family rule in modern times. In Stalinist North Korea, the Kims brought the necessary accessories of Stalinist rule.[1]

Among these is one of the most feared and heartless poison labs in history. While everything is secret in the Hermit Kingdom, intercepted records, as well as guards and prisoners who have escaped, testify to a deeply chilling story matching, if not exceeding, the Mairanovsky-Beria days of Lab One, at least in cruelty.[2] Former prisoner Lee Soon-Ok describes fifty women being forced to eat poisoned cabbages until they died in great pain. Guard Kwon Hyuk, former head of security at Camp 22, described gas chamber experiments where families of four were watched as they were gassed. The efforts of a father and mother to save their young children through mouth-to mouth resuscitation were carefully noted by the clinicians. Documents from Camp 22 verify the practice.

Guard Ahn Nyung Chi describes practice operations by new doctors on prisoners who are first stunned by hammer blows on the back of the head. When zombies are needed for operations poison testing or target practice, a black van (that prisoners call "the Crow") arrives to pick up more victims, usually at least forty to fifty a month, panicking prisoners with its arrival.[3]

The sophisticated poisons developed by North Korea through human testing have, in fact, been used over and over in poisonings and failed poisonings—most spectacularly in the poisoning of the current ruler's half-brother Kim Jong-Nam in the Kuala Lumpur airport on February 13, 2017.[4] Like Iron Felix and Stalin with their testers, Kim Jong-Nam had an antidote to the poison VX that was used, but died before he realized he had been poisoned.[5] Mairanovsky, Beria, and Stalin taught their North Korean pupils well.

While the Kims have been adept at developing poisons, they have not done as well at vaccines and palliative treatments. Reportedly, North Korea has been one of the countries most devastated by COVID-19 with massive but unknown numbers of dead.

CHAPTER TWENTY-ONE

Big Daddy Xi and the Wuhan Virus

*"I still believe that freedom is the bonus you receive
for telling the truth.
You shall know the truth and the truth shall
set you free."*[1]

—Martin Luther King Jr.

The rivalry between the United States and the allied Stalinist-influenced nations of Russia, North Korea, and China has often been compared to the rivalry of golden-age Athens and Sparta: an open culture of innovation and freedom versus a closed culture of martial discipline and centralized control. Like Athens, whose golden age ended with a plague following unsuccessful foreign adventures, the sun may be setting on the golden age of the United States. If so, future historians will mark the decline by a crippling pandemic. In the wonderful chronologically arranged museum of Athens, visitors move from a surviving statuary of the gods, portraying laughing youth, magical legends, physical beauty and athleticism, to mortuary statues to commemorating the many victims of the Plague of Athens. It might as well have commemorated the end of the Athenian golden age itself. The age of Athens was followed by Spartan hegemony, enabled by Sparta-friendly Athenian aristocrats.

Prior to China's conquest by the Manchus, its abuse by colonial powers, and its rule by fanatic Communist ideologues, China was the world's greatest nation. During the Tang and Ming dynasties, China was innovative, inventing printing as well as sailing large fleets of discovery to faraway Africa, and likely the western coastlines of North and South America.[2] It was also a deeply spiritual and moral nation, giving the world Confucius and Lao Tzu, developing new forms of Buddhism, and cultivating a deep respect for ancestry and history. Its culture had successfully resisted the crude barbarism of the Mongols, who conquered China's territory, but not its mind. In the chaos of the seventeenth through twentieth centuries, much of historical China was forgotten. By the 1920s, China was in revolution, and its Communist Party led by Mao Zedong was closely supported by Stalin and his Soviet Communist Party. With Stalin's support, the Chinese Communist Party (CCP) took over control of China in 1949. One of the world's most ancient civilizations was led by rulers who would quickly prove themselves ruthless and without care for human life.

In the years prior to his death in 1953, Stalin was fêted repeatedly by the Chinese Communist Party and Mao as the foundational figure of communism, placed on a pedestal alongside Marx, Lenin, and Mao himself. Russia's own condemnation of Stalin for his crimes in 1956 produced a sharp break with China, where Stalin would remain enshrined as a demi-god. Mao imitated the slaughters of Stalin with his Great Leap Forward and his own Cultural Revolution. After Mao's death, the new rulers of China surveyed the devastation and opted for a better path. The new ruler, Deng Xiaoping, introduced reason and pragmatism to an exhausted China: "No matter if it is a black cat or a white cat—as long as it can catch mice, it is a good cat."[3]

Although China under Deng would continue to industrialize with a mixed private-state enterprise economy, any real hope of political reform—away from rigid Stalinism—died with the protesting students in Tiananmen Square on June 4, 1989.

The West ignored the lesson of Nazi Germany where increasing prosperity under Hitler validated, strengthened, and radicalized the Nazi butchers. Instead, the West, even after the slaughter of 1989, pretended that the increasing prosperity of Communist China would wean Communist China away from Stalinist, Marxist ideals. Sadly, feeding the tiger makes it more fearsome. *Dane-Geld* once again horribly failed.[4] China shifted back towards the Marxist, Stalinist ideals rejected by Deng.

The History of Chinese Bioweapons

Along with its worship of Stalin, China from the inception of the People's Republic of China (PRC) in 1949 has had an extremely secret, but growing biowar program under supervision of the People's Liberation Army (PLA).[5] Like Russia, its hidden military program secretly parallels and uses its more open and apparently benign civilian biolabs. Every Chinese company is required to fund a parallel shadow Communist Party committee. Each apparently open biolab, like that in Wuhan, China, cooperates with a hidden, secret military biowar lab whose job is the development of weaponized viruses, bacteria, and poisons. The secrecy of its special war capacity is among the most closely guarded information of the PRC. While the West freely provided China with virtually all information on viruses, the Chinese military labs run by the PLA are among the most secretive institutions in the world. Even their existence is denied. The PLA military labs conduct research on both deadly toxins and debilitating viruses like COVID-19.[6] Since the Chinese Communist Party did not collapse like the Soviet Union, but merely reformed itself economically, its secrets have never been revealed. But there are glimpses at what is behind China's commercial façade—the iron fist inside the silk glove.

China's involvement in biowar programs began in the strangest of ways: as a victim of biowar activities in World War II. At the end of the war, the infamous Japanese biowar laboratory at Harbin in China was captured. While some high-ranking officers in Japan regrettably escaped prosecution, other officials in the lab were turned over to the Russians. Some were tried as war criminals while others were disposed of after debriefing "rabbits" as test subjects in Lab One. Likewise Soviet and Chinese biowar officials later cooperated in leveling false biowar charges against the United Nations forces in Korea. After the break in relations between Russia and China following Stalin's death, Russia could only view the Chinese biowar labs which it cooperated in launching from afar.

After long cooperation with Russia, China had a thriving biowar capability by the 1960s. The Soviet defector Ken Alibek related in 2003 that Soviet intelligence learned of two separate leaks of hemorrhagic fever from Chinese biowar labs in Western China in the late 1980s which caused many deaths. Soviet intelligence concluded the Chinese were, in addition, weaponizing Marburg Fever and the Ebola virus at the same site.[7] Likewise, Soviet scientists suggested that the 2003 appearance of the SARS virus in China, never seen before, might have been the result of the leak of a bioweapon.[8] These were minor compared to a 1977 leak and the 2019 leak at Wuhan which would each kill millions.

The world became more aware of China's sophisticated and developed bioweapons capability in 2005—sufficiently developed that, in violation of the Biological Weapons Convention, China assisted Iran with its illegal bioweapons program.[9] China is recognized by U.S. intelligence to currently have at least fifteen massive identified facilities devoted to biological weapons research and development—likely the world's largest and most sophisticated biowar capability. Since these programs are in violation of the 1972 treaty, they remain among China's most guarded secrets.[10] Two of these facilities are located in Wuhan in south-central China. The rapid, illegal growth of China's bioweapons program is ironic. More than any other nation, China has itself been the victim of bioweapons—those employed by the Japanese Empire during World War II which killed many thousands. For this reason, China under Deng Xiaoping was at least superficially an aggressive advocate of the outlawing of bioweapons. But Deng's power was much reduced by the Tiananmen Square slaughter, and his rule ended with his death in 1997.

After a succession of relatively low-profile leaders, Xi Jinping rose to power in 2012. China renewed and accelerated its biowar program.

Five months *before* the outbreak of COVID-19, the Pentagon publicly warned about the vastly expanded Chinese chemical and biowar program.[11] "It's only a matter of when," a general said, and China was singled out as the worldwide leader in such toxins.

Poison, a Family Tradition

In 1927 in Fuping, Shaanxi Province, in central China, a fourteen-year-old boy named Xi Zhongxun, infused with radical ideology, tried to murder his teacher by poisoning him for being too reactionary.[12] Jailed for his crime, he became a hero to Shaanxi's Communists. By 1928 (as the Yasha Gang gathered in Paris to poison others in unrelated crimes), Xi Zhongxun joined the Communist Party while in jail, launching a career of more than seventy years during which, in one period, he was in charge of Chinese propaganda, directing cultural and educational policies. During the 1950s and early 1960s, it was Xi Zhongxun's job to conceal the tens of millions who died in China in the Great Leap Forward. Now Xi Zhongxun's son Xi Jinping is China's absolute ruler. He was affectionately dubbed for a time "Big Daddy Xi" in China's official media. According to Xi Jinping, the elder Xi was the greatest influence in his life. Near Xian in Central China, Xi the Poisoner is honored by a massive sixty-ton granite statue in a large park with a nearby museum.[13] It is now a solemn place of religious pilgrimage where visitors are instructed to "bow three times" before the elder Xi the Poisoner's statue "to show respect to the Leader."[14]

Tiananmen Square

Tiananmen Square has been central to the history of China for many centuries. Located near the so-called Imperial Forbidden City, home of the emperors for five hundred years, its construction was begun in 1415, at the height of China's power during the prolific years of the Ming dynasty. The People's Republic of China was first proclaimed in this square in 1949. It contains a mausoleum for the body of the "Great Helmsman," Mao Zedong, whose mummy, like Lenin's, is displayed as a relic in a kind of strange Communist heaven. For a few weeks in the spring and early summer of 1989, the square would become the hinge of a great door that would change Chinese and world history.

Until the events in the square in 1989, China was a rapidly liberalizing country with an economy embracing the power of free enterprise capitalism, changing at breath-taking speed from a primitive medieval economy to a modern industrial powerhouse. With the economic change promoted by Deng came a great thirst for freedom of thought and culture far different than the rigid, colorless Stalinism embraced by Mao. But although the Communist Party had surrendered economic control, it never surrendered rigid political control.

And so thousands of students, many of them dedicated Communists, gathered in the square in the spring of 1989 (as students are wont to do) demanding reform of the Party, freedom of speech, and political reform. Despite great internal opposition in the CCP itself to repression led by China's then reformer premier and party leader, Zhao Ziyang, the army was unleashed upon the students in the square on June 3–5, 1989, with tanks and automatic weapons, killing thousands of unarmed students in full view of a horrified world. After regular units of the PLA refused orders to begin a massacre of the students, a special unit of the PLA called the Fifteenth Airborne Brigade was unleashed to begin a heartless massacre of the unarmed students. They would be seen again in 2019 in Wuhan.

A symbol of the students' hope for political reform amidst the massacre was "Tank Man"—a courageous, now legendary, young man who stood in front of the armored tank column to block their advance with his body. We should never forget that Tank Man was seized by the police, never identified, and disappeared forever into the Chinese gulag with many thousands of others.

Thus the new regime declared its character to the world. Ziyang was removed from office and imprisoned. Within a short time after the massacre, Xi the poisoner offered his full support to the "brave" troops used for the massacre. Xi's wife, Peng Liyuan, a singer and later major general in the PLA, was featured the morning after the massacre singing congratulations in Tiananmen Square to the troops who slaughtered the students. Xi Jinping was silent until later, offering support for the army's actions. Some of China's best and brightest died in those days. With them also died hope for a moderate China which would shed totalitarianism for a democratic or true collective leadership. Although the actual numbers killed were a fraction of those now being killed now on Xi's orders, because it was done publicly, the massacre was a day of infamy. During those fateful days, China and the Xi family crossed a line from progressivism to Stalinism without regret. Although the West hoped and sometimes pretended that its support of the Chinese economy would result in a more humane China, this was false. Like the growth of Nazi Germany in the 1930s, the growth of the Chinese economy did not humanize the Chinese hardliners. It validated their increasing iron-fist rule over China as German growth in the thirties had consolidated Hitler's monstrous control over Germany. In China, the events at Tiananmen Square have been scrubbed from the internet and all sources of information. If you were born after 1989 in China, you would know nothing of these events or China's better days.

With the death of Deng, the hardliners dedicated to the legacy of Mao and Stalin gained total political control. They consolidated power until 2013 when the hardest of hardliners, Xi Jinping, like Mao and Stalin, became first among equals. With the exception of the bloodthirsty Kim dynasty of North Korea, there is no more ruthless or absolute ruler on earth than Xi. As a "princeling," whose father was an associate of Mao, Xi and his family endured terrible treatment at the hands of the Red Guards during the madness of the Great Cultural Revolution. Far from creating a sense of sympathy and mercy in Xi, persecution built a fierce fanaticism to be more Marxist and Stalinist than his father, or even the Red Guards who had abused them. Beginning in 2013, using now familiar Stalinist tactics, he initiated a vast purge of the Communist Party business, the arts, and the government bureaucracy itself, ostensibly to eliminate corruption, but in reality, directed almost solely at his rivals.

It is estimated that Xi likely has so far eliminated several hundred thousand people—perhaps one-third of the upper echelon of the CCP—many secretly or in mock trials like those of the 1930s with brutally extracted confessions. Sometimes there are no trials, just unmentioned disappearances into "black" jails, or into mobile death vans for execution and organ harvesting (reminiscent of the Nazi gas vans), which are now widespread.[15] With incredible brutality Xi also moved against the Uighurs, a Turkic Muslim people of Xinjiang Province in Western China. Much like Hitler's persecution of the Jews or Stalin's murder of the Kulaks, millions of Uighurs are confined to concentration camps euphemistically called "re-education camps," suffering forced abortions, murder, and brainwashing to eliminate religious belief. This is industrial-scale cruelty and cultural extermination of a kind not seen in a great power since the depravities of Hitler and Stalin.[16]

Xi now promotes himself as a demigod, with his portraits everywhere alongside those of Mao. Books of his rather sterile thoughts and quotes are held up by school kids like the *Mao Little Red Books* or *Mein Kampf* as the words of a god. Increasingly he appears in red or black Mao-style clothing, as opposed to business suits. *Animal Farm* and *1984*, together with many other Western or Christian texts, have been banned in a recent book destruction campaign to eliminate "bad" thoughts, together with access to "confusing" foreign news sources like CNN. Any religion other than that found in state churches is banned as an evil cult, and many prominent ministers have been imprisoned or simply disappeared. As Xi tightened the grip of Stalinism on Chinese life, he has also militarized his country, seizing large portions of the South China Sea, annexing Hong Kong in direct violation of treaty promises, and threatening Vietnam, India, Taiwan, and the Philippines. In order to directly neutralize the threat of United States Navy's carriers to his later adventures, Xi has poured resources into the development of very sophisticated long-range cruise missiles with labels like "Assassin's Mace"—hypersonic carrier killers. He has developed space weapons capable of circling the globe at hypersonic speed to destroy the cities of the West with nuclear weapons. Recently, Vice Chairman of the Joint Chiefs of Staffs John Hyten, pointing to hundreds of new ballistic missile sites being constructed in China, questioned whether it was preparing a first nuclear strike capability against the West. If so, Xi is the only ruler since Stalin to prepare to initiate a worldwide nuclear war.[17]

Like old Uncle Joe Stalin, Xi promotes the image of a kind father, the patriarchal "Big Daddy Xi" (though that name was eventually banned in China as insufficiently reverent). Xi's self-promoted demi-god status was illustrated by the prosecution and torture of twenty-three individuals, including an online forum administrator named Niu Tengyu, accused of posting pictures of Xi's daughter without authorization. After being tortured, Niu was sentenced to fourteen years imprisonment, effectively, a death sentence, for "stirring up trouble."[18] Like Mao, Xi holds up Li Lafan as a role model. Li Lafan was a Tang minster 1400 years ago, "whose mouth drips honey while he holds a knife next to his heart." He has described Putin as his closest foreign friend.[19] Like Stalin's Laboratory One and Putin's vast program, Xi has built an extensive concealed bioweapons capability in order to provide a special weapons alternative to direct nuclear war. Xi, like Stalin, Mao, and Putin, is capable of using bioterror to advance Stalinist objectives. It would be but a continuation of the concentration camps of the Uighurs, the slaughter of many comrades, and the destruction of Hong Kong's freedom to create and use bioweapons.

The Big Daddy "Disappearances" and Murders

Shortly after Big Daddy Xi's assumption of absolute power in China, much like Stalinist Russia of the 1920s and '30s, a vast wave of "disappearances" and suicides began.[20] In 2015 alone, Bloomberg reports more than thirty-four traceable, known, high-level executives disappeared or committed "suicide." Once most victims disappear, they are never again discussed. They become non-persons. Like in Stalinist Russia where the purged were airbrushed from photos, to even mention them is both rude and dangerous. No one is ever safe from Big Daddy Xi's secret terror.

The Phantoms

The most famous and incorrigibly honest of Chinese law enforcement officials is Meng Hongwei, a brilliant police official, so respected even in the West that he was made head of the International Criminal Police Organization (INTERPOL).[21] On a trip to China, he simply disappeared for many months after sending his wife a knife emoji to warn her of the threat. Months later, in a repeat of the Stalinist Show Trials, Meng appeared in a videotaped court appearance, much shaken, to supposedly confess to taking two million dollars in bribes. This in a country led by Xi and wealthy relatives who have accumulated billions of dollars. Meng's brave wife, Grace, still free in France, filed suit against INTERPOL and others for refusing to assist her beaten and tortured husband, whose thirteen-year sentence is effectively a death sentence.[22]

The most famous Chinese entrepreneur and technocrat is Jack Ma, creator of Alibaba, the Chinese version of Amazon. Ma is also famous for his generosity. After Ma delivered a talk modestly critical of Chinese state banks, he suddenly vanished. A critical multi-billion-dollar public offering of Ant, a new Ma company, was cancelled. Ma was removed from the list of China's greatest entrepreneurs. Billions in fines were assessed against Alibaba, now a shrinking shadow of the world's second largest internet company.[23] A business and entrepreneur school started by Ma in China was prohibited from taking any new students.[24] Although Ma survives in the shadows in China and sometimes with supervision abroad, he is now a non-person. Likewise, the heads of almost every large Chinese tech company like JD and Tencent Holdings were forced to resign, becoming like Ma, shadowy silent phantoms. It is supremely dangerous to stand too tall in the land of Xi, who like Stalin, favors making himself a giant by making all others appear small.

Wang Yi of the Early Rain Covenant Church, once a well-regarded lawyer, is likely the most well-known Chinese Christian pastor. A guest at the White House, he has been a speaker in numerous international conferences. In 2018 his church was physically destroyed and he, his wife, and over a hundred members of his church were arrested and criminally charged by the Xi government with "inciting subversion of state power" and "illegal business activities."[25] Recently the Wang Yi and his wife were sentenced to nine years in prison in a secret proceeding, as many "trials" conducted by the Xi government are now secret proceedings. The fate of many of church members who disappeared into Xi's gulag is unknown, but it is likely they are effectively being executed for their belief and are in a world beyond the reach of even Xi's police and jailers.

Among the most famous movie and television stars in China, also enjoying worldwide popularity, is Fan Bingbing, whose stardom is in many ways reminiscent of Anna Pavlova's. Fan started with not only beauty, but great acting talent on display in more than twenty films. She also showed great taste and expertise in style and design. Fan soon became an icon for international fashion and design, like Anna Pavlova, wearing the famous dress "Dragon Robe" at Cannes and later "the Four Beauties of Ancient China," a dress imitating a famous porcelain vase from the great Tang Dynasty. Every respected Western designer sought her endorsement. Like Pavlova, Fan became famous for philanthropy and generosity, for example arranging for the treatment of more than three hundred children with congenital heart disease. It was not only her face, but her heart whose beauty attracted the world. Her most famous roles in China were of ancient princesses and empresses of the old regimes—much like Pavlova in Petipa's great ballets. She became too big a figure, however, for China's Communist masters, just as Pavlova grew too big for Stalin. There was not enough room in a Stalinist country for a great personality playing ancient princesses and empresses, as opposed to revolutionaries, while flying around the world highlighting the great, advanced culture of ancient, Imperial China.

In 2018, she was named in an investigation of the movie industry for "distorting social value." Fan, adored by many as the most beautiful and talented woman in the world, suddenly disappeared without a trace shortly before the scheduled filming of an international spy movie.[26] Three months later, she reappeared to make the standard Stalinist confession of cultural hegemony: "Without the party and the state...there would have been no Fan Bingbing." Unlike the Swan, Fan will never escape Xi's China.

A fine of about $131 million, ostensibly for tax evasion in a country notorious for tax evasion, essentially wiped out her fortune. She remains in China, but closely guarded. Meanwhile, Xi has instituted complete "supervision" of the film industry. Like Pavlova, Fan was simply too free for a Stalinist tyrant's comfort. Stars in Xi's China are to be wheels on a Stalinist train. Following her reappearance as a disgraced non-person, Fan was dropped by her faithless Western sponsors, excluded from new movies, and her fiancé broke off their engagement because of her status as someone officially disgraced.

Among Fan's closest friends was the great young Japanese movie star, Haruma Miura. He recently died in Tokyo under very suspicious circumstances. Haruma was found hanging in a closet in the middle of working on several film projects. His friends did not believe him despondent or even anxious. His death was ruled a suicide because of the presence of an undated and vague suicide note—so reminiscent of many of Stalin's victims whose final acts on this earth were to write dictated suicide notes under coercion.[27] Who was responsible and how did Miura die? Was it an authentic suicide or just another Stalinist-staged suicide? We will likely never know.

In her velvet cage in China, Fan Bingbing could only write a post expressing her great sorrow without identifying Miura's death as its cause (although the world knew it was so).[28] She was instantly attacked by inhumane "influencers" hired by the Chinese government in fulfillment of its cultural hegemony campaign under Big Daddy Xi. Attacks directed at her asked, "Why are you always acting up when something happens?" An estimated 200,000 paid professional social media and internet "influencers" employed by the Chinese Communists for propaganda control are called "Wolf Warriors," a moniker later adopted by China's new generation of belligerent diplomats.[29] Given their cowardly anonymity and swarm attacks, the Wolf Warriors would be better termed "Roach Packs" for their propensity to disappear into the darkness when light is shined upon them. They are constantly present to tear Fan down with false reports and rumors.

China's second most famous movie star is Zhao Wei (also known as Vicky Zhao). She gained fame worldwide playing "Little Swallow" in the television series *My Fair Princess*, but she is also as a singer, producer, and director. Zhao was considered China's first great national film idol. In 2014, she was criticized for having shaken hands with Hillary Clinton. As the internet "Wolf Warriors" closed in, suddenly she became a phantom. All movies, television shows, and songs involving her or with her name abruptly disappeared from the internet in China.[30] Zhao's present location is unknown. Her sin seems to have been playing too many parts of a princess, empress, or a mother, and not nearly enough as a faceless cadre adoring Xi.

Peng Shuai, once the number-one doubles tennis star in the world and China's most-successful tennis player, recently vanished suddenly and inexplicably after accusing former senior vice premier Zhang Gaoli of a vicious sexual assault in a public Weibo blog.[31] Following an international outcry for her protection, Shuai recently and predictably denied making any accusations of assault either vocally or in writing.[32] While she alleges recanting the allegations "completely of [her] own will," the World Tennis Association has continued "significant concerns about her well-being and ability to communicate without censorship or coercion." In a nation without individual rights for anyone, there are no equal rights for women.

The Nobel Laureate

China has had three winners of the Nobel Prize who have actually lived in China when the prize was awarded. Fourteen other Chinese citizens have received the Nobel as refugees or émigrés to other lands. In 2010, poet Liu Xiaobo, the first Chinese recipient of a Nobel Peace Prize was not allowed to travel to Stockholm to accept or even designate a representative in his stead. He had bravely returned to China from comfortable university positions abroad to support the Tiananmen students. Other than an imprisoned concentration camp victim of the Nazis in 1935, Liu is the only Nobel laureate unable to accept his prize because of actual imprisonment in isolation. At his brief trial shortly before the Nobel Awards ceremony, Liu sought to read a statement, but it was suppressed. He told his wife at the trial, "If I am crushed into powder, I will greet you with ashes...and with hope." The statement was later read by a crying Liv Ullmann in Stockholm at the Nobel Awards ceremony awarding him the Nobel Prize for Peace:

> I have no enemies and no hatred [after praising by name each of his guards, interrogators, prosecutors, wardens, and judges as good people, not his enemies].... I, filled with optimism, look forward to the advent of a future free China. For there is no force that can put an end to the human quest for freedom, and China will in the end become a nation...where human rights reign supreme.[33]

He then said goodbye to his wife, "... whose love is the sunlight that leaps over prison walls and penetrates the iron bars of my prison windows."[34]

Liu remained imprisoned, despite international pleas for his release. As he slowly wasted away in prison, the pleas for release and for medical treatment were ignored. Liu was "released" a few days before his death in 2017 and was not allowed to be treated abroad. His health was broken, but his spirit was not. After only a perfunctory notice of his death, all mention of Liu on approved search engines in China was replaced with "results for 'Liu Xiaobo' cannot be displayed." His funeral, small and private, was supervised by the Xi government, ensuring he was cremated with his ashes scattered by the government at sea.

As with so many other victims of Stalinism, the Xi government sought to eliminate forever Liu's memory as effectively as his ashes dissolved into the waves. But like those victims, whether Tikhon, Gorky, Pavlova, or the other Chinese martyrs, his memory remains alive in China, even in the shadow of brutal Big Daddy Xi.[35]

The ongoing purge in China, which extends to many others such as brave newspaper publisher Jimmy Lai (who chose prison over flight), is of very great importance because it is evidence of the utter ruthlessness and duplicity of the Xi government as it leaps forward from a mixed economy to becoming as Mao said, "the tallest tree in the forest."[36] There is no life or lives it values, nor is there a lie it will not tell, no matter how preposterous by the standards of objective reality. Thus, the one hundred twenty-five hypersonic missile sites are "for space exploration."

The 1977 Cover-up

Human history has periodically and repeatedly been interrupted by horrific outbreaks of disease. The Antonine Plague of 165 A.D. of unknown type and origin brought the Roman Empire's greatest days to an end. The Bubonic Plague, called "the Black Death," killed up to two hundred million in the fourteenth century and many more in later outbreaks. Smallpox, Syphillis, and other diseases have decimated cities and nations.

The most recent deadly pandemic was a flu: the so-called Spanish Flu of 1918. Its origin, variously attributed to U.S. troops in Kansas, people in Spain, Asia, and other places is not known with certainty, but is effects were devastating, much like the great wars of the twentieth entury. It particularly targeted the young, but infected a third of mankind's 1.5 billion people, killing 10 percent of them, approximately 50 million victims. The pandemic abated in the early 1920s. Then for unknown reasons it disappeared as mysteriously as it first came. The virus likely survived only in frozen corpses in the Arctic, although people lived in fear of its return for a time. It may also have been recaptured secretly in biolabs in China and Russia.

Since the middle of the twentieth century, the world has been visited by four major flu pandemics. In 1957, the "Asian Flu," believed to have originated in Southeast Asia, spread, killing 1.1 million people worldwide. In 1968, once again out of Southeast Asia, the "Hong Kong Flu" emerged, killing between one and four million victims. Then, in 1977 the most mysterious of all of the pandemics emerged from China.

The 1977 flu, which killed 700,000, was virtually an exact duplicate of the 1957 flu virus from twenty years before—in terms of virology, an impossible occurrence. Flu viruses mutate and change with time and circulation. But like a time traveler or Rip Van Winkle visiting from the past, the 1977 virus was almost indistinguishable from the long-gone 1957 virus that had disappeared from the world twenty years earlier. The two viruses were so identical that the 1977 wave affected primarily only those not yet born in 1957. The 1977 virus also showed a susceptibility to temperature that is typical of stored viruses. Various scientists theorized at the time that the 1977 virus could only be explained by someone's having preserving the 1957 virus in an unknown biolab and then later leaking it. China was silent on the subject, the World Health Organization reached no conclusion, and China's friends denounced those who claimed the virus resulted from a leak in China as conspiracy theorists. It seemed fated to be another unsolved mystery where circumstantial evidence strongly indicated, but did not conclusively prove, the existence of a lab or experiment leak in China.

In 2004, virologist Peter Palese wrote that his close, now deceased friend, Chi-Ming Chu, perhaps the world's most prominent virologist at the time and head of the Chinese virology programs, told him that the spread of the 1977 flu was due to leaks caused by 1957 strain-vaccine trials on several thousand military personnel of China's People's

Liberation Army (PLA).[37] The virus had been preserved in a laboratory. Doctor Chi-Ming's disclosures shortly before his sudden death in 1998 were deeply revealing. China had concealed the source of the 1977 flu while nearly 700,000 people died from it. Why? The reason, like the COVID-19 concealment, was to hide its vast, heartless military bioweapons program. Why develop a vaccine for a long-gone virus that exists only in your own biolab if not in preparation for the virus's use as a debilitating bioweapon for which China alone would have a vaccine? The 1977 flu episode certainly shows the ability of the PLA bioweapons program to leak, and the utter ruthlessness of the PLA to maintain the secrecy of China's bioweapons programs even if many die as a consequence. In most courts, the existence of similar past criminal acts like China's decades-long concealment of the origin of the 1977 virus is powerful evidence of the PLA's current concealment of the origin of COVID-19.[38]

The concealment of the leak's origin was intended to conceal China's military bioweapons program—the other side of civilian labs like the Wuhan Institute of Virology. The bioweapons program symbiotically uses and feeds upon the civilian labs while remaining secret. In 2012 and on later occasions, the French government, which helped to establish the Wuhan lab, warned the United States of Chinese "motivations" and intentions for the Wuhan Lab itself—warnings that were wholly disregarded.[39]

The Wuhan Labs and the Virus

In the spring of 2020, people all over the world and the global economy were paralyzed by the great coronavirus pandemic. It originated in Wuhan, China, and was called "COVID-19." Although the appearance of the virus was clearly fixed in Wuhan on the Yangtze River in Southeast China, roughly midway between Beijing and Hong Kong, its actual origin, whether natural or created, and its transfer to humans was initially largely a mystery.

The Wuhan scientist who disclosed the virus's existence, Dr. Li Wenliang, was arrested and imprisoned for "disclosing state secrets." Shortly after his release, Dr. Li was reported to have died on February 7, 2020, at the age of thirty-three purportedly of the virus itself, though the virus is lethal in less than 1.5 percent of people his age. The initial anger of Xi's government towards Dr. Li is explicable only in terms of what he did to undermine their plot to conceal the origin of the virus. Dr. Li's public disclosures placed the outbreak of the virus near or at the Wuhan biolabs—like locating the murder weapon in a criminal's car. After Li's disclosure, the Xi government, directly or through shills, issued fanciful, often childish stories of a mythical magic pangolin bat never discovered, to distract from the reality that the COVID-19 virus had first appeared next to the labs in Wuhan. These virology labs had been involved in gene enhancement experiments and were holding COVID-19's only close natural relative. Dr. Li had, perhaps, inadvertently divulged something much larger than he realized.

The supposed first patient from the virus identified in *Lancet* in January 2020 as "Patient Zero" (sometimes reported to be a fifty-five-year-old man and sometimes a seventy-seven-year-old man) was concealed for a time. He now says he has Alzheimer's disease and doesn't know how he got it. The early Chinese scientists who spoke out have largely "disappeared" or died, along with the earliest patients. All early samples of blood infected with the virus—the most important forensic evidence of origin—were destroyed in February 2020 by specific order of the Xi government.[40] The strange and unlikely death of Dr. Li occurred at the very same time Xi's government was destroying other inconvenient threads of evidence and every single early forensic sample of COVID-19 collected in Wuhan.

The Wuhan Cover-up

Within a very short time of the virus's appearance in Wuhan, the Chinese government certainly had the full story of what actually happened since the early patients, doctors, witnesses and forensic results were all available to them. Xi must have known within a short time where COVID-19 came from and how it spread. But China cloaked everything with wildly varying and implausible cover stories, while seeking to suppress knowledge of what actually happened by destroying evidence, concealing and disappearing both witnesses and forensic results. It was the story of the Tambov poison gassing and the Ukraine slaughter all over again.

In addition to destroying all early patient forensic samples and "disappearing" early witnesses, the CCP propagated a series of wholly bogus stories to conceal the actual origin of the virus.[41] China uses the lucrative prize of access to its market and advertising by its companies to affect media coverage of its horrific actions all over the world. Cover Big Daddy Xi nicely—or be excluded from China and its economy. Just as Walter Duranty's phony *New York Times* reports denying the Ukrainian massacre shaped public perception of Stalin, fear of displeasing China has left the media, newspapers, and publishers timid and strangely uninterested in the origins of the virus.[42] When the former head of the Centers for Disease Control Dr. Robert Redfield publicly alleged that the coronavirus could have had an artificial origin, the *New York Times* initially ran with the headline, "Ex-CDC Director Favors Debunked Covid-19 Origin Theory."[43] Recently as China's cover-up slowly fell apart, the *Wall Street Journal* called people's reluctance to find the virus's origin "inexcusable group think" led by U.S. cheerleaders with hidden financial conflicts of interest.[44]

China has spun a dark cloud of digital ink. Its concealment of the origin of COVID-19, motivated by its Stalinist ideology and coupled with perverted science, has killed millions of people in almost every country. As with Stalin, many other Western media organizations want to hear no evil, see no evil, and most of all, know no evil. These are well-totaled in a *Tablet* article by Ashley Rindsberg which recounts the inexplicable actions of the U.S. press, who labeled as "fringe theories" actual efforts to question the bizarre CCP explanation of a mythical pangolin-bat cross in a Wuhan wet market.[45]

The Wet Market Theory

The original cover story was a new twist on the anthrax cover story the Soviets used at Sverdlovsk. New words to an old song. China told the world that the virus came from eating infected horseshoe bats sold at an open market, a so-called "wet market" in Wuhan. Like the 1979 Russian cover stories citing "tainted meat," the story combined some truth with some falsehood in order to create a plausible cover. The virus's DNA is 96.2 percent the same as that in horseshoe bats found in Himalayan caves. Some of the early victims, but not all, had been to, worked at, or passed the Wuhan wet market that is immediately next to the Wuhan Institute of Virology (WIV) and on the same rail line as both the WIV and a nearby military biolab, making it a convenient, if implausible, alibi. The virus, which has never been located naturally in its entirety in any animal or natural setting, most closely resembles a virus found in horseshoe bats called RaTG13. The virus that has so tragically ravaged mankind has a 96.2 percent correlation with the horseshoe bat coronavirus found in a species in caves in the Chinese Himalayas, which are 700–1,100 miles from Wuhan. Therefore, the Communist government and their apologists[46] around the world, many with lucrative deals in China, parroted (like Duranty and other "useful idiots" once did for Stalin) a common lie that the virus's origin was unknowable, irrelevant, and likely the result of consumption of horseshoe bats in the Wuhan wet market.[47]

The lack of curiosity has implications. The origin is extraordinarily relevant to the treatment of the pandemic, avoidance of future mutations and pandemics, and the assessment of blame for killing millions of people and wrecking the world economy. The "wet market" story rather quickly dissolves on the simplest examination. The horseshoe bat that lives in Himalayan caves about 700–1,100 miles from Wuhan has a range of about twenty miles. There is no evidence that horseshoe bats were ever in the Wuhan wet market. Indeed, it is irrational to imagine these bats being transported so far for consumption at the wet market. Many of the earliest victims of the virus, in fact, had no connection to the wet market. In addition, one would have to believe that the phantom super-bat flying hundreds of miles to Wuhan had mysteriously mutated in a way no other had ever done. China claimed that a Himalayan horse-shoe bat must have mated or crossed with a pangolin and then been eaten by a Wuhan resident. There are no records of the animals or their DNA ever crossing, or either ever being anywhere close to Wuhan, except in the biolabs. The explanation was like Lysenko genetics or voodoo presented as "science."

About 280 meters from the Wuhan wet market is the Wuhan Institute of Virology, operated by the Chinese Communist government, purportedly to study viruses in the search for cures.[48] There is a second, highly secret military biolab, part of the CCP Bioweapons Network, located within a few miles of the WIV, the purpose and experiments of which are closely guarded secrets. The military lab operated by the People's Liberation Army and often called the PLA Lab is critical to understanding the origin of Covid. Many of the PLA officers are on committees of the WIV. The two labs work together and have a completely symbiotic relationship: one to devise cures and protect life, and the second to devise bioweapons as agents of death.[49] There is no reason for the close duplicative military lab except for designing bioweapons prohibited by the 1972 Biological Weapons Convention. Indeed, the U.S. State Department has direct evidence from defectors that since 2017, the Wuhan Virology Laboratory has worked on military projects with the nearby secret military biolab.[50] In an effort to conceal the close connection between the WIV and the secret military lab, the names of the military personnel working at the Wuhan Institute of Virology were erased from the WIV website after the COVID-19 leak was traced to Wuhan.[51]

For at least seven years, horseshoe bats and their viruses have been brought from the faraway Himalayas to conduct medical experiments at the WIV.[52] The lab experiments were supervised by Shi Zhengli, a scientist nicknamed "Bat Woman," and include study of mutations of the natural RaTG13 coronavirus found in the horseshoe bats, very closely related to the final COVID-19 virus.[53] Until 2015 or later, the U.S. government itself and Australia directly financially supported the "research" at Wuhan. In 2015 because of the obvious danger of unleashing newly created variants of coronavirus from gene alteration experiments, the U.S. withdrew direct support.[54] Although the WIV apparently created a number of new variants of coronavirus, there is no record that it ever created either a genuinely effective cure for the variants or a vaccine against them. It has worked with the nearby military lab on an unknown number of secret joint projects.[55] While many of the activities of the WIV are public, the activities of its sister military labs and details of the joint projects between the WIV and nearby military labs are totally concealed by a Chinese government known for its secrecy and misdirection.

Given the highly-suspicious COVID-19 death (or murder) of Dr. Li and the disappearance of many others, as well as the intentional destruction of the virus specimens collected from the earliest victims—all on orders of the CCP and PLA in February as the news spread—it is presently uncertain whether COVID-19 was created in the Wuhan labs or simply extracted there.[56] A group of doctors, some of whom are financially tied to China, has claimed that the absence of certain tells in that coronavirus proves it was not the result of genetic editing with the CRISPR genetic tool or likewise.[57] Other doctors claim to have found intrinsic evidence of genetic manipulation of this very strange virus.[58] Relying on the testimony of a defecting Hong Kong virologist and vast additional evidence, according to U.S. Secretary of State Mike Pompeo, a great deal of evidence points to the Wuhan labs as originating the virus.[59]

Recently released emails viewed by the House Oversight and Reform Committee reveal that the virologists who publicly sponsored a natural origin theory, privately believed at the same time that COVID-19 was created in and leaked from a Wuhan lab.[60] The virologists pointed to fingerprints of manipulation of the virus, specifically in the furin cleavage site that makes the virus so infectious for human cells. No other member of the Sarbecovirus family, of which COVID-19 is included, possesses a furin cleavage site. Additionally, the furin cleavage site inserted into the virus is precisely the required length of twelve units of RNA—a fine precision unusual in nature, but easily generated in a lab.

There is much evidence in the public domain that shows that the WIV was engaged in so-called chimera experiments: the creation of altered viruses through combinations or gene editing.[61] These included experiments with RaTG13, the precise virus from which 96.2 percent of COVID-19 is derived. The lab obtained RaTG13 from a cave in Yunnan Province in 2013.[62] According to the lab itself, RaTG13 has never been located in any tested animals near Wuhan, only in its own lab.[63] Nor has RaTG13 been located naturally anywhere in the world outside of the Himalayan caves. This proves the falsity of the PRC claims that the virus came from another country. A virus located only in a bat found in a Himalayan cave, whose range is only twenty miles, did not fly thousands of miles over oceans to Wuhan. Its discovery and movement by the Bat Woman to the WIV was its only pre-pandemic trip. Moreover, the 3.8 percent of the virus added to the bat virus to produce COVID-19 has never been located naturally anywhere. And further, the so-called furin cleavage of the COVID-19 spike protein is novel and one-of-a-kind.[64]

The Mythical Pangolin and Frozen Food Theory

As in the 1977 Chinese lab leak, the CCP has devised an ever-changing series of explanations for their disastrous error. A pangolin is a strange armadillo-like creature covered with scales, now largely extinct in China, but whose scales are used for Chinese folk medicine. Since some (but not all) of the 3.8 percent of the Wuhan virus which is missing in the RaTG13 virus resembles a virus found in the pangolin, the CCP contended that the virus crossed from an infected horseshoe bat to a pangolin and thence, genetically evolved to infect man.[65] Unfortunately for the CCP, the pangolin theory suffers from the absence anywhere on earth of the mythical RaTG13 pangolin or a coronavirus-infected pangolin, or any explanation for the portion of the 3.8 percent that cannot be found in bats *or* pangolins. No pangolin has ever been found with such an infection. Even the combination of horseshoe bat and pangolin viruses cannot wholly account for the actual altered RaTG13 virus.[66] Not only does the mythical infected pangolin not exist, there is no genetic record of the evolution of viruses leading to COVID-19 and no parents in the genetic record. Outside of the caves and Wuhan lab, there is no horseshoe bat with RaTG13. The theory thus depends upon two mythical animals' mating on the doorstep of China's biolabs. Amazingly, the Pangolin theory has been presented as a "scientific explanation" by public health experts and large portions of the scientific community.

Another theory advanced by the CCP is the frozen food theory—that the virus for which there is no explanation was somehow slipped into frozen food. China's newest theory, that the virus originated from frozen food, is put forward without evidence. Like the mythical pangolin theory, there is no proof of any such infected frozen food, or a mythical crossed pangolin, or even frozen bat-pangolins.

The WHO "Investigation"

The World Health Organization arrived in China to perform a perfunctory "investigation" into the origins of the virus in January 2021. This was more than one year after the outbreak. WHO, building a reputation as the world's least curious investigator, did not interview the jailed early reporters or many patients. Nor did it examine early samples—not that it could have, since they had all been destroyed. It completely ignored the nearby military PLA lab and the joint projects between the PLA lab and the WIV as if these did not exist. Its reports neither examined nor mentioned the vast Chinese bioweapons programs or the 1977 leak. Instead, following in the footsteps of Walter Duranty, WHO advanced as possibilities the mythical Pangolin and frozen food theories, while concluding that because laboratory accidents are "rare," the chance of a laboratory leak was "remote." This ignored various biolab leaks in China,[67] such as a 2004 SARS outbreak in Beijing, the 1977 flu leak, as well as numerous other leaks from Russia's biowar labs,[68] such as the

Kiev leak and the 1979 bio-Chernobyl that were both the result of the development of biowarfare weapons—a dangerous business. Scientists all over the world denounced the WHO investigation as a cover-up.[69] But the media refused to give meaningful coverage of the objections. Like mentioning those who disappear in China, it would be wholly impolite and not good for either health or pocketbook to mention, much less investigate, the likely source of the alien, one-of-a-kind virus, that appeared near the biowarfare labs.

Whether the coronavirus came directly from extraction from a horseshoe bat at the Wuhan lab or resulted from bat genetic alteration or chimera experiments (using tools like CRISPR) at either the WIV or PLA lab or both is less important than the vast evidence it existed in, and was released from, one of the two Wuhan labs.[70] Repeated accidents in Chinese biolabs have alarmed the scientific world long before the appearance of this virus.[71] In April of 2020, a Five Eyes intelligence report, reflecting the best available intelligence of the United States, Canada, Australia, England, and New Zealand, was leaked.[72] It concluded that it was extremely likely that the virus came from the Wuhan lab.[73] Chinese virologist Dr. Li-Meng Yan, after her escape from Hong Kong, held a press conference announcing she had reached a conclusion based on her knowledge and assessment that COVID-19 came from a military bioweapons laboratory run by the Peoples' Liberation Army, despite the CCP's elaborate cover-up. Wei Jingsheng, a high-ranking CCP defector, revealed that, having been alerted by sources in China, he had warned the U.S. government of the development of the virus in Wuhan.[74] On the basis of this evidence, Secretary of State Pompeo pointed to the lab as the origin of the virus. After Dr. Li-Meng presented her assessment to her boss in Hong Kong that the "wet market" story was being used as a decoy, Dr. Li-Meng was placed in grave danger of disappearing like so many under Stalinist rule. She narrowly escaped to the West as Hong Kong was being seized by Xi. Her family, however, has disappeared—probably forever.

Finally on June 1, 2021, the wall of silence of the U.S. media began to crack as the *Washington Post* expressly retracted its false charge that the lab origin theory was "debunked" and a "conspiracy theory."[75] The COVID cover-up continued to unravel with Nicholas Wade's booklet, *Where COVID Came From*, and Matt Ridley's book, *Viral: The Search for the Origin of COVID-19*.[76] The pajama bloggers around the world uncovered facts before journalists or official investigators, including the financial interests of China's American parrots.[77]

Even the CCP doesn't contest that for several weeks after the virus appeared in Wuhan and was disclosed by Dr. Li (before his imprisonment, release, and subsequent death), China under Xi's direction maintained its silence to the world, only speaking up to deny the emerging truth.[78] For a time after the discovery of the outbreak, China freely allowed travel from Wuhan by air throughout the world without testing, thus seeding an unknowing world with the virus. The response of the CCP to a world in agony has been to continue to deny the virus's origin, seed misinformation, and brag that their response was not only correct, but the sign of a world leader.

China's conduct directed by Xi is only understandable in light of his current Stalinist-Maoist ideology. To a Stalinist, beyond service to the state, life has no value, whether that life is Pavlova's, Wallenberg's, Dr. Li's, or the millions dying of COVID-19. The supreme leader, Xi—like Putin, Mao, and Stalin—cannot make a mistake, being a near divine embodiment of the state. Under the Stalinist doctrine of cultural hegemony, the truth of the origin of the Wuhan virus is now irrelevant and should be adjusted to make a convenient story. What is relevant is the account, whether fictional or not, which best serves the state and can somehow be tied to science. And so a documentary being shown throughout China addresses not at all the origin of the virus, and instead depicts brave workers under the noble leadership of a brave Xi fighting the virus, which Chinese media claimed may have come from U.S. soldiers. The long, dark shadow of Stalinism and the biolabs that he began have created the blueprint for China's response. Stalin's bioweapons legacy set the stage for the leak, and it was Stalin's ideology that allowed the Wuhan airport to remain open, leading to the death of millions.

Even in the United States, China-shills imitating Walter Duranty (many having extensive ties through research or commerce with China) have shamefully echoed the Chinese line that the origin of coronavirus is unknowable, that the lab leak theory is an "alt-right" conspiracy, and that China can be trusted as a "respectable" nation.[79] In China, both the employed and volunteer shills are secretly called "parrots" since they repeat ad nauseum the current Party line. They parroted on as Zhang Zhan, a thirty-seven-year-old female lawyer and journalist, filmed and posted online footage of Wuhan and its hospitals in February of 2020 as the virus terrorized the city. She was soon arrested and sentenced to four years of imprisonment in Xi's gulag, from which it is unlikely she will ever emerge.[80] And other journalists who attempted to report on the virus from Wuhan were arrested or disappeared, likely forever, into the gulag. None were interviewed by WHO or mentioned by China's U.S. shills.

Zhang is currently near death in a Chinese prison, a five-foot-ten-inch female emaciated to eighty-eight pounds. She resembles nothing so much as the long-ago prisoners of Auschwitz or Dachau. Her family is not allowed to see her in person or arrange for medical treatment. And when she dies, they will not even be given her body, which will be disposed of after harvesting any usable organs for sale. Zhang leaves to all of us her videos and stories from Wuhan placed on the internet in early 2020 that tell a story sufficiently chilling for Xi's government to take her life as an "agitator," the Xi bromide for "truthteller." There is no report of her current condition in the *New York Times*. Out of sight, out of mind.[81] Although Zhang's voice is silenced in the dark prison cell she is dying in, her videos speak eloquently for her.

Summation: The Case against Xi

Two evidentiary and legal principles, commonly used by courts, lead to the truth of the origin of COVID-19. Among the most treasured principles of human reasoning is Occam's razor: the simplest explanation is usually the true one.[82] It was first expressed in Roman times as *res ipsa loquitur*, "the thing speaks for itself". Second is a related principle, enshrined for centuries in the common law (as well as the law of most countries and common sense): someone who intentionally conceals or destroys evidence that could have proved incriminating is worthy of suspicion.[83] Why destroy evidence unless it is incriminating? These two principles are particularly useful for finding the truth in the bloody history of Marxism. Consider the facts surrounding the disputed origin of COVID-19 in Wuhan and the frantic efforts of the Xi government and friendly influencers to conceal the true events at Wuhan in light of these two principles.

A summation of the facts:

China is slightly larger in physical size than the United States, with a population more than four times greater. In that vast country, the virus conceded by scientists to be the precursor to COVID-19 (RaTG13) is 96.2 percent identical to COVID-19. It has been located in the wild only once in horseshoe bats in a cave in the Himalayan Mountains in far West China by personnel from the Wuhan Institute of Virology. RaTG13 was moved from the cave many hundreds of miles only once and to one place: the WIV in or before 2016.

Comedian Jon Stewart jokingly points to the obvious conclusion that the "lab leak theory" is correct when asked on *The Late Show with Stephen Colbert* whether he thought the virus could have leaked from the WIV.

> A *chance*? Oh, my God. "There's a novel respiratory coronavirus overtaking Wuhan, China—what do we do?" "Oh, you know who could we ask? The Wuhan Novel Respiratory Coronavirus Lab." The disease is the same name as the lab.... "There's been an outbreak of chocolaty goodness near Hershey, Pennsylvania. What do you think happened?" "Oh, I don't know, maybe a steam shovel mated with a cocoa bean. Or it's the [expletive] chocolate factory! Maybe that's it!"[84]

The very earliest cases of COVID-19 arose in Wuhan near the entrance of the WIV in late November or early December of 2019.[85] A principal difference between the original RaTG13 virus and the COVID-19 virus is a hook—the so-called COVID-19 furin spike protein—which effectively attaches the virus to the nose and lungs, making it both very communicable and sometimes lethal. The WIV from 2016 was conducting "gain of function," enhancement, or wired-up experiments in which the hook or spike protein was attached to the coronavirus in order to make it more communicable among test mice.[86]

The WIV is the largest and best-known virology lab in China, but it is only one of several virology labs in Wuhan, another of which is a highly secret lab run not by scientists, but by the People's Liberation Army. The PLA military lab operates in tandem with the WIV as its hidden brother. Its relationship with the WIV is completely hidden, but deeply symbiotic. Until the outbreak in Wuhan, the WIV listed many PLA officers on its advisory committees.[87] The evidence shows that the coronavirus came from RaTG13 recovered by the WIV, a lab that was itself documented to be conducting very dangerous enhancement experiments.[88] It was cooperating with and conducting unknown joint experiments with the nearby secret army lab.[89] COVID-19 first occurred in the proximity of these labs.

A number of experts believe COVID-19 was a prematurely and inadvertently released engineered bioweapon prepared at the PLA military lab.[90] Although the evidence clearly proves release followed by concealment, we will likely never know the actual details of the release. Those are forever hidden by the intentional destruction of the early forensic samples and other necessary tracing information. But if this theory is true, it would explain the desperation with which the Xi government has both concealed and dissembled information about the release and why they almost immediately destroyed all forensic evidence. True to form for a Stalinist government, they destroy evidence of guilt like criminals—from the secret mass graves of Stalinist Russia and

China, to Stalin's poison labs, to the actual forensic samples and tracing information of the virus from Wuhan.[91]

It is also significant that as soon as brave Dr. Li's disclosure alerted the world, it was biowar officers of the People's Liberation Army—not virologists—who were immediately placed in control of the Wuhan containment operations.[92] It was the PLA that ordered the destruction of the early patient forensic samples that were the best evidence of the early origin of the virus. After all, they were likely most familiar with both the COVID-19 virus and how it was leaked.

When the virus broke out, the Xi government arrested those reporting it. In addition, it halted all public reports and destroyed or concealed all early forensic specimens of COVID-19. Although the virus can spread through symptomless carriers, like lab personnel who don't even realize they are sick, by early December, the so-called "Patient Zero" was identified. He was originally described as a seventy-seven-year-old man who had both Alzheimer's disease and COVID-19.[93] Over the next two months, neither China nor the World Health Organization sounded the pandemic alarm. While the world slept, COVID-19 spread first in Wuhan, and then to Europe with passengers from Wuhan International Airport, and from there to the Western Hemisphere and Africa. By December 16, 2019, the Wuhan hospitals were beginning to see cases.[94] On or before December 30, Dr. Li Wenliang sounded the alarm, and was arrested for "making false comments"[95] and forced to confess after jailing. Although the COVID-19 death rate for Dr. Li's age is below 1.5 percent, he conveniently died of the disease—assuming he was not murdered directly or by neglect. Dr. Ai Fen, a colleague of Dr. Li, publicly denounced the Wuhan conditions and the treatment of pandemic whistle-blowers and also disappeared.[96] Early forensic samples of the COVID-19 virus, necessary with records to trace the actual spread and source of the virus, were destroyed by order of the PLA leadership in early January 2020 and again a month later.[97]

Given the initial appearance of COVID-19 next door to the Wuhan labs, many hundreds of miles from the cave home of the horseshoe bat, a creature never seen in Wuhan except when brought to the WIV, virtually every legal system in the world would apply a principle of law and evidence first found in the law of Rome—*res ipsa loquitur*, "the thing speaks for itself." The circumstances themselves, even without additional evidence like that destroyed on orders of the Xi government, present a case so compelling that it would take extraordinary proof to refute it. The intentional destruction of evidence and disappearance of witnesses make a strong case for guilt on their own. Put together, the circumstances and destruction of evidence make a conclusive case that an inadvertent leak from the Wuhan labs led to the coronavirus pandemic.[98] Any reasonable jury would quickly convict China of the leak as public opinion already has.

Early in 2020—too soon to have investigated any records at Wuhan—two sets of virologists deeply involved with the WIV published papers asserting that the human COVID-19 virus was of natural origin.[99] They claimed it could not have come from the Wuhan Lab.[100] The articles were an early deflection of the theory of lab creation, ignoring the possibility that a natural virus could have been extracted (not created), edited, and inadvertently released at Wuhan. Most significantly, the articles rested on the premise that a designed virus would have been optimized, more efficiently than COVID-19.[101] It is a peculiar argument against the most "optimized" communicable disease in history, which has spread like wildfire through humanity.

The Chinese virologists also argued that they could not see tell-tale signs of gene editing with CRISPR. This ignores other widely used and undetectable means of manipulating a virus such as the "no-see 'em" method, achieved by thousands of repetitious combinations of dangerous experiments in a laboratory.[102] Most importantly, the lab-leak skeptics, a majority of whom are closely tied to the Xi government, offer no real or plausible alternatives to the theory of a leak from one or more of the Wuhan labs. They have never found either the mythical far-flying pangolin bat, nor any close parent to COVID-19 other than the bat transported to the Wuhan labs.

Recently the bizarre, unprecedented, and unexpected rapid mutation of COVID-19, particularly in its spike protein has made even prior cynics point to a Wuhan lab origin.[103] The rapid mutation—different in speed and change from those encountered in most viruses — has made vaccines less effective against it, so this killer of human design may be with us for generations.

A Unicorn Theory

A unicorn theory is a common slang term for a story premised upon something that isn't necessarily possible, but isn't impossible, simply due to the fact that stranger things have happened.[104] It is often used as a device by trial lawyers to try to create doubt in a hopeless case where no doubt actually exists. For example, imagine a criminal defendant is caught standing over a murder victim in his home. He has powder stains on his hands. The smoking murder weapon that he purchased is found with only his fingerprints on it in the trash can loaded with bullets that he bought and which match the lethal bullet. Hopeless? No. Invent a Unicorn Story—the never identified "actual" killer who mysteriously entered and left undetected who is never found except in a lawyer's desperate imagination. The CCP's mythical bat-pangolin virus creation theory in which a bat who mated with a near-extinct pangolin coincidentally flew a thousand miles to the doorstep of the biowar labs in Wuhan is the ultimate unicorn story created by the perpetrator of one of history's greatest crimes. With the virus's breaking out on the labs' doorstep, as discovered and reported by a brave doctor, both the closest natural relative and the experiments altering it traced directly to the labs, and efforts to destroy early samples, witnesses, and records having only partly hidden the truth, Xi marched out his parrots with history's most audacious unicorn story. Like all unicorn stories it is based on proof never quite found and just beyond reach. Instead of one death it seeks to explain away perhaps ten million or more worldwide.

The Myth of Infallibility

The primary argument against the leak theory is that leaks are impossible because labs never leak. The people advancing the opposition are "enhancement" scientists who themselves enhance the lethality and communicability of viruses to predict and defend against future threats. But labs do leak.[105] Richard Ebright, a former Howard Hughes Medical Institute investigator and current laboratory director at Rutgers University, has long opposed the expansion of preventative research into dangerous pathogens. In support of his position, he cites a *USA Today* investigation that concluded there were more than 1,100 lab accidents involving dangerous pathogens or toxins in the U.S. alone between 2008 and 2012.[106]

Many warnings have been advanced predicting the exact calamity produced by COVID-19 across the world. Lynn Klotz, a former Harvard University faculty member, biotechnology company executive, and senior science fellow at the Center for Arms Control and Non-Proliferation, warned in 2012 that there was an 80 percent chance that a leak of a potential pandemic pathogen would occur sometime in the next twelve years from one of the many laboratories then handling virulent viro-varietals.[107] Two years later, infectious disease experts Marc Lipsitch and Thomas Inglesby warned the intentional creation of new microbes that combine virulence with heightened transmissibility "poses extraordinary risks to the public."[108]

Historical leaks have repeated themselves time and again with infamous examples resulting in catastrophes in Shanghai, Kiev, Yekaterinburg, and other places. Enhancement scientists are human, and therefore supremely fallible. Biolabs, like nuclear power plants, sometimes fail. In the case of a bioweapons lab engaged in the enhancement of a virus, the consequences of failure are disastrous, including a pandemic that can kill millions and a virus that stays with mankind for centuries.[109]

While America and WHO Slept

The WHO failed to isolate the Great Pandemic in Wuhan because of a combination of non-cooperation by the Xi government, its own lack of preparedness, and its deep fear of offending the Xi government. Although it learned of the appearance of the new virus on December 31, 2019, WHO did not send the alarm through an emergency declaration of pandemic until January 30, 2020—nearly seven weeks after the earliest cases and four weeks after the virus had been again isolated in China. It was during those critical weeks that hundreds of thousands of passengers from Wuhan took international flights, infecting the world. WHO's ineptitude stands in contrast to its earlier better efforts against Ebola and other potential pandemics.

Whatever the explanation for WHO's delay as the watchman in sounding the alarm, its later actions as "investigator" in determining the origin of the virus look craven, even by Walter Duranty standards. Prior to the investigation, WHO negotiated an agreement with China, giving the Xi government a veto over the selection of each investigator.[110] All investigators suggested by the U.S. government were rejected out of hand. The primary U.S. "investigator," named by China and not the U.S., had been deeply involved with the Wuhan labs for many years. He had declared a lab leak impossible a year before the WHO investigation began. At Wuhan, WHO "investigators" were not allowed to meet privately with the Chinese, and their requests for raw data were rejected. The millions of dead and dying from COVID have been buried without truth or justice, like the millions of dead who preceded them in Russia and China.

After a year of total non-cooperation from the Xi regime, during which numerous records and samples were destroyed and witnesses died or were jailed, WHO conducted a largely sham investigation, desperately seeking a cause other than the obvious lab leak. More than half of the "investigators" were nominated not by victims or independent sources, but by the PRC itself, the target of the investigation.[111] Most of the remaining "investigators" involved with the Wuhan Labs in virus enhancement signed a letter within a few weeks of the release declaring it couldn't be a leak, long before any investigation took place.[112]

Other than speaking to a few people presented by the Chinese as early patients and a few doctors at the WIV in China in the presence of Chinese officials (where they and their families were vulnerable to imprisonment already dealt out to so many), the "investigators" essentially did nothing in Wuhan. They suggested no certain or probable cause, discarding the original wet market alibi, and called the frozen food theory offered by the Xi government unlikely. They ignored the destruction of evidence and the arrest of witnesses. They pretended to be wholly unaware of the existence and likely purpose of the nearby secret military virology lab in Wuhan. They made no detailed examination of the records of the gene editing and chimera experiments in which the WIV cooperated with the military lab.

Where are the records tracking the RaTG13 virus from its 2016 arrival through experiments and possible transfer to the military virology lab? What could that lab do that could not be done in the WIV? What did the labs do together? How did the predecessor virus make it to the Wuhan Military Lab? With no such questions asked or answered, the WHO "investigation" was denounced by many virologists as a "charade to appease China."[113] Experts from nations and universities all over the world condemned the WHO "inquiry" as a "masquerade"—political, not scientific—performed to appease China. It was the ultimate gaslighting. Like the concealment of numerous Stalinist atrocities, the Xi government unleashed legions of influencers to conceal its actions after erasing its tracks.

With the 1972 Biological Weapons Convention, the United States, unlike Russia and China, abandoned its offensive capacity for chemical and biological warfare while still retaining a defensive capability. Despite the expenditure of many billions ostensibly to defend our country against biowarfare or inadvertent pandemics, COVID-19 revealed that our nation was completely unprepared—even against a coronavirus far less lethal than many vastly more frightening viruses in the biowar laboratories of China, North Korea, and Russia. Confronted with the coronavirus, there were no vaccines or accepted medical treatments, or even masks and ventilators, despite the expenditure of billions each year.

When a crisis actually occurred with the outbreak of a highly communicable coronavirus, there was only a variety of conflicting advice over whether masks would or would not help, whether the virus would fade in the summer, whether hydrocortisone could prove prophylactic, and the like. We even, as a matter of policy in some states, mixed infected patients with the aged and infirm in elderly care facilities. Like at Pearl Harbor, we slept despite many warnings of the impending crisis. Meanwhile, both Russia and China had carried out disingenuous propaganda campaigns denouncing the United States' limited biolab efforts, which were aimed strictly (and ultimately ineffectively) at planned or inadvertent pandemics. Because America slept, perhaps a million Americans will ultimately die from this disease. That is all of our fault, regardless of party. We relied on the World Health Organization to be the watchman at the gate only to find during the crisis that the watchman slept and then looked the other way.

Zhang's Videos

Although reporter Zhang Zhan is dying in prison, unable even to raise her head, her videos from the early days of the outbreak survive.[114] They reflect a vast bio-complex much larger than simply the WIV that is its only public face. The WIV itself had numerous military officers on its advisory committees, but these were quickly deleted from its records in late 2019. Various other bio-facilities including an Institute of Biological Products next door, never reviewed by WHO, are of military origin. Zhang's videos show that as soon as the outbreak was revealed by the now deceased Dr. Li, a special unit of the PLA known as the Fifteenth Airborne Brigade was immediately placed in charge of Wuhan. The unit was stationed near Wuhan and brought into Wuhan no later than January 2020, almost contemporaneously with the virus. They were portrayed by the government as simply passing out charitable contributions, yet in reality, the unit placed an iron lock on the city and any information leaving it. This was no Dr. Fauci placed in charge of Wuhan, but PLA Major General Chen Wei of the Military Bioengineering Research Institute. There is little more compelling evidence than Zhang's videos of the immediate military takeover of Wuhan by special warfare units under General Wei.

While China played down the gravity of the epidemic globally, it increased its import of medical supplies and cut exports of the same items.[115] Subsequent evidence reveals massive orders of protective equipment and vaccine components by the PLA in early 2019 and 2020.[116] In addition, in a short period of time by the early summer of 2020 and many months ahead of the West, Chinese troops were receiving a vaccine.[117] What happened at Wuhan? While it is certain that the COVID-19 virus was created there, almost certainly in the military labs (and not from a mythical, far-flying pangolin-bat or a unicorn), how it leaked remains unclear. The most probable scenario is that there was a repeat of the 1957/1977 flu situation.

The COVID-19 virus can spread asymptomatically. It is likely that after manufacture of COVID-19 as a bioweapon for future use, efforts began, as in 1977, to develop a vaccine. In the course of these efforts, the vaccine trial likely using military recruits or prisoners, perhaps China's "rabbits," inadvertently leaked, thus creating an uncontrollable pandemic similar to 1977, but much worse. This would explain the early Chinese release of a vaccine to the PLA, the early Chinese purchase of protective equipment, the instant military control by special warfare units, and the frantic and heartless efforts by the Xi government to conceal the nature of the origin of the virus lest its entire illegal biowar program be revealed to the world. It was a bullet that was meant to be fired, but was likely fired by mistake sooner than intended, at the wrong place, and in the wrong way. And the back story of terrible diseases, criminal human testing, and preparation for worldwide biological war is almost certainly a terribly shocking one.

Xi's conduct in producing and then concealing the nature and origin of the COVID-19 virus is not a small infraction. It has killed more Americans than died in the Civil War or in all other American wars combined. Worldwide, uncounted millions have died. Xi thus joins

Hitler, Stalin, and Mao as one of the greatest killers of human history. The enormity of his crime against humanity and its consequences is almost beyond human comprehension. It was the heartless action of a ghoulish, heartless state, which enslaves and kills its own citizens, and now has killed many millions beyond its borders.

CHAPTER TWENTY-TWO

The Last Dance

"This is the way the world ends.
This is the way the world ends.
This is the way the world ends.
Not with a bang, but with a whimper."[1]
—T. S. Eliot
The Hollow Men, 1924

Anonymous poison is the weapon of cowards. Bioweapons are the tools of madmen indiscriminate in their killings. Poisoners and bio-warriors are detested by true warriors, and even by their masters like Stalin, who destroyed generations of Lab One workers. But not by Vladimir Putin. In 2017, Putin began a speech to the KGB by recognizing some of those he said were among Russia's greatest heroes.[2] Amazingly, first on his list was not General Zhukov, who defeated Hitler, or brave Yuri Gagarin, the first man in space who died at a tragically young age. Putin did not name the famous Russian women who were World War II snipers at Stalingrad or flew the dangerous Russian night biplanes used to torment the Nazis. True to his KGB roots, Putin's list of greatest heroes began with Uncle Yasha, the "baker" and poisoner of Paris who murdered hundreds and likely poisoned Diaghilev and Pavlova.[3] In Putin's mind, Yasha the poisoner ranks first among Russia's KGB heroes. Indeed, despite their reported poses as strong men and Marxist heroes, neither Stalin, nor Putin, nor Xi was ever involved in a minute of personal combat, nor carried out any notable act of personal courage. This contrasts strikingly with their victims like Navalny, Xiaobo, Li, and Romzha returning to certain death, or Wallenberg defying two totalitarian dictatorships: those are true heroes all.

In 2012, while running for president of Russia, Putin assured the public that he would neutralize any western advantage in technology by investing in genetics research.[4] Indeed, a Russian genetics research program is appropriately called "Hunter."[5] Using genetic splicing techniques developed in the West to combat disease, the Russian "Hunter" project programs horrific viruses and bacteria to attack people with specified genes.[6] During their long journey through history, groups of people—whether Jewish, Irish, Japanese, or African—have picked up a certain small number of genes peculiar to their group and descent. By keying in these genes, the aim of Hunter is to ensure the death of specified ethnic groups.[7]

In keeping with his style and motto of smiling while plunging the knife deeper, Xi has never threated the use of bioweapons or even commented on them. Instead, he has participated in at least the creation and cover-up of the leak of a virus so communicable and given to mutation that it may be humanity's lethal companion for centuries. It may be Communist China's most important contribution to the world—perhaps killing millions for years to come. Given Xi's suppression of records and witnesses, it is likely that COVID-19 was a Frankenstein created with other Frankensteins that exist in the Chinese military bioweapons labs, or less likely simply an extract from a mutant one-of-a-kind horseshoe bat in the Wuhan labs. There is, even with Xi's concealment, powerful evidence of its origin by extraction or creation in the Wuhan Military Bioweapons Labs. Because of easy avenues that would have been available to Chinese bio-warriors to use this bioweapon in a less traceable place and manner, it is quite likely that the leak of the virus was inadvertent and unintended—discovered and disclosed by Dr. Li Wenliang in an equally unexpected and unauthorized manner. The coronavirus proved to be a cunningly deadly and uncontrollable weapon fired by mistake like Russia's 1979 anthrax leak or China's own 1977 virus. Though unintended, the premature use of this virus has proven to be the most destructive, debilitating poison in our lifetimes. It has killed many millions and weakened to near collapse many of China's rivals, while Xi's China has prospered and used the crisis to extend its economic and military power. Its rapid mutations are not explainable and make rapid extinction very unlikely. For China, it turned out to be a convenient and ultimately useful mistake. For every other nation, it is a human tragedy and an economic cataclysm. It is an unwelcome invader dealing death all over the world.

In 2016, the United States belatedly added biological warfare to its list of primary terrorist threats to the world.[8] Nuclear war threatens the end of all organized civilization, while global warming threatens slow change into a much less desirable world. Biological warfare threatens a quick end of man's troubled stay on this earth.[9] Ninety years ago, Anna Pavlova danced her final public performance, including *Autumn Leaves* about a flower killed by the evil North Wind. It proved a prophecy of her death, but one hopes it is not one for the future of the world.

The poison experiments launched by Stalin to kill priests, a ballerina, and inconvenient old men morphed into a much larger legacy: a threat to nations and even to man himself. The poisons of Laboratory One wiped out not only innocent victims but also its founders—Iron Felix, Lenin, and Stalin themselves. The horrific bioweapons program of Russia, North Korea, and China with selective, mutating diseases with Hunter and gene splicing, threatens us all.

The naïveté of consecutive presidents towards Putin and Xi threatens U.S. and world security. No, Stalin was not a kindly "Uncle Joe," nor are Putin and Xi our friends, nor are their ghoulish directed murders excusable as cultural norms. Their bioweapons using CRISPR can deliver death by undetectable means in many forms, not with a missile or gun, but with a cough or a kiss. The world must awaken to the magnitude of these threats.

Symbols

Marxism proposes a collective government of working classes, but in practice irrationally exalts concentration of all power in a single "Great Leader." It promises equality and freedom but delivers slavery. This contradiction makes Marxism and Stalinist leaders like Putin and Xi unable to fairly debate and defend their philosophy against any opponent, whether a Bukharin with Stalin, or Navalny with Putin, or the Nobel Prize winner Liu who was imprisoned by Xi. Marxism in actual practice is sufficiently ridiculous and odious that it will win only when it is the only fighter in the ring. That is why Marxism requires poison and bioweapons to eliminate its opponents. It is itself the ultimate cowardly ideology, strutting with considerable ceremony on the stage of history while trembling with terror over a sick prisoner, a poisoned opponent, an imprisoned reporter, or even a tiny ballerina. It must control free thought and free spirits because it can neither answer nor survive them.

It is indeed a very dangerous thing in a tumultuous, often violent world to be a symbol. In 2001, the World Trade Center buildings in New York were destroyed by jihadi fanatics determined to eliminate these symbols of American economic freedom. Pavlova and Diaghilev were likewise murdered by Stalin as heretical symbols of both freedom and an older, better time. Tank Man and Fan Bingbing could not be allowed free in Xi's silk prison. The great golden dome of Christ the Saviour Cathedral, as well as the Gate of the Resurrection, were torn down in Moscow for being symbols of a spiritual world wholly denied by Stalin. In his murders of these symbols, Stalin, like the later Putin and Xi, recognized the truth of Lincoln's wisdom—that a house cannot survive half-slave and half-free. And Stalin, like Xi, was determined to impose total control over a slave nation.

The symbol of the Soviet Union, now used by Xi's China, was the hammer and sickle, supposedly representing the Union of Workers and Farmers. It was adopted by Russia in 1923. The Poison Lab had opened, and the slaughter of churchmen commenced. After a half-century of the slaughter of millions of those farmers and workers by Russia and then China, that symbol is now taken as an illustration of brutality and death. It was officially abandoned by Russia in 1993. Even still, Putin has nonetheless encouraged retention of this hated symbol on all Russian airline Aeroflot planes. Likewise in China, it remains the emblem of the Chinese Communist Party. A far better symbol of Putin's Russia or Communist China would be a vial of poison, or a sprig of hemlock, or a warfarin pill, or the spiked beachball of COVID-19.

But even in Putin's Russia, other older and better symbols remain despite almost a century Soviet effort to destroy them. While the Russian center of ballet moved to the Bolshoi under Stalin, the great Mariinsky Theater in Saint Petersburg has been restored to its appearance in pre-Soviet times. It even has its old name back. Though it is joined now in Saint Petersburg by a 700-million-dollar super-theater named Mariinsky II with excellent acoustics, Petipa and Pavlova would be happy to know that most ballerinas still prefer to dance in the Old Mariinsky—and not in annoying Stalinist productions that torture taste—but, in the current season, to *Swan Lake*, *The Nutcracker*, *Sleeping Beauty*, and other ballets once danced by Pavlova. Overlooking the stage, fully restored from the destruction and graffiti of Soviet times, is not a Stalin dealing life and death based upon the performances, but rather the Tsar's Box where the young Romanov princesses, prince, and Tsar Nicholas once watched the ballets. In the Mariinsky, one can sense the spirits and echoes of those times. In a throw-back to Stalinist times, Putin recently installed a Minister of Culture, Olga Lyubimova—a loyal but singularly stupid Marxist Putinite who has declared she hates ballet, opera, and museums.[10] Despite her hatred of ballet and banning of the comic film *The Death of Stalin*, her tentacles have not yet reached the Mariinsky (perhaps because the minister of culture does not even know it exists).

In Saint Petersburg, a memorial to Pavlova has now been built at her last home at Italian Street Number 5, and her statue still flies atop the Palace Theater in London. In Moscow, the great Cathedral of Christ the Saviour was rebuilt in the brief years of freedom pre-Putin. Like a rainbow on the Moscow skyline, it promises again redemption and the return of better times. The great golden dome, which so offended Stalin, is restored and easily visible from Putin's office in the Kremlin and from Stalin's now quite modest grave in the Kremlin necropolis. It is perhaps why Putin so often retreats to conduct meetings in Stalin's dacha outside Moscow.

Even in Xi's China, ruthlessly ruled by his iron hand in a silk glove, brave souls, some in prison, some in hiding, have proven ready to give up everything, including their lives and families, to bring knowledge of the fiendish biowarfare labs and their terrible virus to the world. Like Tank Man and Anna Akhmatova, their day will come, and the sun will set on Xi's brutality. And there is a strange serendipity or providence in the world that seems to protect us from overwhelming evil and encourages the seed of good to grow and bloom another day.

Postscript

In the ballet, *Danse Macabre, Opus 40*, by Saint-Saens, which was turned into a film in 1922 by Adolph Bohn, the old dance is converted into a Halloween dance in which the dead arise one by one on that night to confront the devil.[11] If, as Stalin suggested to Churchill, the Devil is a good Communist, perhaps in a just universe it will be so. And as for sick and starving Anna Akhmatova, her poetry preserved by memory alone, her words resonate today:

"Give me bitter years of sickness, suffocation, insomnia, fever—
Take my child and my lover, and my mysterious gift of song.
This I pray at your liturgy after so many tormented days,
so that the storm cloud over darkened Russia
might become a cloud of glorious rays."[12]

A century of communism could not destroy the love of poetry and ballet and the respect for religion found in the Russian and

Chinese souls. With all his thugs and poisons Stalin could not steal Akhmatova's song, nor the faith of Tikhon and Romzha, nor Wallenberg's nobility of sacrifice, nor even tiny Pavlova's dance. Xi could not break Liu Xiaobo, who died for freedom, loving even his captors, with his spirit now beyond the reach of even Xi's jails. Songs still play at Diaghilev's grave, and a firefly statue flies in the London garden, near Pavlova's ashes. It is a safe bet that no songs of joy are played near Stalin's dreary grave. And some day, the darkness of Stalin and his fellow monsters will give way, as Akhmatova prayed, to a brighter day looked upon by the golden dome of Christ the Saviour which Stalin ultimately could not destroy and which all Moscow sees each and every day. To Christians, free thinkers, and others, that dome is the symbol of a long-ago promise of a better time for Russia. And in China, there will be memories of Dr. Li, Dr. Liu, and Tank Man as the Xi and Mao statues tumble down like the legendary *Ozymandias*, the *Colossus of Nero*, and Stalin's statues.[13] Like Akhmatova, we are each of us called upon to remember . . . to remember their stories and teachings until that different day.

Gandhi, in his own desperate time around the time of the murders of Pavlova and Diaghilev, counseled, "When I despair, I remember that all through history, the way of truth and love have always won. There have been tyrants and murderers and for a time, they seem invincible, but in the end, they always fail. Think of it—always."[14]

Hope

As Gandhi predicted the seeds of hope may be sprouting in the world. In Russia, opposition to the tyrannical poisoner Putin grows as many brave Navalnys take the prisoner's place.[15] Once-popular Putin now rules like Hitler, only through terror and the promise of conquest of weaker nations. In China, the butcher Xi seems to be seriously injuring the vast growing economy that is the foundation of China's prosperity and Communist power. He is irrationally shredding Alibaba and other Chinese companies with a purported "equity" program that never quite aids the poor. Instead, thousands of poor have lost their homes or down payments from the collapse of Evergrande and other developers, ranking among history's largest failures.[16] Meanwhile the Chinese stock market is crashing with many businesses and investors redlining China as a bad place to do business since it is without dependable laws and subject to the fits and fists of a tyrant.[17] And even the dreaded Wuhan virus—killer of many millions, yet slowed by vaccines—may finally bow to nature and the hand of God, as well as new vaccines and therapeutics. The new Omicron mutation likely to become the dominant strain appears more contagious, but milder.[18] This pattern of deadly viruses mutating into more contagious, but less deadly, strains has reccurred many times in the history of diseases.[19] Think of it as God's little joke on the PLA biowarriors. A French legend of the late fourth century, as Europe was being ravaged by the Huns, compared the martyrs (like Wallenberg and Xiaobo) to leaves or bells in the trees that called men to look up beyond the dark, unhappy present to the far horizon knowing that change and miracles lie between there and here. And as Gandhi said they still do. Pavlova, Diaghilev, Romzha, Liu, and Navalny are the lights whose lives guide us past Marxism's dreary road.

As Doctor King quoted Saint John's Gospel before his own murder, we must know the truth, and the truth will set us free. The truth is that Stalin and Putin secretly used deniable poison and bioweapons to murder many innocents whose words and ideas they could neither successful debate, nor control. And the truth is that Xi and Communist China played with fire, and the world is burning.

But the ashes of burned flowers and blackened forests leave seeds long after the fire is forgotten. They grow and bloom, bringing new flowers and forests that spring from the cataclysm. Although there really are no sufficient words for brave spirits like Pavlova and Zhang, the whole earth is the tomb of such heroes:[20]

"The wild swan's death hymn took the soul
Of that waste place with joy
Hidden in sorrow: at first to the ear
The warble was low and full and clear....
But anon her awful jubilant voice,
With a music strange and manifold,
Flowed forth on a carol free and bold;
As when a mighty people rejoice...." [21]

The Dying Swan

Alfred Lord Tennyson

APPENDIX I

The Poisoning of Anna Pavlova

D id Stalin direct the murder of Anna Pavlova through poisoning? There are more than forty different biographies of Anna Pavlova, mostly in English and Russian. They are almost all admirable, but three stand out. First and foremost is Keith Money's exhaustive biography, *Anna Pavlova*.[1] Also very valuable are the great Margot Fonteyn's wonderful, *Pavlova, Portrait of a Dancer*[2] (from the perspective of a great dancer), and Victor D'André's, *Anna Pavlova in Art and Life*[3] (a first-hand account shortly after her death by her manager/husband). None of these propose or discuss the Soviet poisoning of Pavlova, although each note Pavlova's repeated assertion that she had been poisoned by her food in Paris. Until the 1990s, the existence of the Soviet poisoning and liquidation unit known as "Uncle Yasha's Group" headquartered in Paris in the late 1920s and 1930s, responsible for many such liquidations, was wholly unknown to the world and these biographers.

What is the evidence then for the Soviet poisoning of Pavlova?

1. Pavlova, a trained ballerina very much in touch with her own body, told her doctors, her husband, and everyone who would listen that she had been poisoned by the food she ate in Paris before boarding the train. Although she, no doubt, could not state who had poisoned her or with what, her dying declaration that she had been poisoned in Paris is of considerable weight.

2. Joseph Stalin, the dictator of Russia, was deeply infatuated with ballet and believed strongly in cultural

hegemony—the control of all culture in service to the Soviet State.

3. With Stalin's approval, Anatoly Lunacharsky, the Soviet minister of culture, invited Diaghilev to return to Russia. Likewise, Pavlova's long-lost mother appeared in 1924 to lure her to return. It was a serious enough matter that Lunacharsky himself visited Diaghilev in 1926 in Paris to personally extend the invitation of Stalin.

4. When neither returned, Lunacharsky personally (and certainly with Stalin's approval) condemned both in 1927 as class enemies of the Soviet people in a widely circulated article.[4] Diaghilev's family were secretly arrested and sent to Soviet labor camps. The status of Pavlova's mother post-1926 is unknown. The Diaghilev family was executed a short time after Diaghilev's death. Likewise in 1927, defection from Russia or refusal to return when summoned was made a capital offense.

5. After 1925 at Stalin's direction, the Yasha Group was organized in Paris with its own poison lab. They began actively liquidating White Russian émigrés, often with poison. On occasion, like the Black Baron, the poisons simulated pneumonia or lung disease. The Yasha Group and its targets were sufficiently important that by 1929, Sergey Spigelglas, the most notorious and skilled of all high-level secret liquidators, was posted in Paris.

6. There were a number of later confessed Russian poisonings, both in Russia and in the West, which had been disguised to mimic natural causes. Those symptoms and the methodology were virtually identical to the Pavlova poisoning. See, for example, the confessed poisonings of each of the Gorkys (induced lung failure). The death of Diaghilev, while different from Pavlova's pleurisy, was itself highly suspicious and resembled the effects of many poisons then being tested in Russia. Pathologists indicate

there are a number of poisons capable of producing Pavlova's symptoms. The most obvious suspect is anthrax, now a Soviet favorite.

7. While not overtly political, Pavlova, a favorite of the Russian royal family, was the most prominent and loved symbol of old Imperial Russia in the world. She was much beloved by the White Russian émigrés and responded with benefits for the destitute. In Cannes a few days before her death, she visited and prayed over the grave of the last Romanov recognized by some as the tsar and Stalin's most deadly enemy. She had danced at his last birthday earlier in 1928.

8. In August 1929, the Russian government seized all assets in Russia of Pavlova's charity for destitute ballerinas. The assets were distributed to the Red Army. Pavlova was again declared a class enemy of the Russian people. This produced worldwide condemnation of the Soviet government making any more overt action against Pavlova difficult. This practically coincided with Diaghilev's suspicious death.

9. As Pavlova danced in Europe in 1930, the Russian government sought through its ambassadors to prevent her performances. Thus, the diary of Anna Kollontai in 1930 reflects her frustration at her failed efforts, at Stalin's direction, to get Norway to block Anna Pavlova's performance. Kollantai was among the most important Soviet diplomats in the world and very close to Stalin. Pavlova knew of the pressure and implicit threat.

10. In a world which loved Pavlova, there was no one other than Stalin who had both the motive and the instruments in place to poison Pavlova. Such an action would have to be approved by Stalin as with so many others.

11. As a result of these actions, Pavlova told her friends shortly before her poisoning in the fall of 1930 that she

felt "a sword of Damocles" poised over her, no doubt referring to the actions of the Soviets. She begged one friend to pray for her.

12. The circumstances preceding her death strongly support Pavlova's belief that she was poisoned. She was a superb athlete in wonderful condition who had never been seriously ill. Immediately after taking lunch in her Paris hotel room, while boarding a train to begin her 1931 tour—the performances which Stalin ordered stopped—she suddenly and inexplicably felt very ill, inexorably spiraling down to death a few days later despite medical care. Her death appeared to those present to be caused by pneumonia and then blood poisoning. The Soviets had developed and were using poisons which mimicked those diseases.[5] Within a short time, the Soviet government contested her estate in London, ostensibly on behalf of her ancient mother, with the inside knowledge that her marriage to D'André, publicly announced many times by Pavlova, had actually never been legally formalized. Through the ring in Paris, and with cooperation from several of Pavlova's friends, Yasha had inside knowledge of everything she did.

13. The Soviets had available and were using poisons which closely mimicked the symptoms of Pavlova's last hours.[6] They later acknowledged their use in a number of murders. They also had a superb team of poisoners at the location where Pavlova said she was poisoned. Shortly before her death, they dispatched Sergey Spigelglas, the greatest of liternoye killers, to Paris.

14. The timing of the poisoning (immediately before a scheduled train trip with a meal in her room) reflects the brilliance of the Yasha liquidators. They had easy access to her meal, and her travel separated the victim from the forensic evidence and witnesses who might have aided in

an investigation. The site of the crime was additionally located at the convenient headquarter city of Uncle Yasha and Spigelglas. The poisoning occurred immediately before the commencement of her 1931 tour that would take her into Poland, close to Russia whose dictator she was defying. It was an opportune moment to end the prohibited tour.

15. The reader must in the end decide whether Stalin poisoned Anna Pavlova, as he murdered so many others, and whether Pavlova's long-ago plea that she was poisoned in Paris should finally be heeded or whether she will remain simply another convenient death by symptoms without a cause. Purges in the late 1930s completed by Yasha's being beaten to death in 1955 sealed all lips which could have provided additional information. Like the records on Wallenberg, the KGB archives on Pavlova will never be opened until Putin's control of Russia collapses and Russia is freed, as Akhmatova prayed. The refusal of Putin's government to make the applicable records available long after the deaths of Pavlova and Wallenberg speaks loudly of their guilt.

Sample Suspicious Russian Poisonings and Deaths

I t has often been claimed that Stalin's regime killed tens of millions of people, even more people than were horrifically killed by Hitler in the Holocaust.[1] The vast majority of these deaths passed into history without being recorded, and in many instances, were not attributed to Stalin's hit-men. The abundance of suspicious deaths and Russia's ability to get away with murder did not die with Stalin but continues today under Putin's rule.

Former Scotland Yard counter-terror commander Richard Walton, acknowledges that investigating these deaths is "very, very dangerous territory" and "completely out of the scope of local police" who have no experience with sophisticated Soviet poisons and other tactics.[2] Walton also notes Russian assassins' adept ability to "disguise murder" through staged suicides, planted evidence, or murders designed to kill undetectably to give the appearance of natural death. Putin's accumulation of "a suite of chemical and biological agents that were developed for targeted assassinations" leaves scant evidence even if law enforcement were savvy enough to prosecute.[3] A very small sampling of suspicious deaths pointing back to Stalin or Putin follows.

1. Alexei Navalny, an anti-corruption blogger currently known as "Putin's most prominent adversary," was very recently poisoned with a Novichok nerve agent and hospitalized in a coma after falling ill aboard a plane bound for Moscow.[4] His assistant and press secretary

who was with him at the time stated that Navalny had only consumed tea that morning and suspects that is how he was poisoned. Typically, Putin has imprisoned brave Navalny for failing to report to parole authorities while he was critically ill in a German hospital.

2. Alexander Litvinenko, a Russian Secret Service defector who made allegations about an FSB plot to kill oligarch Boris Berezovsky, was poisoned in London after fleeing from his home country. A public inquiry determined that he was killed by two FSB assassins who put radioactive polonium 210 into his tea.[5]

3. Anatoly Sobchak, a leading Soviet-era reformer and former mayor of Saint Petersburg, died suddenly in his hotel room of a massive, yet allegedly natural, heart attack. He was on an urgent trip to Kaliningrad at the time at Putin's direction. Both of Sobchak's bodyguards, two fit young men, also had to be treated for simultaneous "heart attacks" and poisoning after his death.[6]

4. Alexander Kutepov was a leading commander in the White Army who became chairman of the Russian All Military Union in opposition to the Bolsheviks after fleeing Russia. According to the memoirs of former Soviet spy Pavel Sudoplatov, Kutepova was approached on the street and led to a car by two agents dressed as French policemen. After a struggle and shouts in Russian were overheard, Kutepova suddenly died of a heart attack.[7]

5. Stepan Bandera, a Western Ukrainian freedom fighter who led anti-Polish and anti-Soviet movements, was ambushed by KGB agent Bohdan Stashinsky in front of his building. Stashinsky shot Bandera with a syringe gun loaded with cyanide hidden inside of a newspaper. After defecting to Western Germany and asking for

political asylum, Stashinksy confessed to the murder previously believed a natural death.

6. Scot Young was a multimillionaire who was impaled through the chest on the spikes of a wrought-iron fence after falling from a fifth-floor window. Young had been telling friends, family, and the police for years after a mysterious Moscow property deal that he was being targeted by Russian hit-men. His death was the ninth in a string of suspicious deaths among his friends and business associates.[8]

7. Nikolai Khokhlov, a Bulgarian playwright who became an enemy of the Soviet state after broadcasting reports critical of the Bulgarian government on Radio Free Europe, was poisoned with an umbrella gun while walking across Waterloo Bridge and died four days later. Russian-British double agent Oleg Gordievsky claimed the KGB had supplied an umbrella which could deliver ricin to the Bulgarian spy services that was used on Khoklov.[9]

8. Yevhen Konovalets was a Ukraine émigré leader who was killed by a booby-trapped box of chocolates given to him by Pavel Sudoplatov, a friend and under-cover Soviet spy.[10] Sudoplatov was also involved in the murder of Raoul Wallenberg and many others, confessing much later to the crime.

9. Yevgeny-Ludwig Miller, an exiled White Russian general and prominent anti-Communist figure, was tortured and shot after being drugged and kidnapped in Paris and smuggled to Moscow aboard a Soviet freighter.[11] He simply disappeared—fate unknown—until the 1990s when the truth was discovered.

10. Ignace Reiss, alias Poretsky, was an undercover spy working in Europe in the 1920s who made the mistake

of angering the Soviet regime by condemning the purges in a letter to Stalin. His bullet-ridden body was discovered near Lausanne a few months later. A French investigation described his death as "an excellent example of the observation, surveillance and liquidation of a 'deserter' from the Soviet secret service."[12]

11. Mikhail Lesin, founder of *Russia Today Television Network*, died of blunt force trauma to the head, neck, legs, arms, and torso in a Washington, D.C., hotel room. Investigators claimed he received his fatal injuries by falling when drunk, however a former senior national security officer said the death was "suspicious." Further, he stated concern that the Russian government would "start doing [in the United States] what they do with some regularity in London."[13]

12. Nikita Kamaev was the former executive director of the Russian Anti-Doping Agency and was involved in a scandal resulting in the temporary suspension of Russia's track and field team. He died suddenly of a heart attack at fifty-two years old.[14]

13. Vladimir Evdokimov, former executive director of Roscosmos space agency, was found dead with stab wounds in his jail cell. He was awaiting trial on embezzlement charges.[15]

14. Nikolai Volkoff, head of construction of Russia's Interior Ministry, was shot dead in his home two weeks after reporting $170 billion embezzled from his department.[16]

15. Vadim Tyulpanov, a Russian senator overseeing World Cup preparations "slipped in a bathhouse and hit his head" one day after the Saint Petersberg metro bombing.[17]

16. Petr Polshikov, chief advisor to the Latin America department at the Russian Foreign Ministry was found dead

from a gunshot wound to the head in his apartment immediately after the shooting murder of Andrei Karlov, Russia's ambassador to Turkey.[18]

17. Vitaly Churkin was a Russian ambassador to the U.N. and died at work of an apparent heart attack. Citing diplomatic protocol, the U.S. State Department asked the New York City medical examiner not to release the autopsy results.[19]

18. Boris Nemtsov, a former deputy prime minister and out-spoken Putin critic was shot on a bridge near the Kremlin.[20]

19. Pavel Sheremet was a Russian journalist killed in a car bombing in Kiev.[21]

20. Vladimir Shreydler, an outspoken pro-Ukraine activist who spoke out against Stalin on Russian talk shows, died of an apparent heart attack.[22]

21. Denis Voronenkov, a former Russian parliament member, was shot and killed in front of a hotel in Kiev.[23]

22. Yevgeny Khamaganov was an opposition journalist who criticized the Russian government. He died in a hospital in Ulan-Ude. Some reports claim he was beaten to death, while others claim he died from complications from diabetes.[24]

And finally, perhaps most ironically, Stalin's own grandson Yevgeny Dzhugashvili was found dead of unknown causes in 2016 shortly after accusing Vladimir Putin of "being without brains."[25]

Lab One Time Line

1917–1922	Russian Revolution
1919–1920	Soviets kill thousands with poison gases at Tambov to "kill the rats," then hide evidence
1922–1924	Lab One started by Stalin with Dr. Death, Yagoda (Kazakov)
1924	Probable poisoning of Lenin by Stalin (cf Final Testament)
1925	Tikhon poisoned; Iron Felix poisoned
	Stalin begins Russia Bioweapons Program at Lab One, Saratov, and various camps
1926	Yasha's Gang started in Paris
1926–1939	Many "natural" deaths in Russia, Paris, and elsewhere
1927	Diaghilev and Pavlova refuse Stalin's invitation via Lunacharsky to return, now a Soviet offense punishable by death
1928	Wrangel poisoned; Soviet "Cultural Revolution" begins.
1929	Diaghilev dies of "blood poisoning," likely poisoned; his family is then executed
	Pavlova declared Enemy of the People and her charity seized
1930	General Kutenov kidnapped and poisoned in Paris
	Attempted murder of Boris Bazhanov in Paris
	Assassins Spigelglas, Stalin's Sword, Eitingon, Abel, and Maly assigned to Paris.
	Noe Ramishvili assassinated in Paris

1930	Poison Dwarf assigned to Lab One
	Stalin consort Kollontai attempts to block Pavlova tour
	Musicians (Kobzars) killed en masse in Ukraine
1931	Pavlova poisoned in Paris
1935	Gorky and son poisoned by Lab One at Stalin's direction
1937	Yasha assassinates Ignace Reiss and Yevgeny Miller in Paris
1937–1940	Trial of the Twenty-One
	Entire upper staff of Lab One (excluding Yasha after confessing some poisonings) executed by the Poison Dwarf, who is himself then executed
1939	Bioweapons Leak of Pnuemonic Plague from Saratov via sick experimenter Abram Berlin who travels to Moscow for high-level meeting
1940–1951	Mairanovsky appointed head of Lab One and uses human "birdies" for experiments
1947	Bishop Romzha is poisoned by Mairanovsky by order of Stalin and Khrushchev
	Wallenberg is poisoned as a test animal in Lab One
1951–1953	Stalin claims "Doctors' Plot" involving Lab One was set up to poison himself and others
	Beria poisons Stalin and himself is later executed
1954–1956	Entire upper staff of Lab One imprisoned or executed
	Yasha has "heart attack" in Lubyanka
1956–1972	Scattered use of poisons by Russians, mostly against defectors
1961	Mairanovsky has sudden, lethal "heart attack" after claiming he poisoned hundreds as directed
1972	Biological Weapons Convention (BWC) banning bioweapons signed by USSR
	USSR immediately begins vast bioweapons projects (Hunter, Chimera, Rebirth Island)

1977	The Chinese Bioweapons Program leaks the 1957 flu virus preserved only in the labs during secret People's Liberation Army vaccine development, causing a worldwide pandemic
1979	The "bioweapons Chernobyl" at Yekaterinburg involving Anthrax earlier leaked at Kirov
Early 1980s	According to Russian intelligence, Chinese bioweapons facilities involved in developing Marberg and other viruses leak causing many deaths
1986–1998	Efforts by Gorbachev and Yeltsin to limit and reduce poison labs and bioweapons
2000	Putin begins immense "other weapons" biowarfare projects at numerous locations
2001–2019	Many "natural" deaths of Putin enemies
	In violation of BWC, Putin begins gene editing and other bioweapons development
2005	State Department White Paper on the vast fifteen-plus Chinese Biowar Labs created after China helps Iran with their bioweapons program
	Russian intelligence says SARS is leaked from a Chinese biowar lab
2007	Leak of SARS virus from a Chinese biowar lab in Beijing kills one and infects eight
2013	Horseshoe bats are trapped in Yunnan cave by Bat Woman and brought 1100 miles to Wuhan lab. Extraction of virus from bat
2015	Wuhan labs engaged in Chimera experiments altering horseshoe bat viruses. U.S. withdraws support because "too dangerous"
2017	Wuhan lab conducting experiments with nearby Chinese military biowar lab
2019 (August)	U.S. Homeland Security general says a Chinese biowar leak is "almost inevitable"

2019 (November)	Earliest case of COVID-19 appears in Wuhan. Many of the early patients, but not all, in the vicinity of the Wuhan Virology Lab, that has employees sick of concealed causes
Late 2019	Vast Chinese purchase of vaccine components and protective equipment begins. Special Airborne Unit under control of Chinese biowar general takes over control of Wuhan
2019 (December)	Dr. Li Wenliang puts information on the internet about a powerful new coronavirus in Wuhan on December 30, 2019. He is arrested, imprisoned, and subsequently permanently silenced, supposedly dying of COVID-19 although the fatality rate is below 1.5 percent for his age
2020 (February)	All early forensic samples destroyed by order of the CCP. All travel within China to and from Wuhan barred by China, but Wuhan International Airport is left open, seeding the world with COVID-19. All references to military on WIV advisory committees removed from WIV website
2020 (May or June)	PLA units begin to be vaccinated against COVID-19 with vaccine under development for some unknown period— many months before any vaccine was available in the West
Present	Millions continue to die as COVID-19 virus mutates at an amazing speed. Other than a 96.2 percent relative that was brought to Wuhan, no other natural sample or parent located anywhere prior to the Wuhan outbreak

Alleged People's Republic of China Biological Warfare Research Organizations[1]

Factory appellation	Location	Production details	Notes
Yan'an Bacteriological Factory	Yan'an, Xishan	Four types of bacteriological bombs: • Smoke-type bacteria bomb [may refer to aerosol] • Paper canister type, bacteriological container • Malignant *shayan* bacteria[125] grenade • Tetanus bacteria bomb	Potentially one of the larger scale biological research and production sites
Dalian Biological Products Factory	Dalian	• Tetanus/cholera mix vaccine • Diphtheria vaccine. • Rabies virus vaccine • Tetanus vaccine [toxoid] • Typhus vaccine • ABC vaccines	Potentially one of the larger scale biological research and production sites
Changchun Biological Products Factory	Changchun	Cultivation and experimentation of various BW agents	Potentially one of the larger scale biological research and production sites
Wuhan Biological Products Factory	Wuchang	Cultivation of various BW agents	
Chongqing Biological Products Factory	Chongqing	Research and cultivation of various BW agents	
Kunming Biological Products Factory	Kunming	Research and cultivation of various BW agents	
Beijing Biological Products Factory	Beijing	Cultivation and research in various bacteria	
Central Biological Products Testing Laboratory	Beijing	Liquid vaccines, testing of antimicrobial products in sera and bacteriological products	
BW agent production facility [unnamed]	Shenyang	Cultivation of various BW agents	
BW agent production facility [unnamed]	Shanghai	Cultivation of various BW agents	
BW agent production facility [unnamed]	Lanzhou	Cultivation of various BW agents	
BW agent production facility [unnamed]	Guangzhou	Cultivation of various BW agents	

U.S. State Department Report Fact Sheet: Activity at the Wuhan Institute of Virology

FACT SHEET
OFFICE OF THE SPOKESPERSON
JANUARY 15, 2021

For more than a year, the Chinese Communist Party (CCP) has systematically prevented a transparent and thorough investigation of the COVID-19 pandemic's origin, choosing instead to devote enormous resources to deceit and disinformation. Nearly two million people have died. Their families deserve to know the truth. Only through transparency can we learn what caused this pandemic and how to prevent the next one.

The U.S. government does not know exactly where, when, or how the COVID-19 virus—known as SARS-CoV-2—was transmitted initially to humans. We have not determined whether the outbreak began through contact with infected animals or was the result of an accident at a laboratory in Wuhan, China.

The virus could have emerged naturally from human contact with infected animals, spreading in a pattern consistent with a natural epidemic. Alternatively, a laboratory accident could resemble a natural outbreak if the initial exposure included only a few individuals and was compounded by asymptomatic infection. Scientists in China have researched animal-derived coronaviruses under conditions that increased the risk for accidental and potentially unwitting exposure.

The CCP's deadly obsession with secrecy and control comes at the expense of public health in China and around the world. The previously undisclosed information in this fact sheet, combined with open-source reporting, highlights three elements about COVID-19's origin that deserve greater scrutiny:

1. Illnesses inside the Wuhan Institute of Virology (WIV):
   - The U.S. government has reason to believe that several researchers inside the WIV became sick in autumn 2019, before the first identified case of the outbreak, with symptoms consistent with both COVID-19 and common seasonal illnesses. This raises questions about the credibility of WIV senior researcher Shi Zhengli's public claim that there was "zero infection" among the WIV's staff and students of SARS-CoV-2 or SARS-related viruses.
   - Accidental infections in labs have caused several previous virus outbreaks in China and elsewhere, including a 2004 SARS outbreak in Beijing that infected nine people, killing one.
   - The CCP has prevented independent journalists, investigators, and global health authorities from interviewing researchers at the WIV, including those who were ill in the fall of 2019. Any credible inquiry into the origin of the virus must include interviews with these researchers and a full accounting of their previously unreported illness.

2. Research at the WIV:
   - Starting in at least 2016 – and with no indication of a stop prior to the COVID-19 outbreak – WIV researchers conducted experiments involving RaTG13, the bat coronavirus identified by the WIV in January 2020 as its closest sample to SARS-CoV-2 (96.2% similar). The WIV became a focal point for international coronavirus research after the 2003

SARS outbreak and has since studied animals including mice, bats, and pangolins.
- The WIV has a published record of conducting "gain-of-function" research to engineer chimeric viruses. But the WIV has not been transparent or consistent about its record of studying viruses most similar to the COVID-19 virus, including "RaTG13," which it sampled from a cave in Yunnan Province in 2013 after several miners died of SARS-like illness.
- WHO investigators must have access to the records of the WIV's work on bat and other coronaviruses before the COVID-19 outbreak. As part of a thorough inquiry, they must have a full accounting of why the WIV altered and then removed online records of its work with RaTG13 and other viruses.

3. Secret military activity at the WIV:
- Secrecy and non-disclosure are standard practice for Beijing. For many years the United States has publicly raised concerns about China's past biological weapons work, which Beijing has neither documented nor demonstrably eliminated, despite its clear obligations under the Biological Weapons Convention.
- Despite the WIV presenting itself as a civilian institution, the United States has determined that the WIV has collaborated on publications and secret projects with China's military. The WIV has engaged in classified research, including laboratory animal experiments, on behalf of the Chinese military since at least 2017.
- The United States and other donors who funded or collaborated on civilian research at the WIV have a right and obligation to determine whether any of our research funding was diverted to secret Chinese military projects at the WIV.

Today's revelations just scratch the surface of what is still hidden about COVID-19's origin in China. Any credible investigation into the origin of COVID-19 demands complete, transparent access to the research labs in Wuhan, including their facilities, samples, personnel, and records.

As the world continues to battle this pandemic—and as WHO investigators begin their work, after more than a year of delays—the virus's origin remains uncertain. The United States will continue to do everything it can to support a credible and thorough investigation, including by continuing to demand transparency on the part of Chinese authorities.

Anna Pavlova in Houston and India

Houston

Pavlova visited Houston several times between her first visit in 1917 and 1928.[1] It was then just a small Texas city with a population of fewer than 150,000 people. Her visit marked the first time ballet had been introduced to Houston or Texas. She would likely have visited again during her planned 1931–32 tour had she lived. And as her visits did in so many cities, Pavlova's visit to Houston seeded ballet. It was followed quickly by a visit from the Ballet Russes. Houston grew from a small city into a metropolitan area of 6 million, with its own great ballet company. The Houston Ballet now performs both notable original works and those which Pavlova danced so long ago in the Mariinsky. Those early visits, no doubt, helped to inspire both the symphony's move to the Palace Theater shortly after Pavlova's death and the Ballet Russes of Monte Carlo's first visits to Houston.

The notable ballerina Anna Ludmilla, living in Houston, reminisced in 1990 about watching and meeting Anna Pavlova in 1916 as the seminal event that changed her entire life.[2] Efrem Kurtz, the early Houston Symphony director, was quoted in his obituary saying that conducting for Anna Pavlova more than sixty years earlier was one of the highlights of his career.[3] Similar stories of Pavlova's life-changing impact upon the lives of people can be found in many cities around the world.

In Texas, Anna Pavlova left behind some other legacies. In debutante balls, a test of grace, poise, and balance called the "Texas Dip" must be performed by each debutante. The debutante bows almost to the floor with arms outstretched while mothers, fathers, and audiences hold their breath, hoping the young lady does not collapse. This act began as an homage to Anna Pavlova. The Dying Swan marks debutante balls all over Texas and elsewhere at their climatic moment with her moment of near death.

In Houston, far from the country clubs and debutante balls, in parks, churches, and in the streets, particularly on the Cinco de Mayo, lovers of Mexican music dance the great "Jarabe Tapatío"—first danced by Anna Pavlova in the Plaza de Los Toros in Mexico City a hundred years ago. It is now danced in Houston and all over the world and is the national dance of Mexico. Dance schools advertise that they can teach students to dance it like Anna Pavlova.

India

Pavlova had a surprisingly profound and lasting effect on the dance of India. She had a deep interest in Indian dancing as a young ballerina. Visiting India on an Asian Tour in 1922, Pavlova performed in Bombay. One trip east of the city, she saw the ancient Indian cave drawings of Ajanta—2,000-year-old images of Hindu dancers. She fell in love with these and determined to incorporate Hindu dance into her performances. In London in 1923, Pavlova found and employed Indian dance fusionist Uday Shankar. Together, they choreographed two famous Indian dances—*Hindu Wedding* and *Krashna/Radha*, the story of a milkmaid who became one of God's beloved. She performed these all over the world, but more importantly, Shankar was inspired by Pavlova to abandon Western dance and return to Indian dance. He became one of the two greatest figures of modern Indian dance, attributing this to the influence of Pavlova.[4]

Leaving Bombay on a ship, Pavlova met and became a close friend of dancer Rukmini Devi Arundale. She inspired Devi to concentrate on Indian dance and asked members of her troupe to counsel Devi on the intricacies of modern dance. Like Shankar, Devi attributed her lifelong pursuit of Indian dance to the inspiration of Anna Pavlova. Long after Pavlova's death, Shankar in the north of India, and Devi in the south, remained the greatest forces repopularizing modern dance.[5]

India and Houston are just two examples. As the music ripples through hearts from Texas country clubs, to the barrio, and across India, it is quite clear that while Stalin stopped the Swan, he did not, and never will, stop her dance.

"Who will grieve for this woman?
Does she not seem too insignificant for our concern?
Yet in my heart I never will deny her...."
—Anna Akhmatova
Lot's Wife

Epigraphs

1. "Quotations: Communist Leaders and Ideas," Alpha History, https://alphahistory
   .com/coldwar/quotations-communist-leaders-ideas/.
2. Thomas Grove, "Alexei Navalny, Russian Opposition Politician, Given 3 ½-Year
   Sentence," *Wall Street Journal*, February 3, 2021, www.wsj.com/articles/alexei
   -navalny-russian-opposition-politician-sentenced-to-2-years-in-prison
   -11612287803.
3. Trefor Moss, "Anger at China's Covid-19 Response Smolders in Wuhan," *Wall
   Street Journal*, January 22, 2021, www.wsj.com/articles/anger-at-chinas-covid-19
   -response-smolders-in-wuhan-11611336335; Ken Moritsuga, "China Rebuffs
   WHO's Terms for Further COVID-19 Origins Study," AP News, July 20, 2021,
   https://apnews.com/article/health-china-coronavirus-pandemic-united-
   nations-a20391afec60601f3d666efc3c18b61d.
4. Moss, "Anger at China's Covid-19 Response Smolders in Wuhan."

Chapter One: Pavlova's Candle in the Wind

1. George Balanchine and Francis Mason, *101 Stories of the Great Ballets* (New
   York: Anchor Books, 1975), 138.
2. Victor D'André quoting Russian poet, Aleksey Plescheev, "Pavlova's artistic
   personality now seems to us limitless" in his book *Anna Pavlova* (New York:
   Benjamin Blom, Inc., 1972), 147; "Her unique position in the history of dance is
   established beyond doubt; it is hers for all time—Pavlova, the incomparable." Jane
   Pritchard, *Anna Pavlova, Twentieth Century Ballerina* (London: Booth-Clibborn
   Editions, 2013); "Famous Dancers of All Time: Anna Pavlova (1881–1931)," *Dance
   Academy USA*, September 15, 2105, www.danceacademyusa.com/2015/09/15/
   famous-dancers-of-all-time-anna-pavlova-1881-1931/.
3. Upon arriving in Paris, Dr. Zalevsky examined Pavlova and determined that she
   was in "excellent condition for the beginning of the new season." D'André, *Anna
   Pavlova*, 358.
4. The Soviets often used respiratory poisons which mimicked lung failure similar to
   Pavlova's in her last hours. *See* Igor J. Polianski, "Bolshevik Disease and Stalinist
   Terror: On the Historical Casuistry of Artificial Pneumothorax," *United States
   Institutes of Health Library of Medicine*, January 2015, www.ncbi.nlm.nih.gov
   /pmc/articles/PMC4304549/.
5. "Anna Pavlova Dies at Height of Fame," *New York Times Magazine*, January 23,
   1931, https://archive.nytimes.com/www.nytimes.com/specials/magazine4/articles
   /pavlova1.html.

6. Upon becoming ill, Pavlova stated, "Just imagine, I must have been poisoned by something I ate in Paris, and the doctor, instead of treating me for that, says I have pleurisy." D'André, *Anna Pavlova*, 359; Keith Money, *Anna Pavlova, Her Life and Art* (New York: Alfred A. Knopf, 1982), 391.

7. Money, *Anna Pavlova, Her Life and Art*.

8. Victor D'Andre, "D'Andre's Letters to Adja," Adolph Bolm, June 9, 1931, www.adolphbolm.com/html/Articles/Contemporaries/DAndre.html.

9. D'André, *Anna Pavlova*, 360; Tijana Radeska, "Last Words of Dying Prima Ballerina, Anna Pavlova: 'Get My Swan Costume Ready,'" The Vintage News, November 28, 2017, www.thevintagenews.com/2017/11/28/prima-ballerina-anna-pavlova/.

10. Anne de Courcy, "The Scheming Lover Who Drove the World's Top Dancer to Her Grave," *Daily Mail*, January 6, 1995, https://d6d56550-a-62cb3a1a-s-sites.googlegroups.com/site/lastjudgmenttriptyc/more-about-return-ashes-anna-pavlova-2001/Daily%20Mail%201996%20anna%20Pavlova%201.jpg?attachauth=ANoY7cq7QuAIIaqAsiAv-80yhN5WGYbmrTnYD168mjaPEQmmH3Nn8vSmDGB00ADMMQVRF8XthXxoV0uUVgFrJMg6bo9DiOBRBq8jv7d0ouWumpwA_yG5jGEomt02wHhQLVN2PSMxYyEM4_knoFDPBX6XNi_h84VV9MySdv0PovL0MojjASSDbqdPmFKbo1ooWGyCYkh6Ia2KoGRTBF_zBRYxu_mSuxBM93ayW1BNTB6i3VuJH3oQ8EUpxAP3euFcT1803Ler3Cg MqzMLo52fNk9gOQ1VMLsSL3sfcDDUm1vgTg1C_8NVyUZMQNRNqVCTXywoRN_dLVOm&attredirects=0.

11. "More About Anna Pavlova: Return of Ashes to Moscow," Genius or Lunatic, https://sites.google.com/site/jeanthomassenlunaticorgenius/anna-pavlova.

12. "The History of Ballet Flats," October 15, 2019, https://www.crfashionbook.com/fashion/a24663992/the-history-of-ballet-flats/.

13. Ashton described Pavlova, "She injected the poison in my veins." The poison was the desire to dance. *See* Clement Crisp, "Frederick Ashton Sees Pavlova Dance," *Financial Times*, January 18, 2008, www.ft.com/content/ac2ebe4c-c3cd-11dc-b083-0000779fd2ac; Ashton of Pavlova: "Every movement was felt through her entire body, through to the tips of her exquisite fingers, through to her large and luminous eyes." *See* Rupert Christiansen, "The Swan Who Danced Herself to Death," *Telegraph*, February 20, 2012, www.telegraph.co.uk/culture/theatre/dance/9093012/The-Swan-who-danced-herself-to-death.html.

14. Pavlova's graceful motions in the *Dying Swan* were described as "not death" and instead "the freeing of the soul from bondage." *See* D'André, *Anna Pavlova*, 134.

15. A Dutch painter and Pavlova fan claimed her dying wish was to "return to her beloved Russia after the communists have fallen." *See* Jennifer Scott, "Ashes to Russia? Ballerina Anna Pavlova's Resting Place May Not Be Final," *Washington Post*, September 26, 1996, www.washingtonpost.com/archive/lifestyle/1996/09/26/ashes-to-russia-ballerina-anna-pavlovas-resting-place-may-not-be-final/4a92b57b-5932-4088-94cd-ff1357d3848c/?utm_term=.ba8f94d59b65.

16. Alexandra Guzeva, "10 Famous Russians Buried Abroad," *Russia Beyond*, April 15, 2021, www.rbth.com/arts/333659-famous-russians-buried-abroad.

17. Thomas Harding, "Pavlova's Ashes Return to Russia," *Telegraph*, September 9, 2000, www.telegraph.co.uk/news/worldnews/europe/russia/1354719/Pavlovas-ashes-return-to-Russia.html.

18. Vincze Miklos, "The Strange History of the Moscow Cathedral That Couldn't Be Destroyed," Gizmodo, February 4, 2013, https://io9.gizmodo.com/the-strange-history-of-the-moscow-cathedral-that-couldn-5981106/amp.

19. *Ibid.*

20. Citing the Decree of May 15, 1932, of The Five-Year Plan of Atheism, "By May 1, 1937, not a single house of prayer shall remain within the territory of the Soviet Union, and the very concept of God must be banished from the Soviet Union." *See* N. de Basily, *Russia Under Soviet Rule—Twenty Years of Bolshevik Experiment* (Crows Nest, Australia: Allen and Unwin Ltd, 1938); *See also* Johannes Jacobse, "Atheistic Five-Year Plan Was Announced in the USSR 80 Years Ago," American Orthodox Institute, May 18, 2012, www.aoiusa.org/atheistic-five-year-plan-was-announced-in-the-ussr-80-years-ago-video/; For a Marxist view, *see* Paul Dixon, "Religion in the Soviet Union," In Defence of Marxism, April 17, 2006, www.marxist.com/religion-soviet-union170406.htm.

21. Felicity Morse, "Who Said It: Joseph Stalin or Oliver Cromwell?" *Independent*, December 20, 2013, www.independent.co.uk/news/people/who-said-it-joseph-stalin-or-oliver-cromwell-9017590.html.

Chapter Two: The Impresario and the Swan

1. Jennifer Homans, *Apollo's Angels* (New York: Random House, 2011).

2. Sjeng Scheijen, *Diaghilev, A Life*, (London: Oxford University Press, 2009); Andrew O'Hagan, "Diaghilev: Lord of the Dance," *Guardian*, October 9, 2010, https://amp.theguardian.com/culture/2010/oct/09/diaghilev-ballets-russes-victoria-albert.

3. Victor D'André, *Anna Pavlova* (New York: Benjamin Blom, Inc., 1972), 38.

4. *Ibid.*, 387.

5. D'André collected stories and clippings from Pavlova's career and placed these in an appendix to his book. *See Ibid.*, 389. Anna Pavlova, "Dancing is my gift and my life . . . God gave me this gift to bring delight to others. I am haunted by the need to dance. It is the purest expression of every emotion, earthly and spiritual. It is happiness." *See* AZ Quotes, www.azquotes.com/quote/532264.

6. D'André, *Anna Pavlova.*, 393.

7. *Ibid.*, 210; Scheijen, *Diaghilev*, 209.

8. Allegra Kent, "Heroine Worship," *New York Times Magazine*, January 1931, https://archive.nytimes.com/www.nytimes.com/specials/magazine4/articles/pavlova.html.

9. Jane Pritchard, *Anna Pavlova, Twentieth Century Ballerina* (London: Booth-Clibborn Editions, 2013), 130.

10. "A missionary for ballet, [Pavlova] took ballet out of the bastions of high art and was unashamed to share the bill with variety performers." *See* Bonnie G. Smith,

The Oxford Encyclopedia of Women in World History, (London: Oxford University Press, 2008), 1:425; "[Pavlova] was increasingly obsessed with transmitting the beauty of art to everyone in the wide world." *See* Margot Fonteyn, *Pavlova, Portrait of a Dancer* (New York: Viking, 1984).

11. Pavlova "was the first prima ballerina to take her art around the world. Margaret E. Willis, "Anna Pavlova," The Christian Science Monitor, July 2, 1981. www.csmonitor.com/layout/set/amphtml/1981/0702/070200.html.

12. Pritchard, *Anna Pavlova, Twentieth Century Ballerina*, 98.

13. D'André, *Anna Pavlova*, 105.

14. *Ibid.*, 106.

15. Pritchard, *Anna Pavlova, Twentieth Century Ballerina*, 17.

16. Rhian Deutrom, "Australia's Favorite Cake Is Not Actually a Cake at All," News. com, July 23, 2019, www.news.com.au/lifestyle/food/eat/australias-favourite-cake -is-not-actually-a-cake-at-all/news-story/20592692e2d2232c027b6fb7f859fb57.

17. "She was in her time the most famous dancer in the world; and for all the extraordinary numbers of people who actually saw her dance, there were countless others who knew her name and what she stood for." Keith Money, *Anna Pavlova, Her Life and Art* (New York: Alfred A. Knopf, 1982); Pritchard, *Anna Pavlova, Twentieth Century Ballerina*, 7.

18. "Diaghilev appealed to the elite, Pavlova to the masses—and to the elite, in spite of themselves." Pritchard, citing Arnold Haskell, in *Anna Pavlova, Twentieth Century Ballerina*, 29.

19. For example, she was warned by U.S. citizens in 1919 that if she continued to Mexico she would likely be killed by Mexican rebels who were then threatening the government. William Harrison Richardson, *Mexico through Russian Eyes, 1806–1940* (Pittsburg: University of Pittsburg Press, 1988).

Chapter Three: The Last Ball and the Day of the Soviets

1. Aleksandra Shilovskaia, "The Most Famous Ball of the Last Russian Emperor, 1903," Meet Russia Online, July 9, 2019, https://meetrussia.online/the-most -famous-ball-of-the-last-russian-emperor-1903/.

2. A recent *Star Wars* film designed the costume of Queen Amadala after a costume at the Imperial Ball of 1903. *See* Alexandra Guzera, "8 Fascinating Facts about Kokoshnik—The Quintessential Russian Headdress," Russia Beyond, July 18, 2018, www.rbth.com/arts/328784-russian-kokoshnik-headdress.

3. *Ibid.*

4. Amy Growcot, "Matilda Kschessinskaya," Marius Petipa Society, https:// petipasociety.com/matilda-kschessinskaya/.

5. Arthur O'Shaughnessy, "Ode," The Poetry Foundation, www.poetryfoundation .org/poems/54933/ode-.

6. Zoe Anderson, *The Ballet Lover's Companion* (New Haven: Yale University Press, 2015).

7. Jennifer Homans, *Apollo's Angels* (New York: Random House, 2011), 294; KellyAnn Colby, "The Dying Swan—Anna Pavlova," *Prezi.com*, June 12, 2013, https://prezi.com/dpl4bqtqr84g/the-dying-swan-anna-pavlova/.

8. "Pavlova's performance in the movie is no fluke or stunt—it's a fully realized, deeply committed performance that reveals Pavlova to be, from the very start, one of the greatest movie actors, a charismatic and expressive actor who's as forceful in repose as in action, as vital in quiet scenes as she is screen-bursting in melodramatic ones." Richard Brody, "A Great Ballerina's Explosive Movie Performance," *New Yorker*, December 15, 2016, www.newyorker.com/culture/richard-brody/a-great -ballerinas-explosive-movie-performance; "But it is her acting that is the reason to see this movie." Joan Acocella, "Silent Thunder," *New Yorker*, October 24, 2012, www.newyorker.com/culture/culture-desk/silent-thunder/amp.

9. Homans, *Apollo's Angels*, 330.

10. "For each age is a dream that is dying or one that is coming to birth." O'Shaughnessy, "Ode."

11. Robert Wilton, *The Last Days of the Romanovs* (Torrance, California: Noontide Press, 1993).

12. Sergei Nosov, "Forgetting the Purges, Official Claims Russia Has 'Never' Targeted Dissidents," *Moscow Times*, January 11, 2019, www.themoscowtimes.com/2019 /01/11/forgetting-the-purges-official-claims-russia-has-never-targeted-dissidents -a64111; During the Great Terror of 1937-38, the secret police killed thousands of people every day, but hid this fact from the victims' families. *See* Masha Gessen, "Under Russian Terror, All Exiles Are Fearful and All Deaths Are Suspicious," *New Yorker*, April 13, 2018, www.newyorker.com/news/our-columnists/under -russian-terror-all-exiles-are-fearful-and-all-deaths-are-suspicious/amp.

Chapter Four: Their Greatest Days: 1910–1920

1. Jane Pritchard, *Anna Pavlova, Twentieth Century Ballerina* (London: Booth-Clibborn, 2013), 68.

2. Victor D'André, *Anna Pavlova* (New York: Benjamin Blom, Inc., 1972), 319.

3. *Ibid.*, 304.

4. "Pavlova's voyages were global, and the effect she had on the history of dancing is incalculable. . . . In the age of the airplane, can we begin to imagine traveling over 400,000 miles by train and steamer?" Keith Money, *Anna Pavlova, Her Life and Art* (New York: HarperCollins, 1983), 7; After her death, Pavlova was described in headlines around the world as "Idol of Prince and Pauper." *Ibid.*, 393; Pavlova danced in 44 countries across the globe. *See* Dante, *Anna Pavlova*, 142.

5. Pritchard, *Anna Pavlova, Twentieth Century Ballerina*, 27.

6. Stephen D. Press, *Prokoviev's Ballets for Diaghilev* (Farnham, UK: Ashgate Publishing, 2016), 100; Lizzy Davies, "Batten Down the Hatches—Sergei Diaghilev's Back in Paris," *Guardian*, June 17, 2009, https://amp.theguardian.com/world /2009/jun/17/sergei-diaghilev-paris-ballets-russes.

7. Olga Taranova, "Narcissus Marsh, the Theatre Impresario, and the Bolshevik Revolution," Marsh's Library, www.marshlibrary.ie/diaghilev/.

8. Laura Keller, "The Ballets Russes in Paris," Chamber Music Society of Lincoln Center, May 2019, www.chambermusicsociety.org/about/news/the-ballets-russes-in-paris/.

9. Jennifer Homans, *Apollo's Angels* (New York: Random House, 2011), 339.

10. Stephen Walsh, *Stravinsky: A Creative Spring (Russia and France, 1882–1934)* (New York: Alfred A. Knopf, 1999); Nicholas Slonimsky, *Slonimsky's Book of Musical Anecdotes* (New York: Routledge, 2002).

11. Ivan Hewett, "Did the *Rite of Spring* Really Spark a Riot?" BBC News, May 29, 2013, www.bbc.com/news/magazine-22691267.

12. Nancy D. Hargrove, "The Great Parade: Cocteau, Picasso, Satie, Massine, Diaghilev—and T. S. Eliot." *Mosaic: An Interdisciplinary Critical Journal* 31, no. 1 (1998): 83–106, www.jstor.org/stable/44029725.

13. John Richardson, *A Life of Picasso: The Triumphant Years: 1917–1932* (New York: Alfred A. Knopf, 2010), 262.

14. Josh Jones, "Watch the 1917 Ballet "Parade": Created by Erik Satie, Pablo Picasso & Jean Cocteau, It Provoked a Riot and Inspired the Word 'Surrealism,'" Open Culture, May 10, 2017, www.openculture.com/2017/05/the-1917-ballet-parade-created-by-erik-satie-pablo-picasso-jean-cocteau.html; "Beginnings of Surrealism," The Art Story, www.theartstory.org/movement/surrealism/history-and-concepts/.

Chapter Five: Années Folles, "The Crazy Years"

1. Jennifer Fisher, *Ballet Matters: A Cultural Memoir of Dance Dreams and Empowering Realities* (Jefferson, North Carolina: McFarland & Co., 2018), 58.

Chapter Six: The Devil

1. Robert C. Smith, "The Greatest Trick the Devil Ever Pulled," Tracing Curves, July 30, 2015, https://tracingcurves.wordpress.com/2015/07/30/the-greatest-trick-the-devil-ever-pulled-was-convincing-the-world-he-didnt-exist/.

2. "Charles Baudelaire," Goodreads, www.goodreads.com/quotes/8784723-the-greatest-trick-the-devil-ever-pulled-was-convincing-the.

3. John Hooper, "Father Gabriele Amorth Obituary," *Guardian*, September 26, 2016, www.theguardian.com/world/2016/sep/26/father-gabriele-amorth-obituary; Archbishop Charles Chaput, "Sympathy for the Devil," Catholic Philly, June 5, 2017, https://catholicphilly.com/2017/06/archbishop-chaput-column/sympathy-for-the-devil/.

4. Roman Brackman, *The Secret File of Joseph Stalin* (London: Frank Cass Publishers, 2001), 122–23.

5. Brackman, *The Secret File of Joseph Stalin*, 4.

6. *Ibid.*, 11.

7. *Ibid.*, 12.

8. Arkadi Vaksberg, *Toxic Politics* (Westport, Connecticut: Praeger, 2007), 129.
9. *Ibid.*
10. *Ibid.*
11. Brackman, *The Secret File of Joseph Stalin*, 73.
12. *Ibid.*, 19, 122–23.
13. Stalin is a likely suspect in Sverdlov's poisoning. *See* Brackman, *The Secret File of Joseph Stalin*, 162–63.
14. Citing a 1964 CIA report called Soviet Use of Assassination and Kidnapping, "Even in cases where the Soviet hand is obvious, investigation often produces only fragmentary information, due to the KGB ability to camouflage its trial." Ben Macintyre, "All of Russia's Enemies Have Lived in Fear of the Assassin," *The Times*, March 10, 2018, www.thetimes.co.uk/article/all-of-russias-enemies-have-lived-in-fear-of-the-assassin-shhzbm9q6.
15. It was reported that Stalin "howled with laughter when told of final moments of an associate who Stalin had offered clemency for a false confession and who kept asking to contact Stalin." Cathy Young, "A Troubling After-Image of Stalin, 60 Years after His Death," RealClearPolitics, March 13, 2013, www.realclear politics.com/articles/2013/03/13/a_troubling_after-image_of_stalin_60_years_after_his_death__117396.html.
16. Brackman, *The Secret File of Joseph Stalin*, 321.
17. *Ibid.*
18. *Ibid.*, 373.

Chapter Seven: Stalin's "Special" Weapons Are Born

1. Anna Akhmatova, *Requiem*, Poem Hunter, April 1, 1957, www.poemhunter.com/poem/requiem/.
2. Robert Conquest, *The Great Terror: A Reassessment* (Oxford: Oxford University Press, 2007).
3. The century-old marriage between Marxism and what Putin and the Chinese Communists call "special" weapons—poisons, poison gas, and biowar weapons—began a century ago at an unlikely spot. Tambov is an extremely fertile agricultural area of central Russia best known for its farm products and chocolates. In 1920–21, the farmers of Tambov, formerly supporters of the 1917 Revolution, resisted the confiscation of their grain by troops taking even seed sacks. Initially they resisted with shovels and pitchforks, and later captured weapons. To answer this resistance, the Soviets authorized the massive use of poison gases, including both mustard and chlorine gases, upon the farm families in their villages and even those hiding in the woods. *See* Robert Conquest, *The Harvest of Sorrow: Soviet Collectivization and the Terror-famine* (Oxford: Oxford University Press, 1986), 51–53; Somewhere between 15,000–85,000 men, women and children were killed, and Soviet papers celebrated "rooting out" the "rats" with gas. The remaining "rats," perhaps as many as 250,000 who survived the gassing, were sent to extermination camps to die. After the Geneva Convention, these poison gassing activities became

less-fashionable, even among the Soviets. All information about the Tambov massacre gassings was suppressed in Russia. Knowledge of the tens of thousands gassed at Tambov would have vanished but for the chance discovery by Boris Sennikov in 1982. While engaged in archeological study of a monastery seized by the KGB, he found buried half-burned KGB records of the massacre. Sennikov was charged with treason by the KGB for his discovery, but lost only his job, not his life. *See* Nicholas Werth, *The Black Book of Communism: Crimes, Terror, Repression* (Cambridge, Massachusetts: Harvard University Press, 1999), 33–628; The pattern of Tambov-scale indiscriminate death followed by denial, secreting of records, and imprisonment or death of truth-seekers would occur over and over in Marxist countries, most recently in China's concealment of the origin of COVID-19 and its own bioweapons programs. *See* Robert Conquest, *The Harvest of Sorrow: Soviet Collectivization and the Terror-Famine* (Oxford: Oxford University Press, 1986), 51–53; Nicholas Werth, "Crimes and Mass Violence of the Russian Civil Wars (1918–1921)," Sciences Po, March 21, 2008, www.sciencespo.fr/mass-violence-war-massacre-resistance/en/document/crimes-and-mass-violence-russian-civil-wars-1918-1921.html..

4.   Donald Rayfield, *Stalin and His Hangmen* (New York: Random House, 2005), 315.

5.   Arkady Vaksberg, *Toxic Politics* (Westport, Connecticut: Praeger, 2011), 160.

6.   Leninskiy Rayon, "The Kamera (The Chamber)," Atlas Obscura, www.atlasobscura.com/places/the-kamera-the-chamber-leninskiy-rayon-russia.

7.   The use of poison as a murder weapon goes back many centuries in Russia. *See* Ben Macintyre, "All of Russia's Enemies Have Lived in Fear of the Assassin," *The Times*, March 10, 2018, www.thetimes.co.uk/article/all-of-russias-enemies-have-lived-in-fear-of-the-assassin-shhzbm9q6; Heidi Blake, "From Russia with Blood," BuzzFeed News, June 15, 2017, www.buzzfeed.com/heidiblake/from-russia-with-blood-14-suspected-hits-on-british-soil; Ron Synovitz, "Name Your Poison: Exotic Toxins Fell Kremlin Foes," RadioFreeEurope/RadioLiberty, September 18, 2018, www.rferl.org/amp/russia-skripal-kremlin-foes-exotic-toxins/29083216.html.

8.   Felicity Morse, "Who Said It: Joseph Stalin or Oliver Cromwell?" *The Independent*, December 20, 2013, www.independent.co.uk/news/people/who-said-it-joseph-stalin-or-oliver-cromwell-9017590.html; Stalin was responsible for the deaths of at least 20 million people. *See* Cathy Young, "A Troubling After-Image of Stalin, 60 Years after His Death," RealClearPolitics, March 13, 2013, https://www.realclearpolitics.com/articles/2013/03/13/a_troubling_after-image_of_stalin_60_years_after_his_death__117396.html.

9.   Gulbarshyn Bozheyera, Yerlan Kunakbayev, and Dastan Yelenkenov, "OP #1: Former Soviet Biological Weapons Facilities in Kazakhstan: Past, Present, and Future," Middlebury Institute of International Studies at Monterey, June 1999, https://nonproliferation.org/former-soviet-biological-weapons-facilities-in-kazakhstan/.

10.   Investigations in 1968, 1977, and 1990 revealed that [the poison lab] was established not by Beria, but by order of Lenin (it began as a special section—*spetsialny*

cabinet—in his secretariat. *See* Pavel Sudoplatov, *Special Tasks* 283–84; Boris Volodarsky, *The KGB's Poison Factory, From Lenin to Litvinenko*, (Beverly, Massachusetts: Zenith Press, 2010), 32–33.

11. Vadim Birstein, *The Perversion of Knowledge* (New York: Basic Books, 2004), 115.

12. *Ibid.*, 48, 99.

13. "From the early 1920s . . . biochemists, chemists, and toxicologists working for the security services researched deadly chemicals used in executions and assassinations and conducted deadly poison tests on humans." Poison was administered through "food, various drinks . . . hypodermic needles, a cane, a fountain pen and other sharp objects outfitted for the job." *Ibid.*, 81, 101, 117, 120, 127.

14. *Ibid.*, 117–19 citing various 1954 confessions; "Chemicals used in cases known to be Soviet-instigated include arsenic, potassium cyanide, scopolamine, and thallium. Other likely substances are atropine, barbiturates, chloral hydrate, paraldehyde and warfarin. Combinations of two or more substances may also be used, which further complicates diagnosis and tracing." Macintyre, "All of Russia's Enemies."

15. Birstein, *The Perversion of Knowledge*, 149–50.

16. Mark J. Porubcansky, "Stalin's Henchmen Tested Poisons, Murder Methods, on Condemned," *AP News*, June 8, 1990, https://apnews.com/5d65f2e4e9dc7ffcb3b5fb496259c4a1; Carey Scott, "Poisons Tested on Stalin's Prisoners," *Sunday Times UK*, October 15, 1995.

17. Boris Volodarsky, *The KGB's Poison Factory*, 35.

18. Paul Callan, "Stalin's Poison Dwarf," Express.co.uk, June 21, 2008, www.express.co.uk/expressyourself/49304/Stalin-s-poison-dwarf.

19. "Bukharin and Rykov Defend Themselves. Bukharin Was Shot Not Innocently Bukharin's Trial," iia-rf, April 9, 2020, https://iia-rf.ru/en/databasenya-for-children/buharin-i-rykov-zashchishchayutsya-buharin-byl-rasstrelyan-nebezvinno/.

20. Boris Nicolaevsky, *Letter of an Old Bolshevik* (Crows Nest, Australia: George Allen & Unwin, 1938).

21. Alan Wood, *Stalin and Stalinism* (New York: Routledge, 1990), 39.

22. Harold Denny, "Russians Confess Murders by Poison; Doctor Describes Killing of Gorky and Son—A Secret Virus for Menzhinsky," *New York Times*, March 9, 1938, www.nytimes.com/1938/03/09/archives/russians-confess-murders-by-poison-doctor-describes-killing-of.html.

23. "The Great Terror," *Museum of Communist Terror*, www.museumofcommunistterror.com/single-post/The-Great-Terror.

24. Bernstein, *The Perversion of Knowledge*, 163, 165; Colin Shindler, "The Russian Taste for Poison," *Jewish Chronicle*, March 14, 2018, https://www.thejc.com/news/news/the-russian-taste-for-poison-1.460725.

25. Birstein, *The Perversion of Knowledge*, 120.

26. *Ibid.*, 116.

27. "Soviet Use of Assassination and Kidnapping," Central Intelligence Agency, 1964, https://www.cia.gov/static/cdf1ae53dae899a8b8f27e827e6ac22c/Soviet-Use-of -Assassination.pdf.
28. Those opposed to Communism were called the "Whites" because of their white flags, while the Communists or "Reds" were marked by their red flags.
29. This didn't include, for example, the Russian Imperial family, whom they executed (adults and children).
30. Trotsky's last words were reportedly, "I will not survive this attack. Stalin has finally accomplished the task he attempted unsuccessfully before." *See* MacIntyre, "All of Russia's Enemies Have Lived in Fear of the Assassin,"; "NKVD Black Work," The True Crime Database, 2019, http://thetruecrimedatabase.com/case_file/nkvd-black-work/; Birstein, *The Perversion of Knowledge*, 100; Sudoplatov, *Special Tasks*, ix.
31. Sudoplatov, *Special Tasks*.
32. *Ibid.*

Chapter Eight: Strange Deaths at Home and Abroad

1. Roman Brackman, *The Secret File of Joseph Stalin*, (New York: Routledge, 2003), 173.
2. "Lenin, Stalin, and Trotsky—Personality and Views," Neodemocracy, April 22, 2017, https://neodemocracy.blogspot.com/2017/04/lenin-stalin-and-trotsky -personality.html.
3. Alan Nafzger, "Lenin: The Apotheosis of a God," Lenin's Body Blog, https:// leninsbody.wordpress.com/2016/03/30/lenin-the-apotheosis-of-a-god/.
4. Brackman, *The Secret File of Joseph Stalin*, 176.; Vadim J. Birstein, *The Perversion of Knowledge* (Boulder, Colorado: Westview Press, 2001), 39.
5. Gina Kolata, "Lenin's Stroke: Doctor Has a Theory (and a Suspect)," *New York Times*, May 8, 2012. www.nytimes.com/2012/05/08/health/research/lenins-death -remains-a-mystery-for-doctors.html.
6. *Ibid.*
7. Max Eastman, "Lenin 'Testament' at Last Revealed," *New York Times*, October 18, 1926, https://timesmachine.nytimes.com/timesmachine/1926/10/18/98398850 .html?pageNumber=1; V. A. Sakharov, "The Forgery of 'Lenin's Testament.'" Revolutionary Democracy, April 2001, https://revolutionarydemocracy.org/rdv7n1 /LenTest.htm; Discrediting claims that Lenin's Testament was a forgery, John Kappes, "Stephen Kotkin Argues for a Radically Revised Portrait of the Soviet Dictator in the New Biography 'Stalin.'" Cleveland.org, December 29, 2014, www .cleveland.com/books/2014/12/stephen_kotkin_argues_for_a_ra.html.
8. Kolata, "Lenin's Stroke: Doctor Has a Theory (and a Suspect.)"
9. "Was Lenin Poisoned by Stalin?" Firstpost, May 4, 2012, www.firstpost.com /world/was-lenins-poisoned-by-stalin-298095.html/amp.; "Was Lenin Poisoned to Death by Stalin?" NDTV, May 6, 2012, www.ndtv.com/world-news/was-lenin -poisoned-to-death-by-stalin-481030?amp=1&akamai-rum=off.

10. Kolata, "Lenin's Stroke: Doctor Has a Theory (and a Suspect)"; David Niesel and Norbert Herzog, "What Killed Lenin?" Medical Discovery News, 2012, www .medicaldiscoverynews.com/shows/299-lenin.html; Citing Lenin on his deathbed, "I have been poisoned . . . Go fetch Nadia [Krupskaya] at once . . . Tell Trotsky . . . Tell everyone you can," Brackman, *The Secret File of Joseph Stalin*, 174; Alan Nafzger, "The Murder of Lenin."

11. "Lenin's brain, the source of the Bolshevik revolution will endure—sliced like prosciutto into 31,000 slivers, mounted on glass and stored behind three locked doors, each reinforced with metal and fitted with an alarm, in Room 19 of the Moscow Brain Institute," Andrew Higgins, "Lenin's Brain," The Independent, November 1, 1993, www.independent.co.uk/life-style/lenins-brain-they-took-it -out-to-understand-the-source-of-a-revolution-they-now-reject-but-they-tend -1501441.html.

12. Suspicious Russian deaths continue today under Putin. *See* Sarah Hurst, Oren Dorrell, and George Petros, "Suspicious Russian Deaths: Sacrificial Pawns or Coincidence?" *USA Today*, May 2, 2017, www.usatoday.com/pages/interactives /suspicious-russian-deaths-sacrificial-pawns-or-coincidence/; Masha Gessen, "Under Russian Terror, All Exiles Are Fearful and All Deaths Are Suspicious" *New Yorker*, April 13, 2018, www.newyorker.com/news/our-columnists/under -russian-terror-all-exiles-are-fearful-and-all-deaths-are-suspicious/amp.

13. Yeryomina Anastasia, "Lenin's on Sale Again: Life as a Lookalike Leader on Red Square," *Russia Beyond*, June 9, 2016, www.rbth.com/arts/2016/06/09/lenins-on -sale-again-life-as-a-lookalike-leader-on-red-square_601693.

14. Pavel Sudoplatov and Anatoli Sudoplatov, *Special Tasks* (New York: Back Bay Books, 1994), 280.

15. John Simkin, "Walter Krivitsky," Spartacus Educational, September 1997, https:// spartacus-educational.com/SSkrivitsky.htm.

16. Sudoplatov states that Krivitsky was found dead in his hotel room in Washington, D.C. "It was assumed that he was assassinated by the NKVD, although the police verdict was that his death was a suicide. . . . It was not through our efforts that he died. We believe he shot himself in despair as a result of a nervous breakdown." Sudoplatov, *Special Tasks*, 49.

17. CIA memorandum prepared in February 1964 for the President's Commission on the Assassination of President Kennedy (the Warren Commission) and declassified in 1971. Approved for release in September 1993. "Soviet Use of Assassination and Kidnapping: A 1964 View of KGB Methods," Central Intelligence Agency, 1964, www.cia.gov/library/center-for-the-study-of-intelligence/kent-csi/vol19no3/html /v19i3a01p_0001.htm.

18. *Ibid.*

19. Igor J. Polianski, "Bolshevik Disease and Stalinist Terror: On the Historical Casuistry of Artificial Pneumothorax," United States Institutes of Health Library of Medicine, January 2015, www.ncbi.nlm.nih.gov/pmc/articles/PMC4304549/.

20. Ivan M. Andreev, "The Trial of Patriarch Tikhon," *Orthodox Christianity*, October 10, 2013, http://orthochristian.com/64798.html.

21. Brackman, *The Secret File of Joseph Stalin*, 192.
22. "The Show Trials," Masterandmargarita.eu, www.masterandmargarita.eu/en
/09context/processen.html; Christopher Andrew, "Secret History of Drugs and
Poison Arsenal, *The Times*, October 29, 2002, www.thetimes.co.uk/article/secret
-history-of-drugs-and-poison-arsenal-rdkwb26928c; Harold Denny, "Russians
Confess Murders by Poison; Doctor Describes Killing of Gorky and Son—A Secret
Virus for Menzhinsky," *New York Times*, March 9, 1938, https://timesmachine
.nytimes.com/timesmachine/1938/03/09/issue.html.
23. Svetlana Lokhova, *The Spy Who Changed History: The Untold Story of How the
Soviet Union Stole America's Top Secrets* (New York: Pegasus Books, 2019).
24. Citing rumors Wrangel had been poisoned by the OGPU, the secret police who
had deeply infiltrated émigré circles, Anthony Kroner, "Searching for Peter
Wrangel," Stanford University Hoover Institution, January 23, 2012, www.hoover
.org/research/searching-peter-wrangel.
25. Brackman, *The Secret File of Joseph Stalin*, 213; Birstein, *The Perversion of
Knowledge*, 85.
26. Sudoplatov, *Special Tasks*, 91.
27. Birstein, *The Perversion of Knowledge*, 85.
28. Adrian Bryttan, "Film Review: Secret Diary of Symon Petliura," *Ukrainian
Weekly*, November 16, 2018, www.ukrweekly.com/uwwp/film-review-secret-diary
-of-symon-petliura/.
29. Eric Lee, "Georgia: Another Revolution Was Possible," openDemocracy.net,
November 27, 2017, www.opendemocracy.net/en/odr/another-revolution-was
-possible/; Nucleus, "Case File #0121: NKVD Black Work," The True Crime
Database, http://thetruecrimedatabase.com/case_file/nkvd-black-work.
30. Keith Money, *Anna Pavlova, Her Life and Art* (New York: HarperCollins, 1982),
385.
31. David S. Shields, "Andreas Pavley Biography," *Broadway Photographs*, https://
broadway.cas.sc.edu/content/andreas-pavley; "Andreas Pavley Leaps to Death in
Chicago," *New York Times*, June 27, 1931, https://timesmachine.nytimes.com/tim
esmachine/1931/06/27/102246707.pdf.
32. Describing victims of the NKVD, prima ballerina Maya Plisetskaya stated,
"Nobody knew what NKVD did to people in their camps; the truth was hidden
and lied about. I think there were more victims, many more," Anna Nemtsova, in
"Russia's Greatest Ballerina Remembered in the War Zone," Daily Beast, May 6,
2015, www.thedailybeast.com/russias-greatest-ballerina-remembered-in-t
he-war-zone?ref=scroll.
33. "Soviet Use of Assassination and Kidnapping," Central Intelligence Agency.
34. Arnold Beichman, "Death of the Butcher," Hoover Institution, April 30, 2003,
www.hoover.org/research/death-butcher.

Chapter Nine: Stalin, Music, and Ballet

1. Antonio Gramsci, *Letters from Prison*, (New York: Columbia University Press, 2011).
2. Andrew Fedynksky, "Perspectives," *The Ukrainian Weekly*, July 27, 1997, www .ukrweekly.com/old/archive/1997/309720.shtml; Eimear McBride, "It Gets People Killed: Osip Mandelstam and the Perils of Writing Poetry under Stalin," New Statesman America, May 9, 2017, www.newstatesman.com/culture/poetry/ 2017/05/it-gets-people-killed-osip-mandelstam-and-perils-writing-poetry-under-stalin; David Morse, "Enemies of the People: Poetry and Politics in the Time of Stalin," Social Studies, www.socialstudies.org/sites/default/files/publications/ se/6504/650401.html.
3. Donald Rayfield, "On Stalin's Team by Sheila Fitzpatrick Review—Soviet Bunglers and Sadists," *The Guardian*, April 27, 2016, www.theguardian.com/books/2016 /apr/27/on-stalins-team-sheila-fitzpatrick-review-living-dangerously-soviet-union.
4. Alexandra Guzeva, "5 Russian Poets with the Most Tragic Lives," Russia Beyond, November 11, 2019, www.rbth.com/arts/331305-tragic-russian-poets.
5. Olga Savka, "The Death of the Poet of Communism, Vladimir Mayakovsky, Remains Mysterious," Pravda, October 26, 2005, www.pravdareport.com/business /9129-mayakovsky/.
6. Constantin V. Ponomareff, *The Time Before Death: Twentieth-Century Memoirs* (Amsterdam: Editions Rodopi, 2013), 45.
7. Fedynsky, "Perspectives."
8. "In Memoriam. Night of Executed Poets in Minsk," Gencat TV, Belsat, October 30, 2017, https://belsat.eu/en/news/in-memoriam-night-of-executed-poets-in-minsk/.
9. Valeriy Anikeyenko, "The Destruction of Ukraine's Folk Singers," *Euromaiden Press*, December 9, 2015, http://euromaidanpress.com/2015/12/09/the-destruction-of-ukraines-folk-singers/.
10. Taras Shevchenko, *Kobzar: The Poetry of Taras Shevchenko* (Oosterhout, Netherlands: Glagoslav Publications, 2013).
11. Soloman Volkov, *Shostakovich and Stalin: The Extraordinary Relationship Between the Great Composer and the Brutal Dictator* (New York: Alfred A. Knopf, 2004).
12. Jennifer Homans, *Apollo's Angels* (New York: Random House, 2011), 341; Stalin sent flowers to Olga Lepeshinskaya. *See* Yekaterina Sinelschikova, "Stalin's Women: Who Shared a Bed with the Soviet Leader?" Russia Beyond, www.rbth.com/history/329366-stalins-women-shared-bed/amp.
13. Anna Nemtsova, "Russia's Greatest Ballerina Remembered in the War Zone," The Daily Beast, May 6, 2015, www.thedailybeast.com/russias-greatest-ballerina -remembered-in-the-war-zone.
14. Masha Gessen, "Under Russian Terror, All Exiles Are Fearful and All Deaths Are Suspicious," *New Yorker*, April 13, 2018, www.newyorker.com/news/our -columnists/under-russian-terror-all-exiles-are-fearful-and-all-deaths-are -suspicious/amp.

15. James Wolcott, "The Gone Girl of Ballet," *Vanity Fair*, October 12, 2014, www .vanityfair.com/culture/2014/10/the-gone-girl-of-ballet.

16. Gennady Smakov, "Theater of Cruelty," *New York Review of Books*, September 1978, www.nybooks.com/articles/1978/09/28/theater-of-cruelty/.

17. Wendy Perron, "Who Is the Girl Who Arches Up to the Heavens at the End of Serenade?" *Dance Magazine*, June 2013, www.dancemagazine.com/who_is_the _girl_who_arches_up_to_the_heavens_at_the_end_of_serenade-2306913833 .html.

18. Smakov, "Theater of Cruelty."

19. Sjeng Scheijen, *Diaghilev, A Life* (London: Oxford University Press, 2009), 395–417.

20. *Ibid.*, 414.

21. *Ibid*; Andrew O'Hagan, "Diaghilev: Lord of the dance," *The Guardian*, October 9, 2010, https://amp.theguardian.com/culture/2010/oct/09/diaghilev-ballets-russes -victoria-albert.

22. Keith Money, *Anna Pavlova, Her Life and Art* (New York: Alfred A. Knopf, 1982), 332.

23. Victor D'André, *Anna Pavlova* (New York: Benjamin Blom, Inc., 1972), 225.

24. Birstein, *The Perversion of Knowledge*, 94.

Chapter Ten: Into the Storm

1. Keith Money, *Anna Pavlova, Her Life and Art* (New York: Alfred A. Knopf, 1982), 385.

2. Sheila Fitzpatrick, "Cultural Revolution in Russia 1928–32." Journal of Contemporary History, January 1974, www.jstor.org/stable/260267.

Chapter Eleven: Death of the Ballet Russes

1. John Keats, "Endymion," The Poetry Foundation, www.poetryfoundation.org /poems/44469/endymion-56d2239287ca5.

2. Sjeng Scheijen, *Diaghilev, A Life* (London: Oxford University Press, 2009), 440.

3. For discussion of the execution of Diaghilev's family, *see* Olga Taranova, "Narcissus Marsh, The Theatre Impresario, and The Bolshevik Revolution," Marsh's Library, https://www.marshlibrary.ie/diaghilev/.

4. Arkadi Vaksberg, *The Murder of Maxim Gorky, A Secret Execution*, (West Point, Kentucky: Enigma Books, 2006), ch. 12; Markov developed high fever and died shortly after being poisoned by ricin-laced umbrella tip. Richard Edwards, "Poison-Rip Umbrella Assassin of Georgi Markov Reinvestigated," *The Telegraph*, June 19, 2008, www.telegraph.co.uk/news/2158765/Poison-tip-umbrella-assassination-of-Georgi-Markov-reinvestigated.html; Philip Whiteside, "10 Ways Spies Have Tried to Poison Targets," *Sky News*, September 6, 2018, https://news.sky.com/story/amp/10-ways-spies-have-tried-to-poison-people-11490974; Matthew Weaver, "Poisoned Umbrellas and Polonium: Russian-Linked UK Deaths," *The Guardian*, March 6, 2018, https:// amp.theguardian.com/world/2018/mar/06/poisoned-umbrellas-and -polonium-russian-linked-uk-deaths.

5. Sjeng Scheijen, *Diaghilev, A Life* (London: Oxford University Press, 2009), 444.

6. Sjeng Scheijen, *Diaghilev, A Life* (London: Oxford University Press, 2009), 440; Bonnie Cuthbert *et al.*, "Dissection of the Molecular Circuitry Controlling Virulence in Francisella tularensis," *Genes & Development,* Duke University School of Medicine, September 13, 2017, https://medschool.duke.edu/about-us/news-and-communications/med-school-blog/molecular-map-shows-how-disable-dangerous-bioweapon.

7. Michael Steinberg, *Choral Masterworks: A Listener's Guide* (Oxford: Oxford University Press, 2008), 274.

8. Christine Stevenson, "Grave Encounters—Diaghilev and Stravinsky," Notes From a Pianist, May 21, 2013, https://notesfromapianist.wordpress.com/2013/05/21/grave-encounters-diaghilev-and-stravinsky/.

9. Michael Kennedy and Joyce Bourne, *The Concise Oxford Dictionary of Music* (Oxford: Oxford University Press, 2004), 707.

10. Simon Karlinsky, "Transformer of the Arts," *New York Times*, October 7, 1979, www.nytimes.com/1979/10/07/archives/transformer-of-the-arts-diaghilev.html.

11. Isabelle Fokine, "Michel Fokine: Choreographer," The Sarasota Ballet, www.sarasotaballet.org/michel-fokine.

12. Boris Pasternak, "Boris Pasternak Quotes," Brainyquote, www.brainyquote.com/quotes/boris_pasternak_116674.

Chapter Twelve: Swan Song

1. Elton John, "Candle in the Wind," Genius, October 5, 1973, https://genius.com/Elton-john-candle-in-the-wind-lyrics.

2. Quoting Kollontai's diary, Donald Rayfield, *Stalin and His Hangmen* (New York: Random House, 2005), 261.

3. *Ibid.*

4. Patricia Clavin and Glenda Sluga, *Internationalisms: A Twentieth-Century History* (Cambridge: Cambridge University Press, 2016), 69.

5. Keith Money, *Anna Pavlova, Her Life and Art* (New York: HarperCollins, 385).

6. Colin Shindler, "The Russian Taste for Poison," *Jewish Chronicle*, March 14, 2018, https://www.thejc.com/news/news/the-russian-taste-for-poison-1.460725.

7. Boris Volodarsky, *The KGB's Poison Factory, From Lenin to Litvinenko* (London: Zenith Press, 2010).

8. *Ibid.*

9. Money, *Anna Pavlova, Her Life and Art*, 385, 391. In antiquity, the Sword of Damocles was a heavy sword hanging by a thread over one's head.

10. *Ibid.*, 390.

11. Anna Pavlova's husband, Victor D'André, wrote of her: "She always bore slight illnesses so easily, that the idea that there could be any danger never entered anybody's head" in *Anna Pavlova* (New York: Benjamin Blom, Inc., 1972), 359.

12. *Ibid.*, 359; Money, *Anna Pavlova, Her Life and Art*, 391.

13. Margot Fonteyn, *Pavlova, Portrait of a Dancer* (New York: Viking, 1984), 146.

14. Alexandra Guzeva, "10 Famous Russians Buried Abroad," *Russia Beyond*, April 15, 2021, www.rbth.com/arts/333659-famous-russians-buried-abroad.

15. DeAndre, *Anna Pavlova, 359*; Money, *Anna Pavlova, Her Life and Art*, 393.

16. *Ibid*. Pavlova was adamant that there should be no cancellation of the tour, stating, "My company is the work of twenty years. It must outlive me."

17. *Ibid*.

18. Alfred Lord Tennyson, "The Dying Swan," Bartleby, 1830. www.bartleby.com/360/5/230.html.

19. Don McLean, "American Pie," United Artists, 1971. The song commemorated the death of Buddy Holly and others.

20. D'André, *Anna Pavlova*, 363.

21. Jane Pritchard, *Anna Pavlova, Twentieth Century Ballerina*, (London: Booth-Clibborn Editions, 2013), 48.

22. Peggy Turchette, "London," *Pavlova Project, A Dancer and Her Dressmaker*, https://pavlovaproject.com/gallery/london/.

23. Fonteyn, *Pavlova, Portrait of a Dancer*, 94.

24. "Anna Pavlova and the Dying Swan Drama Essay," *UKEssays.com*, May 12, 2016, www.ukessays.com/essays/drama/anna-pavlova-and-the-dying-swan-drama-essay.php#citethis.

25. Ekaterina Loushnikova, "Comrade Stalin's Secret Prison," openDemocracy, January 13, 2015, www.opendemocracy.net/en/odr/comrade-stalins-secret-prison/.

26. D'André, *Anna Pavlova*, 359.

27. "All the obituary notices as well as all the articles inspired by her death, have emphasized one important, outstanding fact: Pavlova was verily the best-loved person of her time, was truly idolized." *Ibid.*, 364.

28. Joris Nieuwint, "Maria Limanskaya—Anna Pavlova Directing Traffic at the Brandenburg Gate, 1945," War History Online, September 24, 2015, www.warhistoryonline.com/featured/soviet-fearless-female-fighters-that-killed-nazis.html/attachment/maria_limanskaya-anna_pavlova_directing_traffic_at_the_brandenburg_gate_1945.

29. Jennifer Fisher, Jennifer, *Ballet Matters: A Cultural Memoir of Dance Dreams and Empowering Realities,* (McFarland & Co., 2018), 58; See also the numerous dolls of Anna Pavlova in *Swan Lake* and Pavlova jewelry boxes available on Ebay and other sites.

30. Anna Akhmatova, *Rosary: Poetry of Anna Akhmatova*, trans. Andrey Kneller (Scotts Valley, California: Createspace Independent Publishing Platform, 2014).

Chapter Thirteen: Stalin's Legacy

1. Arkadi Vaksberg, *The Murder of Maxim Gorky, A Secret Execution*, (West Point, Kentucky: Enigma, 2006), 349–52.

2. "Soviets Told Stalin Drove His Wife to Suicide," *Los Angeles Times*, April 13, 1988, www.latimes.com/archives/la-xpm-1988-04-13-mn-1090-story.html.

3. Vaksberg, *The Murder of Maxim Gorky*, 233, 390.

4. *Ibid.*, 390.

5. *Ibid.*, 312.

6. Yolanda Delgado, "The Final Days of Russian Writers: Maxim Gorky," *Russia Beyond*, July 15, 2014, www.rbth.com/arts/2014/07/15/the_final_days_of_russian _writers_maxim_gorky_36685.

7. *Ibid.*

8. Alexander Novikov, a former NKVD officer taken prisoner by the Germans during WWII, told a French prisoner of war, a fellow inmate in the Buckenwald camp, that Stalin had poisoned Gorky. A German Communist, Brigitte Gerland, after being released from the Gulag and allowed to return learned from him that Gorky's health had suddenly deteriorated as a result of eating poisoned candies that Stalin had sent to him as a present, and that two medical orderlies, who were on duty that day and whom Gorky treated to the candies, also suddenly died. In the 1938 Show Trial of the Twenty-One, doctors and KGB officials confessed to poisoning the Gorkys, although presenting it as a rogue operation. *See* Roman Brackman, *The Secret File of Joseph Stalin* (New York: Routledge, 2003), 251.

9. Simon Sebag Montefiore, *Stalin, The Court of the Red Tsar* (Visalia, California: Vintage, 2005), 222.

10. Pavel Sudoplatov and Anatoli Sudoplatov, *Special Tasks* (New York: Back Bay Books: 1994), 137.

11. Rayfield. Stalin and His Hangmen, 279.

12. Boris Egorov, "How the USSR Fought Deadly Epidemics," Russia Beyond, March 27, 2020, www.rbth.com/history/331901-how-ussr-fought-deadly-epidemics; Casey W. Mahoney, James W. Toppin, and Raymond A. Zilinskas, "Stories of the Soviet Anti-Plague System," Middlebury Institute of International Studies at Monterrey, September 2013, http://www.nonproliferation.org/wp-content/uploads/2017/10/op18-soviet-antiplague.pdf; Milton Leitenberg, Raymond A. Zilinskas, and Jens H. Kuhn, *The Soviet Biological Weapons Program*, (Cambridge, Massachusetts: Harvard University Press, 2012), 20.

13. Mahoney, Toppin, and Zilinskas, "Stories of the Soviet Anti-Plague System." This is a detailed and thoughtful compilation of the Soviet bioweapons programs featuring many brave scientists who, risking their careers and their lives, refused to participate.

Chapter Fourteen: The Murder of a Saint

1. Frederick William Faber, "Faith of our Fathers," Hymnary.org, 1849, https:// hymnary.org/text/faith_of_our_fathers_living_still.

2. Yezhov, a four-foot-eleven crippled man, was head of the secret police and second in power only to Stalin during the height of the great purges in 1937–38. He was aptly nicknamed, "The Poison Dwarf." Paul Callan, "Stalin's Poison Dwarf," Express, June 21, 2008, www.express.co.uk/expressyourself/49304/Stalin-s-poison-dwarf.

3. Arkadi Vaksberg, *Toxic Politics* (Westport, Connecticut: Praeger, 2011), 95.

4. Vadim Birstein, *The Perversion of Knowledge* (New York: Basic Books, 2004), 149.
5. Antony Percy, "Homage to Ruthenia," Coldspur, March 2014, www.coldspur .com/reviews/homage-to-ruthenia/.
6. Father Robert F. McNamara, "BL. Theodore Romzha, Bishop and Martyr." Saint Kateri, 2001, www.kateriirondequoit.org/resources/saints-alive/tarsicius-toribio/ bl-theodore-romzha-bishop-and-martyr/.
7. *Ibid.*
8. Sudoplatov, *Special Tasks*, 408.
9. Morgan Lee, "Sorry, Tertullian," *Christianity Today*, December 4, 2014, www .christianitytoday.com/ct/2014/december/sorry-tertullian.html.
10. "Blessed Theodore Romzha (1911–1947)," Saint Nicholas of Myra Byzantine Catholic Church, www.ak-byz-cath.org/blesswed_romzha.

Chapter Fifteen: The Missing Man, Prisoner Number Seven—1947

1. Richard Lovelace, "To Althea, From Prison," Poetry Foundation, www .poetryfoundation.org/poems/44657/to-althea-from-prison.
2. Kati Marton, *Wallenberg* (New York: Arcade Publishing, 2011), 160.
3. *Izvestia* publication is referenced in the Wallenberg book, but not for the proposition that the Germans killed him. See Marton, *Wallenberg*, 220.
4. Marton, *Wallenberg*, 191; On Wallenberg's death, Sudoplatov stated, "My best estimate is that Wallenberg was killed by Mairanovsky, who was ordered to inject him with poison under the guise of medical treatment." Sudoplatov, *Special Tasks*, 270, 274; "Russia engaged in an active campaign of disinformation during the 1990s and through the 2000s, in order to influence the Wallenberg investigation at crucial moments." Susanne Beger and Vadim Birstein, "Why Do Swedish Officials Stall the Raoul Wallenberg Investigation?" *Russian Retrospective*, August 27, 2019, www.vbirstein.com/why-do-swedish-officials-stall-the-raoul-wallenberg-investigation/; Sergei Bertov, "Russian Authorities Seal Stalin-Era NKVD Archives," Moscow Times, March 14, 2019, www.themoscowtimes.com/2019/03/14/authorities-seal-stalin-era-nkvd-archives-reports-a64804; Jonathan Brent, *Inside the Stalin Archives* (London: Atlas and Co., 2008), 201–2.
5. Ingrid Carlberg, "Raoul Wallenberg's Biographer Uncovers Important Clues to What Happened in His Final Days," Smithsonian Institution, January 15, 2016, www.smithsonianmag.com/smithsonian-institution/raoul-wallenbergs-biographer -uncovers-important-clues-his-final-days-180957837/.
6. Vaksberg, *Toxic Politics*, 98; Wallenberg's only cell mate who knew the details of Wallenberg's case died suddenly in the Lubyanka in a similar manner. Birstein, *The Perversion of Knowledge*, 137; Luke Harding, "Russia's Lab X: Poison Factory That Helped Silence Soviets' Critics," The Guardian, March 9, 2018, https:// amp.theguardian.com/world/2018/mar/09/russia-lab-x-poison-factory-that-helped -silence-soviets-critics.
7. Carlberg, "Raoul Wallenberg's Biographer."

8. Daria Litvinova, "Soviet Prisoner No. 7: The Mysterious Case of Raoul Wallenberg," *Moscow Times*, September 30, 2016, www.themoscowtimes.com /2016/09/30/the-mysterious-case-of-raoul-wallenberg-soviet-prisoner-a55533; "Moscow Court Rejects Wallenberg Suit against FSB to Declassify Files," *Moscow Times*, September 18, 2017, www.themoscowtimes.com/2017/09/18/moscow-court-rejects-wallenberg-suit-against-fsb-to-declassify-files-a58979.

9. Birstein, *The Perversion of Knowledge*, 120.

Chapter Sixteen: The Poet—"A Former Person"

1. Anna Akhmatova, "Loneliness," *Peter and the Hare*, https://peterandthehare .wordpress.com/2007/08/30/loneliness-by-anna-akhmatova/.

2. Anna Akhmatova, *The Word That Causes Death's Defeat: Poems of Memory (Annals of Communism)* (New Haven, Connecticut: Yale University Press, 2004), 156.

3. Victor D'André quoting Russian poet Aleksey Plescheev, "Pavlova's artistic personality now seems to us limitless" in *Anna Pavlova* (New York: Benjamin Blom, Inc., 1972), 147; "Her unique position in the history of dance is established beyond doubt; it is hers for all time—Pavlova, the incomparable." Jane Pritchard, *Anna Pavlova, Twentieth Century Ballerina* (London: Booth-Clibborn, 2013), 171; "Famous Dancers of All Time: Anna Pavlova (1881–1931)," Dance Academy USA, September 15, 2105, www.danceacademyusa.com/2015/09/15/famous-dancers-of-all-time-anna-pavlova-1881-1931/; Dutch painter and Pavlova fan claims her dying wish was to "return to her beloved Russia after the communists have fallen." Jennifer Scott, "Ashes to Russia? Ballerina Anna Pavlova's Resting Place May Not Be Final," *Washington Post*, September 26, 1996, www.washingtonpost.com/archive/lifestyle/1996/09/26/ashes-to-russia-ballerina-anna-pavlovas-resting-place-may-not-be-final/4a92b57b-5932-4088-94cd-ff1357d3848c/?utm_term=.ba8f94d59b65; Thomas Harding, "Pavlova's Ashes Return to Russia." *The Telegraph*, September 9, 2000, www.telegraph.co.uk/news/worldnews/ europe/russia/1354719/Pavlovas-ashes-return-to-Russia.html; Amor Towles, *A Gentleman in Moscow* (New York: Viking Press, 2016).

Chapter Seventeen: Poison Makers, Stalin's Himmler, and Yasha's Gang

1. Ola Cichowlas, "Russian Historians Use Nazi Photo to Locate Stalin-Era Mass Graves," *Times of Israel*, October 9, 2018, www.timesofisrael.com/russian -historians-use-nazi-photo-to-locate-stalin-era-mass-graves/.

2. Sean Keach, "Soviets' Most Twisted Science Experiments," Northern Star, March 21, 2018, www.northernstar.com.au/news/the-twisted-history-of-soviet-science -human-apes-t/3366652/.

3. Yun Zhang, citing Vladimir Bobryonev, "Doktor Smert." *Ili Varsonofievskie prizraki* ["Doctor Death," or the Ghosts of Varsonofyevsky Lane], (Moscow: Olimp, 1997), 409–411 in "A Reciprocal Reaction: The USSR Chemical Weapons Program and Its Influence on Soviet Society through Three Civilian Groups," Colby College, 2019,

39, https://digitalcommons.colby.edu/cgi/viewcontent.cgi?article=1951& context=honorstheses.

4. Helen Womack, "Mass Grave May Hold Beria's Sex Victims," *Independent*, April 4, 1993, www.independent.co.uk/news/world/mass-grave-may-hold-berias-sex -victims-1453126.html.

5. Sergo Beria, *Beria—My Father: Inside Stalin's Kremlin* (London: Bloomsbury Publishing, 2002).

6. Colin Shindler, "The Russian Taste for Poison," *Jewish Chronicle*, March 14, 2018, https://www.thejc.com/news/news/the-russian-taste-for-poison-1.460725.

7. Robert W. Pringle, *Historical Dictionary of Russian and Soviet Intelligence* (Lanham, Maryland: Scarecrow Press, Inc., 2006), 234.

8. Andrey Vedyaev, "Yakov Serebryansky. Master of Illegal Intelligence," *Voennoye Obozreniye*, December 25, 2016, https://en.topwar.ru/106213-yakov-serebryanskiy -magistr-nelegalnoy-razvedki.html.

9. Ville-Juhani Sutinen, "Unknown Victim, Kommunarka, Moscow," Postcards from Gulag, May 19, 2018, https://postcardsfromgulag.wordpress.com/tag/ orthodox-church/.

Chapter Eighteen: Stalin's Last Day

1. Vadim Birstein relates the story of Oggins in *The Perversion of Knowledge* (New York: Basic Books, 2004), 132–39.

2. *Ibid.*, 135.

3. Oggins's falsified death certificate states "death was caused by a heart paralysis aggravated by angiospasm and papillar cancer of the uninary bladder." He actually died from an injection of curare. *Ibid.*, 136.

4. Jonathan Brent and Vladimir P. Naumov, *Stalin's Last Crime* (New York: HarperCollins, 2003), 4.

5. Jonathan Brent quoting Stalin, "And when we are finished with this idiotic sickness, we will be able to say with complete confidence that we are afraid of no enemy, neither internal nor external; their attacks do not frighten us, because we will destroy them in the future as we destroy them now, as we destroyed them in the past" in *Inside the Stalin Archives* (London: Atlas and Co., 2008), 293; "Joseph Stalin," Atomic Heritage Foundation, www.atomicheritage.org/profile/joseph-stalin; Sarah Pruitt, "The Hiroshima Bombing Didn't Just End WWII—It Kick-Started the Cold War," History, www.history.com/news/hiroshima-nagasaki-bombing-wwii-cold-war.

6. "Joseph Stalin's Dacha: The Riches of Power Beyond Authority," The Urban Imagination, https://hum54-15.omeka.fas.harvard.edu/exhibits/show/russian _dacha/joseph-stalin-s-dacha—the-ric.

7. See generally Yuri Druzhnikov or *Druzhnikov.com*. The author as a young student visited the dacha when it was to be opened in 1954–55 as a Stalin museum—plans were cancelled after Khrushchev's denunciation of Stalin. It has been closed to the public since then, although it was used by Putin in 2000. Yuri Druzhnikov,

"Contemporary Russian Myths. A Skeptical View of the Literary Past: Visiting Stalin's, Uninvited," Yuri Druzhnikov, www.druzhnikov.com/english/text/vizit1.html.

8. *Ibid.*

9. *Ibid.*

10. Simon Sebag Monetfiore, "Stalin, His Father and the Rabbit," New Statesman, September 6, 2007, www.newstatesman.com/politics/2007/09/stalin-father-egnatashvili.

11. Adam Ramos, "Top 10 Wild Facts about the Death of Joseph Stalin," Listverse, February 2, 2018, https://listverse.com/2018/02/02/top-10-wild-facts-about-the-death-of-joseph-stalin/.

12. Miguel A. Faria, "Stalin's Mysterious Death," Surgical Neurology International Journal, November 14, 2011, www.ncbi.nlm.nih.gov/pmc/articles/PMC3228382/.

13. *Ibid.*

14. "Lavrentiy Beria: A Look into a Different Post Stalin Soviet Union," The New Soviet Republic, April 20, 2020, https://blogs.lt.vt.edu/andrewp18/2020/04/20/lavrentiy-beria-a-look-into-a-different-post-stalin-soviet-union/#comments.

15. Jackie Mansky, "The True Story of the Death of Stalin," *Smithsonian Magazine*, October 10, 2020, www.smithsonianmag.com/history/true-story-death-stalin-180965119/.

16. Svetlana Alliuzeva, *Twenty Letters to a Friend*, (New York: HarperCollins, 1967), 7–9; *See also* Nikita Sergeevich Khrushchev, *Khrushchev Remembers* (Little Brown & Co., 1970).

17. Miguel A. Faria, "Stalin's Mysterious Death."

18. Alliuzeva, *Twenty Letters to a Friend.*

19. Khrushchev, *Khrushchev Remembers.*

20. Molotov, a Stalinist until the end and willing "to roll innocent heads," was the last leaf on the Soviet tree. *See* V.M. Molotov, *Molotov Remembers: Inside Kremlin Politics* (Chicago: Ivan R. Dee, 2007).

21. Miguel A. Faria, "The Death of Stalin—Was It Natural Death or Poisoning," National Center for Biotechnology Information, July 30, 2015, www.ncbi.nlm.nih.gov/pmc/articles/PMC4524003/; Jonathan Brent, *Stalin's Last Crime* (London: Atlas and Co, 2008), 320–21.

22. Mansky, "The True Story of the Death of Stalin..

23. Kile Smith, "When Prokofiev and Stalin Died on the Same Day," WRTI, February 29, 2016, www.wrti.org/post/when-prokofiev-and-stalin-died-same-day.

24. *Ibid.*; Jef Rouner, "How Josef Stalin Stole Sergei Prokofiev's Flowers," Houston Press, April 25, 2011, www.houstonpress.com/music/how-josef-stalin-stole-sergei-prokofievs-flowers-6522832.

25. Robert Coalson, "Prokofiev: The Genius in Stalin's Shadow," Radio Free Europe Radio Liberty, March 5, 2013, www.rferl.org/amp/prokofiev-stalin-deaths/24920002.html.

26. Adam White, "The Death of Stalin: What Really Happened on the Night That Forever Changed Soviet History?" *The Telegraph*, October 19, 2017, w w w . t e l e g r a p h . c o . u k / f i l m s   / 0 /

truth-death-stalin-really-happened-night-forever--changed-soviet/; As reported by Khrushchev's 1970 memoirs, two months after Stalin's death, Beria boasted to Vyacheslav M. Molotov, a Politburo member, "I did him [Stalin] in! I saved all of you." *See* Allan B. Schwartz, "Medical Mystery: What Killed Joseph Stalin?," *Philadelphia Inquirer*, January 15, 2017, www.inquirer.com/philly/health/Medica -mystery-What-killed-Joseph-Stalin.html; Ramos, "*Top 10 Wild Facts about the Death of Joseph Stalin.*"

27. Donald Rayfield, *Stalin and His Hangmen* (New York: Random House, 2005). 453.

28. Lord Byron, "The Destruction of Sennacherib," Poetry Foundation, www .poetryfoundation.org/poems/43827/the-destruction-of-sennacherib.

Chapter Nineteen: Stalin's Shadows

1. In a 1997 interview, Major General Anatoly Khorehko, who ran Compound 19 in Yekaterinburg (Sverdlovsk), stated, "We are restoring what was destroyed between 1986 and 1989." Ken Alibek, *Biohazard, The Chilling True Story of the Largest Covert Biological Weapons Program in the World—Told from Inside by the Man Who Ran It* (McHenry, Illinois: Delta Books, 1999), 263

2. Arkadi Vaksberg, *Toxic Politics* (Westport, Connecticut: Praeger, 2011), 13.

3. Andrew Roth and Tom McCarthy, "'It's Got Me': The Lonely Death of the Soviet Scientist Poisoned by Novichok," *The Guardian*, March 22, 2018, https://amp .theguardian.com/world/2018/mar/22/andrei-zheleznyakov-soviet-scientist -poisoned-novichok; Vladimir Isachenkov, "Russian Says Secret Cold War Lab Developed Poison Used in England," *Boston Globe*, April 23, 2018, www.bostonglobe.com/news/world/2018/04/23/russian-says-secret-cold-war-lab- developed-poison-used-england/zoJIAFi7msQGsCo8Lq7niL/story .html?outputType=amp; Ken Alibek and Stephen Handelman, "Is Russia Still Preparing for Bio-Warfare?" *Wall Street Journal*, February 16, 2000, www.wsj.com/articles/SB950656184355240629; Judith Miller, "U.S. Aid Is Diverted to Germ Warfare, Russian Scientists Say," *New York Times*, January 26, 2000, https://archive.nytimes.com/www.nytimes.com/learning/teachers/featured_ articles/20000126wednesday.html.

4. Filippa Lentzos, *Biological Threats in the 21st Century* (London: Imperial College Press, 2016, 79); The United States announced it would impose restrictions on the export of sensitive technology to Russia because of its use of a nerve agent in the attempted murder of a former Russian spy and his daughter. *See* Julian Borger, "U.S. to Impose Sanctions against Russia over Salisbury Nerve Agent Attack," *The Guardian*, August 8, 2018, www.theguardian.com/world /2018/aug/08/us-russia-sanctions-nerve-agent-attack-salisbury; Eva Gudbergsdottir, "Professor, Alumnus Shed Light on Russia's Secret Bioweapons Program," Middlebury Institute of International Studies, March 27, 2018, www.middlebury.edu/institute/news/professor-alumnus-shed-light-russias-secret-- bioweapons-program; "During the years of Soviet power, surely more money was

spent on developing, producing and equipping chemical weapons than in all public education." Lev Aleksandrovich Fedorov, "Chemical Weapons in Russia: History, Ecology, Politics," Center of Ecological Policy of Russia, July 27, 1994, https://fas.org/nuke/guide/russia/cbw/jptac008_l94001.htm.

5.   Alibek, *Biohazard.*
6.   Similarly, the Chinese have been accused of executing "prisoners of conscience," people killed for their beliefs, and harvesting their organs. *See* Ephrat Livni, "A Chinese Medical Study Is Being Retracted for Relying on Organs Harvested from Executed Prisoners," Quartz, February 9, 2017, https://qz.com/906142/a-chinese-medical-study-is-being-retracted-for-relying-on-organs-harvested-from-executed-prisoners/#:~:text=RARE%20PARTS-,A%20Chinese%20medical%20study%20is%20being%20retracted%20for,organs%20harvested%20from%20executed%20prisoners&text=A%20heavy%20price%20to%20pay.&text=Now%2C%20Liver%20International%20is%20retracting,people%20killed%20for%20their%20beliefs.
7.   *Ibid.*, 18.
8.   Alibek and Handelman, "Is Russia Still Preparing for Bio-Warfare?" ; Judith Miller, "U.S. Aid Is Diverted to Germ Warfare, Russian Scientists Say," *New York Times,* January 26, 2000, https://archive.nytimes.com/www.nytimes.com/learning/teachers/featured_articles/20000126wednesday.html.
9.   Alibek, *Biohazard,* 20.
10.   *Ibid.*, 41.
11.   *Ibid.*, 17.
12.   Boris Egorov, "How the USSR Fought Deadly Epidemics," Russia Today, March 27, 2020, www.rbth.com/history/331901-how-ussr-fought-deadly-epidemics.
13.   Mike Eckel, "U.S. Blacklists Russian Entities For Chemical, Biological Weapon Research," Radio Free Europe, RadioLiberty, August 27, 2020, www.rferl.org/a/us-blacklists-russian-entities-for-chemical-biological-weapon-research/30805564.html.
14.   *Ibid.*, 78.
15.   This was the original "wet" or "meat market" alibi later unoriginally advanced by the Xi government to cover the leak at Wuhan, China.
16.   Colonel Kanatzhan Alibekov is a former Soviet physician, microbiologist and biological warfare expert. He served as the First Deputy Director of Biopreparat, where he oversaw a vast program of BW facilities. In his book Biohazard, written after defection, he states, "In 1997, [it was] reported in the Russian publication *Questions of Virology* that they had successfully inserted a gene for Ebola into the genome of vaccinia. Once again, a benign scientific explanation was put forward: they said it was an important step towards creating an Ebola vaccine. But we had always intended vaccinia to be our surrogate for further smallpox weapons research. There was no doubt in my mind that Vector was following our original plan." *Ibid.*, 261
17.   Ibid., 129.

18. "In addition to the poisoning and assassinations, Putin has been quoted as saying, 'Russia never lost the Cold War…because it never ended.'" Newt Gingrich, "Collusion—The Real Russian Threat," Fox News, May 1, 2019, www.foxnews.com/opinion/newt-gingrich-collusion-the-real-russian-threat.amp.

19. "Soviet scientists combined the knowledge gained from postwar biochemistry and genetic research with modern industrial techniques to develop what are called, 'aerosol' weapons—particles suspended in a mist, like the spray of an insecticide, or a fine dust, like talcum powder." Alibek, *Biohazard*, 20.

20. *Ibid.*, 172.

21. *Ibid.*, 176.

22. Giovanni Catelli, *The Death of Camus* (London: C. Hurst & Co., 2019); Allison Flood, "New Book Claims Albert Camus Was Murdered by the KGB," *The Guardian*, December 5, 2019, https://www.theguardian.com/books/2019/dec/05/albert-camus -murdered-by-the-kgb-giovanni-catelli#:~:text=Sixty%20years%20after%20the %20French,for%20his%20anti%2DSoviet%20rhetoric.&text=Camus%20died %20on%204%20January,it%20crashed%20into%20a%20tree.

23. Jerrold L. Schecter, "Book Review: 'Once Upon a Time in Russia, The Rise of Oligarchs, A True Story of Ambition, Wealth, Betrayal, and Murder' by Ben Mezrich," The European Institute, www.europeaninstitute.org/index.php /component/content/article?id=2054:auto-generate-from-title.

24. Schecter. "Book Review: 'Once Upon a Time in Russia"; Oliver Bullough, "Former Aide Says Putin Has No Strategic Plan," *Time*, November 5, 2014, https:// time.com/3547935/putin-pugachev-oligarchs/.

25. Katya Golubkova, "Putin Says Grandfather Cooked for Stalin and Lenin," Reuters, Mar.ch 11, 2018, https://mobile.reuters.com/article/amp/idUSKCN1GN0OR; "Putin Weeps: Russia's Desire for the World's Admiration Backfires," Ami Magazine, May 13, 2020, www.newstatesman.com/politics/2007/09/ stalin-father-egnatashvili.

26. Andrei Kolesnikov, "Facing a Dim Present, Putin Turns Back to Glorious Stalin," *Washington Post*, May 8, 2020, www.washingtonpost.com/opinions/2020/05/08/ facing-dim-present-putin-turns-back-glorious-stalin/.

27. Tom Robberson, "I Looked the Man (Putin) in the Eye and Saw…the Enemy" *Dallas Morning News*, June 29, 2010, www.dallasnews.com/opinion/2010/06/29 /i-looked-the-man-putin-in-the-eye-and-saw-the-enemy/; H.G. Wells similary mis-described Stalin as "a kindly man…who owes his position to the fact that no one is afraid of him and everyone trusts him." Roman Brackman, *The Secret File of Joseph Stalin* (New York: Routledge, 2003), 249.

28. Malcom Forbes, "How Putin Came to Power," Columbia Journalism Review, March 7, 2012, https://archives.cjr.org/critical_eye/how_vladimir_putin_came_to _power.php.

29. Editorial Board, "Putin Touts Christianity. So Why is Russia Persecuting Christians?" *Washington Post*, June 6, 2019, www.washingtonpost.com /opinions/global-opinions/putin-touts-christianity-so-why-is-russia-persecuting

-christians/2019/06/06/9876523c-87d1-11e9-98c1-e945ae5db8fb_story.html
?outputType=amp.

30. Michael McFaul, "Russia's 2000 Presidential Elections: Implications for Russian
Democracy and U.S.–Russian Relations," Carnegie Endowment for International
Peace, April 1, 2000, https://carnegieendowment.org/2000/04/01/russia-s-2000
-presidential-elections-implications-for-russian-democracy-and-u.s.-russian
-relations-pub-421.

31. John Stonestreet, "The Point: Christian Persecution in Russia," Breakpoint,
www.breakpoint.org/2019/07/the-point-christian-persecution-in-russia/; Max
Seddon, "Putin and the Patriarchs," *Financial Times*, August 21, 2019,
www.breakpoint.org/2019/07/the-point-christian-persecution-in-russia/.

32. Austin Cline, "Karl Marx on Religion as the Opium of the People," Learn
Religions, January 7, 2019, www.learnreligions.com/karl-marx-on-
religion-251019; For the history of this quote, see Andrew M. McKinnon,
"Reading 'Opium of the People': Expression, Protest and the Dialectics of Religion."
Critical Sociology, January 1, 2019, https://journals.sagepub.com/doi/10.1163
/1569163053084360.

33. Damien Sharkov, "Putin Says Communism Comes from the Bible, Compares Lenin
to a Saint," *Newsweek*, January 15, 2018, www.google.com/search?client=safari
&rls=en&q=Newsweek,+January+15,+2018,+Putin+says+Communism+comes+
from+the+bible.+Damien+Sharkov.&ie=UTF-8&oe=UTF-8.

34. "Militant atheism is not merely incidental or marginal to Communist policy. It is
not a side effect, but the central pivot." Giles Fraser, "Why the Soviet Attempt to
Stamp Out Religion Failed," *The Guardian*, October 26, 2017, https://amp
.theguardian.com/commentisfree/belief/2017/oct/26/why-the-soviet-attempt-to
-stamp-out-religion-failed; Kate Shellnutt, "Russia's Newest Law: No Evangelizing
Outside of Church," *Christianity Today*, www.christianitytoday.com/news/2016
/june/no-evangelizing-outside-of-church-russia-proposes.html; Jason Lemon, "Is
Religious Persecution in Russia Escalating? Elderly Baptist Pastor Charged for
'Illegal' Missionary Work," *Newsweek*, April 25, 2019, www.newsweek.com/
religious-persecution-russia-baptist-pastor-1406134?amp=1.

35. Ralph Dumain, "Lenin on God-Concepts, Liberalized Religion, & Political
Orientation," Reason and Society, July 1, 2008, http://reasonsociety.blogspot.com
/2008/07/lenin-on-god-concepts-liberalized.html.

36. Andrew Osborn, "Josef Stalin Statue Removed from Hometown in Georgia," The
Telegraph, June 25, 2010, www.telegraph.co.uk/news/worldnews/europe/georgia
/7854736/Josef-Stalin-statue-removed-from-hometown-in-Georgia.html; Valeria
Luiselli, "A New Love of Stalin," Strangers Guide, February 17, 2019, https://
strangersguide.com/articles/a-new-love-of-stalin/.

37. Cathy Young, "A Troubling After-Image of Stalin, 60 Years after His Death,"
RealClearPolitics, March 13, 2013, www.realclearpolitics.com/articles/2013/03/13
/a_troubling_after-image_of_stalin_60_years_after_his_death__117396.html.

38. Agence France-Presse, "Russia Divided on Stalin 60 Years after His Death," *South China Morning Post*, March 6, 2013, www.scmp.com/news/world/article/1182611 /russia-divided-stalin-60-years-after-his-death.

39. Irina Sherbakova, "Vladimir Putin's Russia Is Rehabilitating Stalin. We Must Not Let It Happen," *The Guardian*, July 10, 2019, www.theguardian.com/commentisfree /2019/jul/10/vladimir-putin-russia-rehabilitating-stalin-soviet-past.

40. Peter Rutland and Neil Shimmield, "Putin's Dangerous Campaign to Rehabilitate Stalin," *Washington Post*, June 13, 2019, www.washingtonpost.com/outlook /2019/06/13/putins-dangerous-campaign-rehabilitate-stalin/; "Stalin's Approval Rating among Russians Hits Record High—Poll," *Moscow Times*, April 16, 2019, www.themoscowtimes.com/2019/04/16/stalins-approval-rating-among-russians-hits-record-high-poll-a65245.

41. Donald Rayfield, *Stalin and His Hangmen* (New York: Random House, 2005), 193, citing Gorky's diary, " …if you magnified an ordinary flea several thousand times, you'd get the most fearful animal on earth which nobody would be strong enough to control… But history's monstrous grimaces produce such magnifications in the real world, too. Stalin is a flea which Bolshevik propaganda and the hypnosis of fear have magnified to unbelievable proportions.".

42. Michael Schwirtz, "How a Poisoning in Bulgaria Exposed Russian Assassins in Europe," *New York Times*, December 22, 2019, www.nytimes.com/2019/12/22 /world/europe/bulgaria-russia-assassination-squad.html.

43. Bellingcat Investigation Team, "Skripal Poisoner Attended GRU Commander Family Wedding," Bellingcat, October 14, 2019, www.bellingcat.com/news/uk -and-europe/2019/10/14/averyanov-chepiga/; Bellingcat Investigation Team, "The Dreadful Eight: GRU's Unit 29155 and the 2015 Poisoning of Emilian Gebrev," Bellingcat, November 23, 2019, www.bellingcat.com/news/uk-and-europe/2019 /11/23/the-dreadful-eight-grus-unit-29155-and-the-2015-poisoning-of-emilian -gebrev/.

44. Bellingcat Investigation Team, "Skripal Poisoner Attended GRU Commander Family Wedding."

45. Lluba Lulko, "GRU Secret Unit: It's a Pity, If It Doesn't Exist," *Pravda*, November 10, 2019, www.pravdareport.com/world/142824-gru/; Michael Schwirtz, "Top Secret Russian Unit Seeks to Destabilize Europe, Security Officials Say," *New York Times*, October 8, 2019, www.nytimes.com/2019/10/08/world/europe/unit-29155- russia-gru.html.

46. Terry Hayes, *I Am Pilgrim: A Thriller* (New York Emily Bestler Books, 2014).

47. Nikolai Litovkin, "Would You Survive a Week in the Russian Army?" Russia Beyond, October 18, 2021, www.rbth.com/lifestyle/334315-would-you-survive- year-in-army.

Chapter Twenty: North Korea's Poison Labs

1. According to Ken Alibek and many other sources, Communist Cuba with Soviet assistance has also been hard at work developing bioweapons. *See* Peter Slevin,

"Cuba Seeks Bioweapons, U.S. Says," *Washington Post*, May 7, 2002, www .washingtonpost.com/archive/politics/2002/05/07/cuba-seeks-bioweapons-us-says /bfa31f3f-b2e2-4ca3-8459-c5d1ac8faa99/.

2. Antony Barnett, "Revealed: The Gas Chamber Horror of North Korea's Gulag," *The Guardian*, January 31, 2004, www.theguardian.com/world/2004/feb/01/northkorea; Robert Windrem, "Death, Terror in N. Korea Gulag," *NBC News*, October 24, 2003, www.nbcnews.com/id/wbna3071466.

3. Nicolas Werth *et al.*, *The Black Book of Communism: Crimes, Terror, Repression*, (Cambridge, Massacusetts: Harvard University Press, 1999).

4. Robert Windrem, Ken Dilanjan, and Abigail Williams, "North Korea Has a History of Assassination Attempts on Foreign Soil," NBC News, November 21, 2017, www.nbcnews.com/news/amp/ncna823016.

5. "Kim Jong Un's Assassinated Half-Brother Carried Antidote to Poison That Killed Him," *DW*, December 1, 2017, https://amp.dw.com/en/kim-jong-uns-assassinated-half-brother-carried-antidote-to-poison-that-killed-him/a-41609274.

Chapter Twenty-One: Big Daddy Xi and the Wuhan Virus

1. Martin Luther King Jr., "The Other America," Grosse Pointe Historical Society, March 14, 1968, https://www.gphistorical.org/mlk/mlkspeech/.

2. Gavin Menzies, *1421: The Year China Discovered America* (New York: William Morrow Paperbacks, 2008); *See also* Edward L. Dreyer, "Zheng He: China and the Oceans in the Early Ming Dynasty, 1405–1433," (New York: Pearson College Div., 2006).

3. "Is the Chinese Growth Model Replicable?" International Monetary Fund, March 2012, https://www.elibrary.imf.org/view/IMF071/12538-9780262017619/12538 -9780262017619/ch18.xml?language=en&redirect=true.

4. Rudyard Kipling, "Dane-Geld," Poetry Lovers Page, www.poetryloverspage.com /poets/kipling/dane_geld.html.

5. Javin Aryan, "A Look at China's Biowarfare Ambitions," Observer Research Foundation, June 2, 2021, www.orfonline.org/expert-speak/a-look-at-chinas -biowarfare-ambitions/.

6. Bill Gertz, "China Conducting Covert Biological Weapons Research, State Dept. Says," *Washington Times*, June 23, 2020, https://m.washingtontimes.com/news /2020/jun/23/china-conducting-covert-biological-weapons-researc/; Eric Croddy, "China's Role in the Chemical and Biological Disarmament Regimes," The Nonproliferation Review (Spring 2002) https://www.nonproliferation.org/wp -content/uploads/npr/91crod.pdf.

7. William J. Broad and Judith Miller, "Soviet Defector Says China Had Accident at a Germ Plant," *New York Times*, April 5, 1999, https://www.nytimes.com /1999/04/05/world/soviet-defector-says-china-had-accident-at-a-germ-plant.html.

8. Richard D. Fisher Jr., "SARS Crisis: Don't Rule Out Linkages to China's Biowarfare," The Jamestown Foundation, April 22, 2003, https://jamestown.org /program/sars-crisis-dont-rule-out-linkages-to-chinas-biowarfare/.

9.   "2005 Adherence to and Compliance with Arms Control, Nonproliferation, and Disarmament Agreements and Commitments," U.S. Department of State, August 2005, https://2009-2017.state.gov/t/avc/rls/rpt/51977.htm.

10. Dany Shoham, "China's Biological Warfare Programme: An Integrative Study with Special Reference to Biological Weapons Capabilities," *Journal of Defence Studies* 9, no. 2 (April–June 2015): 131–56, http://idsa.in/jds/9_2_2015_ChinasBiologica lWarfareProgramme.html.

11. Yasmin Tadjeh, "CBRN Conference News: Defense Officials See Increased Threat from Chinese, Russian Chem-Bio Weapons (UPDATED)," *National Defense Magazine*, September 23, 2019, https://www.nationaldefensemagazine.org/articles/2019 /7/23/defense-officials-see-increased-threat-from-chinese-russian-chembio-weapon #:~:text=CHEM%20BIO%20PROTECTION-,CBRN%20Conference%20News %3A%20Defense%20Officials%20See%20Increased%20Threat%20from %20Chinese,Chem%2DBio%20Weapons%20(UPDATED)&text= WILMINGTON%2C%20Del.,their%20nuclear%20and%20conventional %20forces.&text=But%20China%20is%20the%20leader,%2Dbased%20threats %2C%20Madsen%20said.

12. Alice Su, "Dreams of a Red Emperor: The Relentless Rise of Xi Jinping," *Los Angeles Times*, October 22, 2020, www.latimes.com/world-nation/story/2020-10-22/china-xi-jinping-mao-zedong-communist-party; Pamela Engel, "Chinese President Xi Jinping's Father Tried to Poison a Teacher When He Was 14," *Business Insider*, April 1, 2015, www.businessinsider.com/xi-jinpings-father-tried-to-poison-a-teacher-when-he-was-14-2015-4; Even Osnos, "Born Red: How Xi Jinping, an unremarkable provincial administrator, became China's most authoritarian leader since Mao." *The New Yorker*, 30 Mar. 2015, www.newyorker.com/magazine/2015/04/06/born-red ?source=search_google_dsa_paid&gclid=EAIaIQobChMIps _IzLDx7gIVkobACh1_gwLUEAAYASAAEgJNU_D_BwE. 1.

13. Tom Hancock, "Xi Jinping's Father Elevated to China's Pantheon of Communist Greats," *Financial Times*, August 9, 2018, www.ft.com/content/c4a9fdc8-9c3a-11e8-9702-5946bae86e6d.

14. "President Xi Jinping's Father's Tomb Crown Is China's New Silk Robe Hub," *NDTV*, August 17, 2014, www.ndtv.com/world-news/president-xi-jinpings-fathers -tomb-crown-is-chinas-new-silk-road-hub-649702.

15. Jaime Micklethwaite, "DEATH STATE: Inside China's Brutal Execution System with Mobile Injection Vans & Firing Squads after Killing Most in the World," The U.S. Sun, February 18, 2021, https://www.the-sun.com/news/2358126/china-brutal-execution-death-vans-trials/.

16. Jane Clark Scharl, "For China's Uighurs, the Red Terror Isn't Over," *Crisis Magazine*, August 5, 2020, www.crisismagazine.com/2020/for-chinas-uighurs-the -red-terror-isnt-over.

17. Joby Warrick, "China Is Building More Than 100 New Missile Silos in Its Western Desert, Analysts Say," *Washington Post*, June 30, 2021, www.washingtonpost .com/national-security/china-nuclear-missile-silos/2021/06/30/0fa8debc-d9c2 -11eb-bb9e-70fda8c37057_story.html; Callie Patteson, "Top General Warns China

Could Soon Spring Surprise Nuclear Strike on U.S.," *New York Post*, November 17, 2021, https://nypost.com/2021/11/17/top-general-china -could-spring-surprise-nuke-attack-on-us/.

18. Yitong Wu, "Court in China's Guangdong Jails 24 over Posts on Xi Jinping's Family,"trans. Luisetta Mudie, Radio Free Asia, January 7, 2021, https:// www.rfa.org/english/news/china/family-01272021143721.html.

19. "China's Xi Praises 'Best Friend' Putin during Russia Visit," BBC News, June 6, 2019, www.bbc.com/news/world-europe-48537663.

20. Andreas Illmer, "China Disappearances Show Beijing Sets Its Own Rules," BBC News, October 17, 2018, www.bbc.com/news/amp/world-asia-china-45806904; Ben Chapman, "Chinese Billionaires and CEOs Keep Disappearing in 'State-Sanctioned' Abductions," *Independent*, February 6, 2017, www .independent.co.uk/news/business/news/china-billionaires-ceo-disappearing -missing-station-sanctioned-abductions-beijing-security-agencies-a7564896.html; "HRC42: China Must End All Forms of Enforced Disappearance," *International Service for Human Rights*, September 16, 2019, www.ishr.ch/news/hrc42-l-china-must-end-all-forms-enforced-disappearance; "'Locked Up in Hell:' China's Forced Disappearances," DW News, www.dw.com/en/locked-up-in-hell-chinas-forced-disappearances/av-48092109.

21. Andreas Illmer, "China Disappearances Show Beijing Sets Its Own Rules.".

22. Stuart Lau, "Former Interpol Chief Meng Hongwei's Wife Sues Agency for 'Failing to Assist Her Family,'" Scroll, July 7, 2019, https://scroll.in/latest/929749/former-interpol-chief-meng-hongweis-wife-sues-agency-for-failing-to-assist-her-family.

23. Robert Olsen, "Jack Ma's Alibaba Hit with $2.8 Billion Fine for Abusing Its Dominant Market Position," *Forbes*, April 10, 2021, https://www.forbes.com/sites /robertolsen/2021/04/10/jack-mas-alibaba-hit-with-28-billion-fine-for-abusing-its -dominant-market-position/?sh=b87879937d14.

24. Reuters Staff, "China Halts New Enrollments at Business School Backed by Jack Ma: FT," Reuters, April 9, 2021, www.reuters.com/article/us-alibaba-academy/china-halts-new-enrollments-at-business-school-backed-by-jack-ma-ft -idUSKBN2BW0LT.

25. Amy Gunia, "Prison Sentence for Pastor Shows China Feels Threatened by Spread of Christianity, Experts Say," *Time*, January 2, 2020, https:// time.com/5757591/wang-yi-prison-sentence-china-christianity/.

26. May Jeong, "The Big Error Was That She Was Caught": The Untold Story behind the Mysterious Disappearance of Fan Bingbing, the World's Biggest Movie Star," *Vanity Fair*, March 26, 2019, www.vanityfair.com/hollywood/2019/03/the-untold -story-disappearance-of-fan-bingbing-worlds-biggest-movie-star.

27. "Actor Haruma Miura Dies in Apparent Suicide," *Tokyo Reporter*, July 18, 2020, www.tokyoreporter.com/japan/actor-haruma-miura-found-dead-in-apparent -suicide/.

28. Toh Ziyi, "Fan Bingbing Writes Emo Post Supposedly about Late Japanese Actor Haruma Miura, Gets Attacked by Netizens Instead," 8 Days, July 20, 2020,

https://www.8days.sg/sceneandheard/entertainment/fan-bingbing-writes-emo-post
-supposedly-about-late-japanese-12947648.

29. Carmen Paun and Susannah Luthi, "What China's Vax Trolling Adds Up To," *Politico*, January 28, 2021, www.politico.com/newsletters/global-pulse/2021/01/28 /what-chinas-vax-trolling-adds-up-to-491548.

30. Wenxin Fan, "China's Biggest Movie Star Was Erased from the Internet, and the Mystery Is Why," *Wall Street Journal*, September 15, 2021, www.wsj.com/articles /zhao-wei-china-biggest-movie-star-erased-from-internet-11631713293.

31. Somayeh Malekian, "Fears Grow for Missing Chinese Tennis Star Who Accused Ex-Official of Sexual Abuse," ABC News, November 17, 2021, https:// abcnews.go.com/Sports/fears-grow-missing-chinese-tennis-star-accused-official/story?id=81225830; Michelle Butterfield, "Fears Grow for Missing Chinese Tennis Star Peng Shuai after Email Raises Suspicions," Global News, November 18, 2021, https://globalnews.ca/news/8383540/peng-shuai-china-missing-tennis -star-email/; "China Silent on Tennis Star Peng Shuai despite Growing Concern," France24, November 15, 2021, https://www.france24.com/en/live -news/20211115-china-silent-on-tennis-star-peng-shuai-despite-growing-concern.

32. Helen Regan and Jacob Lev, "Peng Shuai Denies Making Sexual Assault Allegation against Retired Communist Party Leader, but WTA Concerns Persist," CNN, December 20, 2021, https://www.cnn.com/2021/12/20/tennis/peng-shuai-retracts-sexual-assault-allegations-intl-hnk/index.html.

33. Liu Xiaobo, "Nobel Lecture in Absentia—I Have No Enemies: My Final Statement," Nobel Prize Organization, December 10, 2010, https:// www.nobelprize.org/prizes/peace/2010/xiaobo/lecture/.

34. *Ibid.*

35. Like Stalin's Special Tasks and Putin's murderers, the Xi Government has increasingly reached abroad through kidnapping. *See* Emily Feng, "Hong Kong Bookseller Sentenced by China to 10 Years for Passing 'Intelligence,'" NPR, February 25, 2020, www.npr.org/2020/02/25/809163417/hong-kong-bookseller-sentenced-by-china-to-10-years-for-passing-intelligence; Like Yasha's Gang and Putin's Killer Unit, Xi's China has begun to kill and kidnap opponents— particularly Chinese opponents —in other countries. *See* Cathy He, "Chinese Regime Leads the World in Attacking Its Citizens Abroad: Report," The Epoch Times, February 6, 2021, www.theepochtimes.com/chinese-regime-leads-the -world-in-attacking-its-citizens-abroad-report_3687588.html.

36. Philip Short, *Mao: The Man Who Made China* (London: Bloomsbury Publishing, 2016), footnote 101.

37. Peter Palese, "Influenza: Old and New Threats," Nature Medicine, November 30. 2004, www.nature.com/articles/nm1141; Mohana Basu, "Lab Leak Is the Biggest Suspect in 1977 Flu Pandemic. But It Took 3 Decades to Gain Currency," The Print, June 3, 2021, https://theprint.in/science/lab-leak-is-the-biggest-suspect-in-1977-flu-pandemic-but-it-took-3-decades-to-gain-currency/669907/; Michelle Rozo and Gigi Kwik Gronvall, "The Reemergent 1977 H1N1 Strain and the

Gain-of-Function Debate," The National Center for Biotechnology Information, August 18, 2015, www.ncbi.nlm.nih.gov/pmc/articles/PMC4542197/.

38. Zeynep Tufekci, "Where Did the Coronavirus Come From? What We Already Know Is Troubling," *New York Times*, June 25, 2021, www.nytimes.com /2021/06/25/opinion/coronavirus-lab.html.

39. Eleanor Bartow, "France Warned the U.S. in 2015 about the Wuhan Lab It Helped Build, Former COVID-19 Investigator Claims," The Daily Caller, July 26, 2021, https://dailycaller.com/2021/07/26/france-wuhan-lab-david-asher-state-department/; Tyler Durden, "French Intelligence Warned Obama State Department about Wuhan Lab in 2015: Former U.S. Official," ZeroHedge, July 26, 2021, www.zerohedge.com/covid-19/french-intelligence-warned-obama-state-department-about-wuhan-lab-2015-former-official.

40. "China Destroyed Incriminating Documents on Gross Mishandling of Wuhan Virus," Japan Forward, January 11, 2021, https://japan-forward.com/china-destroyed-incriminating-documents-on-gross-mishandling-of-wuhan-virus/; Josh Chin, "China Told Labs to Destroy Coronavirus Samples to Reduce Biosafety Risks," *Wall Street Journal,* May 16, 2020, https://www.wsj.com/articles/china-told-labs-to-destroy-coronavirus-samples-to-reduce-biosafety-risks-11589684291.

41. Javier C. Hernandez, "China Peddles Falsehoods to Obscure Origin of COVID Pandemic," *New York Times*, December 6, 2020, www.nytimes.com/2020/12/06 /world/asia/china-covid-origin-falsehoods.html?auth=login-facebook.

42. Sarah Cook, "The Long Shadow of Chinese Censorship: How the Communist Party's Media Restrictions Affect News Outlets around the World," Freedom House, October 22, 2013, https://freedomhouse.org/sites/default/files/2020-02/Special_Report_Long_Shadow_Chinese_Censorship_2013.pdf.

43. Jerry Dunleavy (@JerryDunleavy), "Also. NYT says 'the message from intel agencies was clear…they had no evidence coronavirus escaped from the lab,'" Twitter, March 27, 2021, 7:45 p.m., https://twitter.com/JerryDunleavy/status/1375957065450057894

44. Editorial Board, "Where Are the Wuhan Subpoenas?" *Wall Street Journal*, October 27, 2021, www.wsj.com/articles/where-are-the-wuhan-subpoenas -ecohealth-alliance-peter-daszak-nih-anthony-fauci-gain-of-function-coronavirus -11635343111.

45. Ashley Rindsberg, "The Lab Leak Fiasco," Tablet, November 15, 2021, www.tabletmag.com/sections/news/articles/lab-leak-fiasco.

46. Monica Showalter, "To Propagandize the West, Lenin Recruited a Corps of 'Useful Idiots,'" *Investors Business Daily*, December 4, 2013, www.investors.com/politics /commentary/lenin-used-useful-idiots-to-spread-propaganda-to-the-west/.

47. David Cyranoski, "Inside the Chinese Lab Poised to Study World's Most Dangerous Pathogens," *Nature*, February 22, 2017, www.nature.com/news/inside-the-chinese-lab-poised-to-study-world-s-most-dangerous-pathogens-1.21487.

48. Nicoletta Lanese, "Only One Lab in China Can Safely Handle the New Coronavirus," Live Science, January 22, 2020, www.livescience.com/china-lab-meets-biosafety-levels-new-coronavirus.html.

49. Philip Willan and Didi Tan, "Wuhan Lab Used Chinese Military as Key Advisors," *The Times*, June 21, 2021, www.thetimes.co.uk/article/china-nominates-lab-leak -wuhan-institute-of-virology-for-top-science-award-37pg72gx5; Minnie Chan, "Coronavirus: Chinese Military Takes Control of Medical Supplies in Wuhan," *South China Morning Post*, February 3, 2020; Steven Carl Quay, "First COVID-19 Genomic Patient Cluster Was at PLA Hospital in Wuhan, China," Zenodo, October 28, 2020, https://zenodo.org/record/4139432#.YZKfmdbMK3I.

50. "Fact Sheet: Activity at the Wuhan Institute of Virology," Office of the Spokesperson, January 15, 2021, https://lb.usembassy.gov/fact-sheet-activity-wuhan-institute-of-virology/#main.

51. Natalie Winters, "Wuhan Institute of Virology Erased Names of Military-Linked Researchers from Website," The National Pulse, May 17, 2021, https:// thenationalpulse.com/breaking/wuhan-lab-erased-military-researchers-from-site/.

52. George Arbuthnott, Jonathan Calvert, and Philip Sherwell, "Revealed: Seven-Year Coronavirus Train from Mine Deaths to a Wuhan Lab," *The Times*, July 4, 2020, www.thetimes.co.uk/article/seven-year-covid-trail-revealed-l5vxt7jqp.

53. Jane Qiu, "How China's 'Bat Woman' Hunted Down Viruses from SARS to the New Coronavirus," *Scientific American*, June 1, 2020, https://www .scientificamerican.com/article/how-chinas-bat-woman-hunted-down-viruses -from-sars-to-the-new-coronavirus1/.

54. There is considerable evidence that the NIH, through intermediaries, continued to support the research, doing indirectly what the law prohibited it from doing directly.

55. "Fact Sheet: Activity at the Wuhan Institute of Virology," Office of the Spokesperson.

56. Philippe Lemoine, "The China Syndrome Part II: Wet Markets and Biolabs," Quillette, September 2, 2020, https://quillette.com/2020/09/02/the-china-syndrome-part-iii-wet-markets-and-biolabs/.

57. K. G. Anderson *et al.,* "The Proximal Origin of SARS-CoV-2," *Nature Medicine*, March 17, 2020, www.nature.com/articles/s41591-020-0820-9.

58. Sakashi Piplani, Puneet Kuman Singh, David A. Winkler, and Nikolai Petrovsky, "In Silico Comparison of Spike Protein-ACE2 Binding Affinities across Species; Significance for the Possible Origin of the SARS-CoV-2 Virus," Cornell University, May 13, 2020, https://arxiv.org/abs/2005.06199.

59. Kenneth Rapoza, "Wuhan Lab as Coronavirus Source Gains Traction," *Forbes*, May 1, 2020, www.forbes.com/sites/kenrapoza/2020/05/01/wuhan-lab-as -coronavirus-source-gains-traction/?sh=62ca0f1d6743; Former researcher at Hong Kong School of Public Heath, Li-Meng Yan, who claimed COVID 19 was "man-made" and "not from nature," fled to the United States in April 2020. Her elderly mother has now been arrested by the Chinese government to punish her daughter's whistleblowing. *See* "Chinese Virologist Who Fled to US after Claiming Coronavirus Was Made in a Military Lab Says Her Mother Has Now Been Arrested by Beijing," *Daily Mail*, October 6, 2020, www.dailymail.co.uk/news /article-8809809/amp/Coronavirus-Chinese-virologist-said-COVID-19-lab-reveals

-mothers-arrest.html; Mihika Basu, "Covid-19 Is an 'Unrestricted Bioweapon'": Virologist Dr. Li-Meng Yan Accuses China of Fabricating Genome Sequence," Meaww, October 9, 2020, https://meaww.com/amp/covid-19-unrestricted-bioweapon-chinese-virologist-dr-li-meng-yan-report-virus-china-genomic-sequence; Barnini Chakraborty and Alex Diaz, "EXCLUSIVE: Chinese Virologist Accuses Beijing of Coronavirus Coverup, Flees Hong Kong. 'I Know How They Treat Whistleblowers,'" *Fox News,* July 10, 2020, www.foxnews.com/world/chinese-virologist-coronavirus-cover-up-flee-hong-kong-whistleblower; Kairvy Grewal, "Covid Virus Developed in Wuhan Lab, Highly Mutant—Hong Kong Virologist Says She Has Evidence," The Print, September 14, 2020, https://theprint.in/world/covid-virus-developed-in-wuhan-lab-highly-mutant-hong-kong-virologist-says-she-has-evidence/502237/?amp; Nicholas Wade, "Origin of Covid-Following the Clues," Nicholas Wade, May 2, 2021, https://nicholaswade.medium.com/origin-of-covid-following-the-clues-6f03564c038; Keith Griffit, "CNN's Sanjay Gupta Breaks with His Network and Backs Former CDC Director Robert Redfield's 'Informed' Theory That COVID Escaped from Wuhan Lab as 'Simplest' Explanation," *Daily Mail,* April 12, 2021, https://www.dailymail.co.uk/news/article-9463153/CNNs-Sanjay-Gupta-breaks-network-BACKS-Wuhan-lab-theory.html?fbclid=IwAR0gpVhFwuBEVt_L-9GCsbhX-9px079sCv2rJz5_9MJp2m0U9_AN897KMmE; Nicholas Wade, "The Origin of COVID: Did People or Nature Open Pandora's Box at Wuhan?" Bulletin of the Atomic Scientists, May 5, 2021, https://thebulletin.org/2021/05/the-origin-of-covid-did-people-or-nature-open-pandoras-box-at-wuhan/.

60. Nicholas Wade, "A Covid Origin Conspiracy?" *City Journal,* January 23, 2022, https://www.city-journal.org/covid-origin-conspiracy?skip=1.

61. Derived from ancient Greek stories, a chimera is a creature which is a combination of animals (such as a lion and a dragon).

62. "Fact Sheet: Activity at the Wuhan institute of Virology," Office of the Spokesperson.

63. Laura Spinney, "Wuhan Virologist Says More Bat Coronaviruses Capable of Crossing Over," *The Guardian,* December 4, 2020, www.theguardian.com/world/2020/dec/04/wuhan-virologist-warns-more-bat-coronaviruses-capable-of-crossing-over-covid-beyond-china.

64. Liping Zhang, "Furin Cleavage of the SARS-CoV-2 Spike Is Modulated by O-glycosylation," Proceedings of the National Academy of Sciences of the United States of America, November 23, 2021, www.pnas.org/content/118/47/e2109905118.

65. "This bat virus would unlikely be able to infect pangolins." Cara Murez, "Did the New Coronavirus Come from Pangolins? New Study Says It's Possible," Heath Day, February 10, 2021, https://consumer.healthday.com/amp/b-2-10-did-the-new-coronavirus-come-from-pangolins-new-study-says-its-possible-2650332416.

66. The ongoing pandemic of Covid-19, caused by the severe acute respiratory syndrome Coronavirus 2 (SARS-CoV-2), has been fueled by a highly infective spike protein. The origin of this protein could have occurred through random insertion mutation, recombination or laboratory insertion. Researchers discard random insertion as an

origin of the protein. *See* Liji Thomas, "The Origin of SARS-CoV-2 Furin Cleavage Site Remains a Mystery," News Medical, February 17, 2021, www.news-medical.net/amp/news/20210217/The-origin-of-SARS-CoV-2-furin-cleavage-site-remains-a-mystery.aspx; Recombination of bat viruses and pangolin viruses is unlikely. *See* Jackson Ryan, "The Twisted, Messy Hunt for Covid-19's Origin and the Lab Leak Theory," CNet, February 6, 2021, www.cnet.com/google-amp/news/the-twisted-messy-hunt-for-covid-19s-origin-and-the-lab-leak-theory/.

67. "Fact Sheet: Activity at the Wuhan institute of Virology." Office of the Spokesperson.

68. *See* Ken Alibek, *Biohazard* (McHenry, Illinois: Delta, 2000), infra.

69. Javier C. Hernandez and James Gorman, "On W.H.O. Trip, China Refused to Hand Over Important Data," *New York Times*, February 12, 2021, www.nytimes.com/2021/02/12/world/asia/china-world-health-organization-coronavirus.html.

70. Ronald Bailey, "Did COVID-19 Leak from a Wuhan Lab?" *Reason*, May 12, 2021, https://reason.com/2021/05/12/did-covid-19-leak-from-a-wuhan-lab/?fbclid=IwAR2cVfMGuHznelwMAle45gc8xE0rBSll-SAeIqyjEqJ18bY2d3nbrsaD1aU&; Joel Zinberg, "The Evidence Mounts," *City Journal*, November 1, 2021, www.city-journal.org/new-evidence-for-lab-leak-hypothesis-of-covid-origins.

71. Dennis Normile, "Mounting Lab Accidents Raise SARS Fears," *Science*, April 30, 2004, https://science.sciencemag.org/content/304/5671/659; David Cyranoski, "Inside the Chinese Lab Poised to Study World's Most Dangerous Pathogens," *Nature*, February 22, 2017, www.nature.com/news/inside-the-chinese-lab-poised-to-study-world-s-most-dangerous-pathogens-1.21487.

72. Sharri Markson, "Coronavirus NSW: Dossier Lays Out Case against China Bat Virus Program," *Daily Telegraph*, May 4, 2020, www.dailytelegraph.com.au/coronavirus/bombshell-dossier-lays-out-case-against-chinese-bat-virus-program/news-story/55add857058731c9c71c0e96ad17da60.

73. Adam Shaw, Gillian Turner, and John Robers, "Leaked 'Five Eyes' Dossier on Alleged Chinese Coronavirus Coverup Consistent with US Findings, Officials Say," Fox News, May 2, 2020, www.foxnews.com/politics/five-eyes-dossier-chinese-coronavirus-coverup-u-s-findings; Henry Holloway, "VIRUS LEAK: Chinese Scientist Who Fled to US Claims Coronavirus Came from a 'Military Lab,'" *The Sun*, August 2, 2020, www.the-sun.com/news/1240870/china-scientist-coronavirus-leak-military-lab/; Eric Mack, "Five Eyes Intelligence Memo Details China COVID-19 Cover-Up," South Asia Journal, May 3, 2020, http://southasiajournal.net/five-eyes-intelligence-memo-details-china-covid-19-cover-up/; Eric Mack, "National Security Group Detail's China's Coronavirus Deceptions," Newsmax, April 4, 2020, www.newsmax.com/politics/pandemic-disinformation-propaganda-center-for-security-policy/2020/04/04/id/961384/.

74. Sharri Markson, "China's Most Famous Defector to America Warned U.S. Intelligence Agencies of Coronavirus in 2019," *New York Post*, September 14, 2021, https://nypost.com/2021/09/14/chinese-defector-warned-us-intelligence-of-covid-19-in-2019/.

75. Olafimihan Oshin, "*Washington Post* Issues Correction on 2020 Report on Tom Cotton, Lab-Leak Theory," *The Hill*, June 1, 2021, https://thehill.com/homenews /media/556418-washington-post-issues-correction-on-2020-report-on-tom-cotton -lab-leak-theory.

76. Nicholas Wade, *Where Covid Came From* (New York: Encounter Books, 2021); Matt Ridley, *Viral: The Search for the Origin of COVID-19* (New York: Harper, 2021).

77. Adam O'Neal, "What Happened in Wuhan?" *Wall Street Journal*, November 26, 2021, www.wsj.com/articles/what-happened-in-wuhan-china-review-four-books -covid-19-origin-controversey-lab-leak-theories-11637964296.

78. Kylie Atwood, "US Intel Agencies Find Wuhan Officials Kept Beijing in the Dark for Weeks about Coronavirus," CNN, August 21, 2020, www.cnn.com/2020/08/21 /politics/us-intel-wuhan-covid/index.html.

79. Madison Dibble, "'Growing into a Respectable Nation': Dianne Feinstein Praises China," *Washington Examiner*, July 30, 2020, www.washingtonexaminer .com/news/growing-into-a-respectable-nation-dianne-feinstein-praises-china.

80. Lily Kuo, "China Sentences Citizen Journalist to Four Years in Prison for Wuhan Lockdown Reports," *Washington Post*, December 28, 2020, www.washingtonpost .com/world/asia_pacific/china-wuhan-journalist-trial-coronavirus/2020/12/28 /01fac40c-48b7-11eb-97b6-4eb9f72ff46b_story.html.

81. Chao Deng, "Chinese Journalist Who Reported from Wuhan Is Gravely Ill after Prison Hunger Strike," *Wall Street Journal*, November 9, 2021, www.wsj.com /articles/chinese-journalist-who-reported-from-wuhan-is-gravely-ill-after-prison -hunger-strike-11636460027.

82. "Occam's Razor," Definition, Merriam Webster Online Dictionary, www .merriam-webster.com/dictionary/Occam%27s%20razor.

83. 2 Wigmore, *Evidence in Trials at Common Law* §291 at 228.

84. Aaron Blake, "Jon Stewart Goes All-In on the Lab Leak Theory," *Washington Post*, June 15, 2021, www.washingtonpost.com/politics/2021/06/15/jon-stewart -lab-leak-colbert/; Matthew Dessem, "Jon Stewart Embraced the Lab Leak Theory on the Late Show with Stephen Colbert. Was He Joking?" *Slate*, June 16, 2021, https://slate.com/culture/2021/06/jon-stewart-stephen-colbert-lab-leak-theory-late-show.html.

85. Steven Quay, "New Research Points to the People's Liberation Army Hospital in Wuhan, China as the Origin for the Worldwide Coronavirus Pandemic," Cision PR Newswire, October 28, 2020, www.prnewswire.com/ae/news-releases/new -research-points-to-the-peoples-liberation-army-hospital-in-wuhan-china-as-the -origin-for-the-worldwide-coronavirus-pandemic-301158985.html; Steven Quay, "First COVID-19 Genomic Patient Cluster Was at PLA Hospital in Wuhan, China," Zenodo, October 28, 2020, https://zenodo.org/record/4139432 #.YZUzLb3MK3I; Gordon, Michael R., Warren P. Strobel, and Drew Hinshaw, "Intelligence on Sick Staff at Wuhan Lab Fuels Debate on Covid-19 Origin," *Wall Street Journal*, May 23, 2021, www.wsj.com/articles/intelligence-on-sick-staff-at -wuhan-lab-fuels-debate-on-covid-19-origin-11621796228.

86. Emily Crane, "NIH Admits US Funded Gain-of-Function in Wuhan—despite Fauci's Denials," *New York Post*, October 21, 2021, https://nypost.com/2021/10/21/nih -admits-us-funded-gain-of-function-in-wuhan-despite-faucis-repeated-denials/.

87. Philip Willan, "Wuhan Lab Used Chinese Military as Key Advisors," *Sunday Times*, June 21, 2021, www.thetimes.co.uk/article/china-nominates-lab-leak -wuhan-institute-of-virology-for-top-science-award-37pg72gx5.

88. Elsa B. Kania and Wilson Vorndick, "Weaponizing Biotech: How China's Military Is Preparing for a 'New Domain of Warfare,'" Defense One, August 14, 2019, www.defenseone.com/ideas/2019/08/chinas-military-pursuing-biotech/159167/.

89. See Appendix III: "Fact Sheet: Activity at the Wuhan institute of Virology," Office of the Spokesperson.

90. Editorial Board, "More Reason to Think Beijing's to Blame for the Pandemic," *New York Post*, March 16, 2021, https://nypost.com/2021/03/16/more-reason-to -think-beijings-to-blame-for-the-pandemic/?utm_source=email_sitebuttons&utm _medium=site%20buttons&utm_campaign=site%20buttons; Sainath Suryanarayanan, "Biohazards News Tracker: Best Articles on SARS-CoV-2 Origins, Biolabs, and Gain of Function Research," U.S. Right to Know, March 18, 2021, https://usrtk.org/biohazards/origins-of-sars-cov-2-risks-of-gain-of -function-research-reading-list/.

91. Jan van der Made, "China's Communist Party Plans Stalinist-Style Purge ahead of Congress," Freedom House, October 22, 2013, https://amp.rfi.fr/en/international /20200714-china-s-communist-party-plans-stalinist-style-purge-ahead-of -congress.

92. Sharri Markson, *What Really Happened in Wuhan: A Virus Like No Other, Countless Infections, Millions of Deaths* (New York: Harper Collins, 2021); Yanzhong Huang, "U.S.—Chinese Distrust Is Inviting Dangerous Coronavirus Conspiracy Theories," *Foreign Affairs*, March 5, 2020, www.foreignaffairs.com/articles/united-states/2020 -03-05/us-chinese-distrust-inviting-dangerous-coronavirus-conspiracy.

93. This is a completely different patient than the one presented to the WHO as "Patient Zero" one year later in China. *See* Fernando Duarte, "Who Is 'Patient Zero' in the Coronavirus Outbreak?" BBC, February 23, 2020, www.bbc.com/future/article/20200221-coronavirus-the-harmful-hunt -for-covid-19s-patient-zero.

94. David Stanway, "1st COVID-19 Case Could Have Emerged in China in 2019-Study," Reuters, June 25, 2021, www.reuters.com/world/china/first-covid-19-case -could-have-hit-china-oct-2019-study-2021-06-25/.

95. Stephanie Hegarty, "The Chinese Doctor Who Tried to Warn Others about Coronavirus," BBC, February 6, 2020, www.bbc.com/news/world-asia-china -51364382.

96. Lily Kuo, "Coronavirus: Wuhan Doctor Speaks Out against Authorities," *The Guardian*, March 11, 2020, https://www.theguardian.com/world/2020/mar/11/ coronavirus-wuhan-doctor-ai-fen-speaks-out-against-authorities.

97. Excellent investigative sources and materials include: Josh Rogin, *Chaos under Heaven: Trump, Xi, and the Battle for the Twenty-First Century* (Houghton

Mifflin Harcourt, 2021); Josh Rogin, "In 2018, Diplomats Warned of Risky Coronavirus Experiments in a Wuhan Lab. No One Listened," *Politico*, March 8, 2021, www.politico.com/news/magazine/2021/03/08/josh-rogin-chaos-under-heaven-wuhan-lab-book-excerpt-474322; Lauren Starke, "On the Cover of *New York Magazine*: The Lab-Leak Hypothesis," *New York Magazine*, January 4, 2021, https://nymag.com/press/2021/01/on-the-cover-of-new-york-magazine-the-lab-leak-hypothesis.html; "Fact Sheet: Activity at the Wuhan institute of Virology," Office of the Spokesperson.

98. Grace Niewijk, "Controversy Aside, Why the Source of Covid-19 Matters," *Genetic Engineering & Biotechnology News*, September 21, 2020, www.genengnews.com/insights/controversy-aside-why-the-source-of-covid-19-matters/; Jamie Metzl, foreign policy expert and author of *Hacking Darwin* states, "Suggesting that an outbreak of a deadly bat coronavirus accidentally occurred near the only level 4 virology institute in all of China—which happened to be studying the closest known relative of that exact virus—strains credulity." Jamie Metzl, "How to Hold Beijing Accountable for the Coronavirus," *Wall Street Journal*, July 28, 2020, www.wsj.com/articles/how-to-hold-beijing-accountable-for-the-coronavirus-11595976973; Jerry Dunleavy, "GOP Report Says Evidence Points to COVID Emerging from Wuhan Lab," *Washington Examiner*, August 2, 2021, www.washingtonexaminer.com/news/gop-report-evidence-proves-covid-emerged-wuhan-lab; Editorial Board, "The 'Wuhan Lab Leak' Theory Looks More Credible Than Ever,'" *New York Post*, May 22, 2021, https://nypost.com/2021/05/22/the-wuhan-lab-leak-theory-looks-more-credible-then-ever/amp/; Ronald Bailey, "Did COVID-19 Leak from a Wuhan Lab?" *Reason*, May 12, 2021, https://reason.com/2021/05/12/did-covid-19-leak-from-a-wuhan-lab/?fbclid=IwAR2cVfMGuHznelwMAle45gc8xE0rBSll-SAeIqyjEqJ18bY2d3nbrsaD1aU&.

99. Ronjiun Lu et al. "Genomic Characteristics and Epidemiology of 2019 Novel Coronavirus Implications for Virus Origins and Receptor Binding," *The Lancet*, Jan.uary 30, 2020, www.thelancet.com/article/S0140-6736(20)30251-8/fulltext.

100. Charles Calisher *et al.*, "Statement in Support of the Scientists, Public Health Professionals, and Medical Professionals of China Combatting COVID-19." *The Lancet*, February 19, 2020, https://www.thelancet.com/journals/lancet/article/PIIS0140-6736(20)30418-9/fulltext.

101. Kristian G. Anderson *et al.*, "The Proximal Origin of SARS-CoV-2," *Nature Medicine*, March 17, 2020, https://www.nature.com/articles/s41591-020-0820-9?utm_medium=affiliate&utm_source=commission_junction&utm_campaign=3_nsn6445_deeplink_PID100072647&utm_content=deeplink#citeas.

102. Eric F. Donaldson, Amy C. Sims, and Ralph S. Baric, "Systematic Assembly and Genetic Manipulation of the Mouse Hepatitis Virus A59 Genome," National Center for Biotechnology Information, November 28, 2007, https://www.ncbi.nlm.nih.gov/pmc/articles/PMC7120124/.

103. Bill Gertz, "Omicron Prompts New Virus Origin Worries," *Washington Times*, December 1, 2021, www.washingtontimes.com/news/2021/dec/1/omicron-prompts-new-virus-origin-worries/.

104. Heckin_Dinosaur, "Unicorn Theory" Definition, Urban Dictionary, October 26, 2020, www.urbandictionary.com/define.php?term=Unicorn%20Theory.

105. Baker, "The Lab-Leak Hypothesis."

106. Alison Young, "Hundreds of Bioterror Lab Mishaps Cloaked in Secrecy," *USA Today*, August 17, 2014, www.usatoday.com/story/news/nation/2014/08/17/reports -of-incidents-at-bioterror-select-agent-labs/14140483/.

107. *Ibid.*

108. Baker, "The Lab-Leak Hypothesis"; Marc Lipsitch and Thomas Inglesby, "Moratorium on Research Intended to Create Novel Potential Pandemic Pathogens," American Society for Microbiology, December 12, 2014, www .centerforhealthsecurity.org/our-work/publications/moratorium-on-research -intended-to-create-novel-potential-pandemic-pathogens.

109. Nathan Levine and Chris Li, "Pathogens Have the World's Attention," *Foreign Affairs*, March 16, 2021, www.foreignaffairs.com/articles/united- states/2021-03-16/pathogens-have-worlds-attention.

110. Jeremy Page, Betsy McKay, and Drew Hinshaw, "How the WHO's Hunt for COVID's Origins Stumbled in China," *Wall Street Journal*, March 17, 2021, www .wsj.com/articles/who-china-hunt-covid-origins-11616004512.

111. Milton Leitenberg, "Did the SARS-CoV-2 Virus Arise from a Bat Coronavirus Research Program in a Chinese Laboratory? Very Possibly," Bulletin of the Atomic Scientists, June 4, 2020, https://thebulletin.org/2020/06/did-the-sars-cov-2-virus -arise-from-a-bat-coronavirus-research-program-in-a-chinese-laboratory-very -possibly/; Baker, "The Lab-Leak Hypothesis"; Dominic Dwyer, "I Was the Australian Doctor on the WHO's COVID-19 Mission to China. Here's What We Found about the Origins of the Coronavirus," The Conversation, February 21, 2021, www.abc.net.au/news/2021-02-22/australian-doctor-on-the-who-covid-19 -mission-china-origin-covid/13180078.

112. Brian McGleenon, "UN Informed China of Human Rights Activists Plan to Attend Meeting, Claims Whistleblower," Express, June 7, 2020, www.express.co.uk /news/world/1292510/un-human-rights-council-emails-sent-to-china-dissident -Uighur-Tibet-hong-kong-Gao-Zhisheng.

113. Ian Birrell, "World Experts Condemn WHO Inquiry as a 'Charade,'" Ian Birrell, February 14, 2021, www.ianbirrell.com/world-experts-condemn-who-inquiry-as -a-charade/; Dr. David A. Relman, professor of medicine and microbiology at Stanford University and a member of the intelligence community studies board at the National Academies of Science, Engineering, and Medicine (an advisory body of the federal government) states, "I completely agree, based on what we know so far, that the W.H.O. investigation appears to be biased, skewed, and insufficient." James Gorman, "Some Scientists Question W.H.O. Inquiry into the Coronavirus Pandemic's Origins," *New York Times*, March 4, 2021, www.nytimes.com/2021/03/04/health/covid-virus- origins.html.

114. Lynn Chaya, "Chinese Journalist Detained in Wuhan for Initial Reporting on COVID Is 'Close to Death,'" *National Post*, November 9, 2021, https://

nationalpost.com/news/chinese-journalist-detained-in-wuhan-for-initial-reporting-on-covid-is-close-to-death.

115. Abigail Williams and Dan De Luce, "DHS Report: China Hid Coronavirus' Severity in Order to Hoard Medical Supplies," NBC News, May 4, 2020, www.nbcnews.com/politics/national-security/dhs-report-china-hid-coronavirus-severity-order-hoard-medical-supplies-n1199221; Isabel Togoh, "China Covered Up Coronavirus to Hoard Medical Supplies, DHS Report Finds," *Forbes*, May 4, 2020, www.forbes.com/sites/isabeltogoh/2020/05/04/china-covered-up-coronavirus-to-hoard-medical-supplies-dhs-report-finds/?sh=44d14fda1dba; Chad P. Bown, "China's Net PPE Exports Plummeted in Early 2020 but Are Recovering," Peterson Institute for International Economics, May 5, 2020, www.piie.com/research/piie-charts/chinas-net-ppe-exports-plummeted-early-2020-are-recovering.

116. Daniel T. Teng, "PCR Sales Soared in Wuhan Before 1st Official COVID-19 Cases Publicized Report," The Epoch Times, October 5, 2021, www.theepochtimes.com/mkt_breakingnews/pcr-sales-soared-in-wuhan-before-first-official-covid-19-cases-publicised-report_4032361.html; Jamie Tarabay, "China PCR Purchases Spiked in Months before First Known Covid Cases, Firm Says," *Bloomberg*, October 4, 2021, www.bloomberg.com/news/articles/2021-10-04/china-pcr-purchases-spiked-in-months-before-first-known-covid-cases-firm-says.

117. "CanSino's COVID-19 Vaccine Candidate Approved for Military Use in China," Reuters, June 28, 2020, www.reuters.com/article/us-health-coronavirus-china-vaccine-idUSKBN2400DZ; Dyani Lewis, "China's Coronavirus Vaccine Shows Military's Growing Role in Medical Research," *Nature*, SeptEMBER 11, 2020, www.nature.com/articles/d41586-020-02523-x.

Chapter Twenty-Two: The Last Dance

1. T. S. Eliot, "The Hollow Men," All Poetry, November 23, 1925, https://allpoetry.com/the-hollow-men.

2. Colin Shindler, "The Russian Taste for Poison," *Jewish Chronicle*, March 15, 2018, www.thejc.com/salisbury-nerve-gas-attack-on-sergei-skripol-russia-s-history-of-poison-plots-1.460725.

3. *Ibid.*

4. Joby Warrick, "Poisoning of Russian Ex-Spy Puts Spotlight on Moscow's Secret Military Labs," *Washington Post*, March 18, 2018, www.washingtonpost.com/world/national-security/poisoning-of-russian-ex-spy-puts-spotlight-on-moscows-secret-military-labs/2018/03/18/9968efb6-2962-11e8-b79d-f3d931db7f68_story.html?outputType=amp; Katherine Charlet, "The New Killer Pathogens: Countering the Coming Bioweapons Threat," Carnegie Endowment for International Peace, April 17, 2018, https://carnegieendowment.org/2018/04/17/new-killer-pathogens-countering-coming-bioweapons-threat-pub-76009; Joby Warrick, "Putin Expands Secret Military Labs for 'Genetic' Bombs

as Powerful as Nukes," *Washington Post* (reprinted in the *Miami Herald*), March 19, 2018, https://amp.miamiherald.com/article205810859.html.

5. A project code-named "Hunter" sought to develop hybrids of bacteria and viruses such that use of an antibiotic to kill the bacteria would trigger release of the virus. Steven Aftergood, "The History of the Soviet Biological Weapons Program." Federation of American Scientists, July 18, 2012, https://fas.org/blogs/secrecy/2012/07/soviet_bw/; Kirk Wolfinger, "Interview with Biowarriors, Sergei Popov," Public Broadcasting Service, November 2001, https://news.un.org/en/story/2018/08/1017352.

6. By employing genetic manipulation and other molecular biology techniques, its scientists were able to breach barriers separating species. *Ibid.*; Pandemics could spread only indiscriminately among targeted populations. *See* Loren Thompson, "The Threat of Biological Warfare Is Increasing, and the U.S. Isn't Ready," *Forbes Magazine*, April 9, 2018, www.forbes.com/sites/lorenthompson/2018/04/09/biowar-a-guide-to-the-coming-plague-years/amp/.

7. Genetic engineering could be used to kill specific ethnic groups. *See* Kurt Nimmo, "The Genocide Bioweapon," Newsbud, November 13, 2019, www.newsbud.com/2017/11/13/the-genocide-bioweapon/.

8. James Clapper, "Statement for the Record Worldwide Threat Assessment of the U.S. Intelligence Community," Senate Armed Services Committee, February 9, 2016, www.dni.gov/files/documents/SASC_Unclassified_2016_ATA_SFR_FINAL.pdf; Antonio Regalado, "Top U.S. Intelligence Official Calls Gene Editing a WMD Threat," MIT Technology Review, February 9, 2016, www.technologyreview.com/s/600774/top-us-intelligence-official-calls-gene-editing-a-wmd-threat/.

9. "Terrorists Potentially Target Millions in Makeshift Biological Weapons 'Laboratories,' UN Forum Hears," UN News, August 17, 2018, https://news.un.org/en/story/2018/08/1017352.

10. "Does Russia's New Culture Minister Hate the Arts?" BBC News, January 23, 2020, www.bbc.com/news/world-europe-51220594.

11. The "Danse Macabre" was first performed in the Middle Ages. Dancers representing a cross section of people would form a circle, all dancing together. In the center, a dancer represented the Devil as death. One by one, he would select and symbolically kill the dancers, sparing neither nobles, nor women, nor children. *See* Ginny Burges, "Dancing to Death's Tune: The 'Danse Macabre.'" Rhap.so.dy in Words, https://rhapsodyinwords.com/tag/sylvia-plath-poem-danse-macabre/; Andrea Warner, "Danse Macabre: A Brief History of Halloween's Haunting Anthem," CBC Music, October 30, 2017, www.cbcmusic.ca/posts/19203/danse-macabre-a-brief-history-of-the-halloweens-ha.

12. Anna Akhmatova, "Anna Akhmatova Quotes," Your Dictionary, https://quotes.yourdictionary.com/author/anna-akhmatova/142785.

13. *See* Percy Bysshe Shelley, "Ozymandias," Poetry Foundation, www.poetryfoundation.org/poems/46565/ozymandias.

14. Mohandas Karamchand Gandhi, *Mohandas K. Gandhi, Autobiography: The Story of My Experiments with Truth* (Mineola, New York: Dover Publications, 1983).

15. "Vladimir Putin Is Growing Ever More Repressive as He Loses Support," *Economist*, April 24, 2021, www.economist.com/briefing/2021/04/23/vladimir-putin-is-growing-ever-more-repressive-as-he-loses-support.

16. Laura He, "Evergrande Can't Pay Its Debts. China Is Scrambling to Contain the Fallout," CNN Business, December 10, 2021, www.cnn.com/2021/12/10/business/evergrande-government-intervention-intl-hnk/index.html; Laura He, "Evergrande Shares Plummet 20% to New Record Low as Default Fears Resurface," CNN Business, December 6, 2021, www.cnn.com/2021/12/06/business/markets-evergrande-intl-hnk/index.html.

17. Jonathan Ponciano, "U.S.-Listed Chinese Stocks Lose $80 Billion in Value As Didi Delisting Crashes Prices," *Forbes*, December 3, 2021, www.forbes.com/sites/jonathanponciano/2021/12/03/us-listed-chinese-stocks-lose-80-billion-in-value-as-didi-delisting-crashes-prices/?sh=43f0cfa92b1e; Julia Horowitz, "Didi's Delisting Could Spell the End for Chinese Stocks on Wall Street," CNN Business, December 3, 2021, www.cnn.com/2021/12/03/investing/premarket-stocks-trading/index.html.

18. Sarah Toy, "Omicron Covid-19 Cases in U.S. Mostly Mild So Far, CDC Data Show," *Wall Street Journal*, December 10, 2021, www.cnn.com/2021/12/03/investing/premarket-stocks-trading/index.html; Sarah Knapton, "Omicron May Be No Worse Than Flu, Says Former Government Adviser," *The Telegraph*, December 14, 2021, www.telegraph.co.uk/news/2021/12/14/omicron-less-severe-covid-delta-variant-two-vaccine-jabs-give/.

19. Frederick Cartwright and Michael Biddiss, *Disease and History: From Ancient Times to Covid-19* (London: Lume Books, 2020).

20. *See Pericles' Funeral Oration over the First Athenian Dead*, recorded by Thucydides.

21. Alfred Lord Tennyson, "The Dying Swan" Bartleby, 1830, www.bartleby.com/360/5/230.html.

Appendix I: The Poisoning Of Anna Pavlova

1. Keith Money, *Anna Pavlova: Her Life and Art* (New York: HarperCollins, 1982).
2. Margot Fonteyn, *Pavlova, Portrait of a Dancer* (New York: Viking, 1984).
3. Victor D'André, *Anna Pavlova* (New York: Benjamin Blom, Inc., 1972).
4. Sjeng Scheijen, *Diaghilev, A Life* (London: Oxford University Press, 2009), 414–15.
5. Igor Polianski, "Bolshevik Disease and Stalinist Terror: On the Historical Casuistry of Artificial Pneumothorax," United States National Library of Medicine, January 2015, www.ncbi.nlm.nih.gov/pmc/articles/PMC4304549/.

Appendix II: Sample Suspicious Russian Poisonings and Deaths

1. Snyder, Timothy. "Hitler vs. Stalin: Who Killed More?" *New York Review of Books*, March 10, 2011, www.nybooks.com/articles/2011/03/10/hitler-vs-stalin-who-killed-more/.

2. Heidi Blake, *From Russia with Blood: The Kremlin's Ruthless Assassination Program and Vladimir Putin's Secret War on the West* (New York: Mulholland Books, 2019.

3. *Ibid.*

4. Masha Gessnen, "The Suspected Poisoning of Alexey Navalny, Putin's Most Prominent Adversary," *New Yorker*, August 20, 2020, www.newyorker.com /news/our-columnists/the-suspected-poisoning-of-alexey-navalny-putins-most -prominent-adversary/amp; Oleg Kashin, "The Russian Opposition Leader Aleksei Navalny Was in Intensive Care after Suffering Symptoms of What His Spokeswoman Called Poisoning," *New York Times*, August 20, 2020, www.nytimes.com/2020/08/21/opinion/navalny-russia-poison.html.

5. Litvinenko issued a brave final statement on November 21, 2006, the day before his death: "This may be the time to say one or two things to the person responsible for my present condition. You may succeed in silencing me, but that silence comes at a price. You have shown yourself to be as barbaric and ruthless as your most hostile critics have claimed. You have shown yourself to have no respect for life, liberty or any civilized value... You may succeed in silencing one man, but the howl of protest from around the world will reverberate, Mr. Putin, in your ears for the rest of your life. May God forgive you ... " Matthew Chance, "Alexander Litvinenko: Why Was Ex-Spy a Marked Man? CNN, January 20, 2016, www.cnn.com/2015/01/28/europe/russia-britain-litvinenko/index.html; In response, Putin issued the following piggish response, "Mr. Litvinenko Is, Unfortunately, Not Lazarus." See Adam Taylor, "Why Would Putin Have Had a Former KGB Operative Murdered?" *Washington Post*, January 21, 2016, www .washingtonpost.com/news/worldviews/wp/2016/01/21/why-would-putin-have -had-a-former-kgb-operative-murdered/.

6. Masha Gessen, "The Best Theory for Explaining the Mysterious Death of Putin's Mentor," *Business Insider*, February 17, 2015, www.businessinsider.com/the- mysterious-death-of-putins-mentor-2015-2.

7. Oleg Yegorov, "Seek and Destroy: 3 Detested Soviet Enemies Hunted and Killed Abroad," Russia Beyond, August 2, 2017, www.rbth.com/politics_and_society/2017 /08/02/seek-and-destroy-3-detested-soviet-enemies-hunted-and-killed-abroad _815294.

8. Blake, "From Russia with Blood."

9. "10 Ways Spies Have Tried to Poison Targets," Sky News, September 6, 2018, https:// news.sky.com/story/amp/10-ways-spies-have-tried-to-poison-people-11490974.

10. Ben Macintyre, "All of Russia's Enemies Have Lived in Fear of the Assassin," *The Times*, March 10, 2018, www.thetimes.co.uk/article/all-of-russias-enemies-have -lived-in-fear-of-the-assassin-shhzbm9q6.

11. *Ibid.*

12. *Ibid.*

13. Blake, "From Russia with Blood."

14. Sarah Hurst, Oren Dorrell, and George Petros. "Suspicious Russian Deaths: Sacrificial Pawns or Coincidence?" *USA Today*, May 2, 2017, www.usatoday.com /pages/interactives/suspicious-russian-deaths-sacrificial-pawns-or-coincidence/.
15. *Ibid.*
16. *Ibid.*
17. *Ibid.*
18. *Ibid.*
19. *Ibid.*
20. *Ibid.*
21. *Ibid.*
22. *Ibid.*
23. *Ibid.*
24. *Ibid.*
25. "Russia Josef Stalin: Outspoken Grandson Is 'Found Dead,'" *BBC News*, December 22, 2016, www.bbc.com/news/world-europe-38410731.

Appendix IV: Alleged People's Republic of China Biological Warfare Research Organizations

1. Eric Croddy, "China's Role in the Chemical and Biological Disarmament Regimes," The Nonproliferation Review, Spring 2002, https://www.nonproliferation.org/wp -content/uploads/npr/91crod.pdf.

Appendix V: U.S. State Department Report Fact Sheet: Activity at the Wuhan Institute of Virology

1. "Fact Sheet: Activity at the Wuhan institute of Virology," Office of the Spokesperson, January 15, 2021, https://lb.usembassy.gov/fact-sheet-activity-wuhan-institute-of-virology/#main; Simrun Sirur, "Days before Trump Goes, U.S. Releases Report Pointing Finger at Wuhan Lab for Covid Origin," The Print, January 17, 2021, https:// theprint.in/world/us-says-wuhan-scientists-fell-sick-with-symptoms-consistent-with-covid-in-autumn-2019/587156/?amp.

Appendix VI: Anna Pavlova in Houston and India

1. Keith L. Bryant Jr., *Culture in the American Southwest: The Earth, the Sky, the People* (College Station, Texas: Texas A&M University Press, 2014); Ann Dunphy Becker, *Houston 1860–1900* (Mount Pleasant, South Carolina: Arcadia Publishing, 2010); Robert I. Giesberg, "Houston Ballet," Handbook of Texas Online, https:// tshaonline.org/handbook/online/articles/kkh01; Heather Brand, "Performance Aplenty:

Theater-Hopping in the Houston Theater District," Texas Highways, October 2016, https://texashighways.com/culture/performance-aplenty-houston-theater-district/.

2. Cynthia Crain, "America's Forgotten Ballerina," Cynthia Crain, January 25, 2019, https://cynthiacrainauthor.com/author/cynthiacrainauthor/.

3. Allan Kozinn, "Efrem Kurtz, 94, a Conductor in Europe, Kansas and Houston," *New York Times*, June 29, 1995, www.nytimes.com/1995/06/29/obituaries/efrem-kurtz-94-a-conductor-in-europe-kansas-and-houston.html.

4. Utpal K. Banerjee, "Anna Pavlova's Anmol Gifts," The Pioneer, April 13, 2017, www.dailypioneer.com/2017/friends-forever/anna-pavlovas-anmol-gifts.html.

5. Suanshu Khurana, "The Collaboration between Uday Shankar and Anna Pavlova Is the Subject of a New Documentary," The Indian Express, January 8, 2020, https://indianexpress.com/article/lifestyle/art-and-culture/uday-shankar-anna-pavlova-protima-chatterjee-meeting-of-two-cultures-documentry-6205211/.